iPad®
For Seniors

FOR

DUMMIES®

A Wiley Brand

6th Edition

iPad® For Seniors

FOR

DUMMIES®

A Wiley Brand

6th Edition

by Nancy Muir

iPad® For Seniors For Dummies®, 6th Edition

Published by:
John Wiley & Sons, Inc.,
111 River Street,
Hoboken, NJ 07030-5774,
www.wiley.com

For general information on our other products and services, please contact our Customer Care Department within the U.S. at 877-762-2974, outside the U.S. at 317-572-3993, or fax 317-572-4002. For technical support, please visit www.wiley.com/techsupport.

Wiley publishes in a variety of print and electronic formats and by print-on-demand. Some material included with standard print versions of this book may not be included in e-books or in print-on-demand. If this book refers to media such as a CD or DVD that is not included in the version you purchased, you may download this material at http://booksupport.wiley.com. For more information about Wiley products, visit www.wiley.com.

Library of Congress Control Number: 2013949067

ISBN 978-1-118-72826-0 (pbk); ISBN 978-1-118-72816-1 (ebk); ISBN 978-1-118-72819-2 (ebk); ISBN 978-1-118-72822-2 (ebk)

Manufactured in the United States of America

10 9 8 7 6 5 4

Contents at a Glance

Table of Contents

*I*f you bought this book (or are even thinking about buying it), you've probably already made the decision to buy an iPad. The iPad is designed to be simple to use, but still, you can spend hours exploring the preinstalled apps, finding out how to change settings, and syncing the device to your computer or through iTunes or iCloud. I've invested those hours so that you don't have to — and I've added advice and tips for getting the most out of your iPad.

This book helps you get going with the iPad quickly and painlessly so that you can move directly to the fun part.

About This Book

This book is specifically written for mature people like you, folks who may be relatively new to using a tablet device and want to discover the basics of buying an iPad, working with its preinstalled apps, and getting on the Internet. In writing this book, I've tried to consider the types of activities that might interest someone who is 50 years old or older and picking up an iPad for the first time.

Conventions used in this book

This book uses certain conventions to help you find your way around, including

➡ Text you type in a text box is in **bold.** Figure references, such as "see **Figure 1-1**," are also in bold, to help you find them.

➡ Whenever I mention a website address, or *URL,* I put it in a different font, `like this`.

➡ Figure callouts draw your attention to actions you need to perform. In some cases, points of interest in a figure might be indicated. The text tells you what to look for; the callout line makes it easy to find.

Tip icons point out insights or helpful suggestions related to tasks in the step lists.

New icons highlight what features of iOS 7 and the iPad Air are new and exciting, in case you're moving up from an earlier version.

Foolish Assumptions

This book is organized by sets of tasks. These tasks start from the beginning, assuming that you've never laid your hands on an iPad, and guide you through basic steps in nontechnical language.

This book was written about the iPad Air (the 9.7-inch model) and iPad mini with Retina Display (the 7.9-inch model). Most material is relevant whether you have an iPad 2, an iPad mini or mini with Retina Display, or a third-gen, fourth-gen, or iPad Air model, though I strongly recommend that you update to iOS 7, which is quick and easy to do (see Chapter 2), because it's the operating system I based this book on.

This book covers both the Wi-Fi–only and the Wi-Fi and 3G/4G iPad features. I'm also assuming that you'll want to download and use the iBooks e-reader app, so I tell you how to do that in Chapter 9 and cover its features in Chapter 10.

Beyond the Book

I've provided additional information about iPad and iOS7 online to help you on your way:

⟶ **Cheat Sheet:** Check out www.dummies.com/ cheatsheet/ipadforseniors to help you figure out various iPad General settings and settings for e-mail and contacts that will come in handy on a regular basis.

⟶ **Online articles:** On several of the pages that open each of this book's parts, you'll find links to what the folks at *For Dummies* call Web Extras, which expand features that I've discussed in that particular section. You'll find them at www.dummies.com/extras/ ipadforseniors. There I've given you a listing of free apps to get you going with your iPad at no cost, info about customizing iTunes Radio channels, and a handy list of Siri commands.

Where to Go from Here

Dive in and get started! You can work through this book from beginning to end, or simply open a chapter to solve a problem or acquire a specific new skill whenever you need it. The steps in every task quickly get you to where you want to go, without a lot of technical explanation.

Note: At the time I wrote this book, all the information it contained was accurate for the Wi-Fi–only and Wi-Fi and 3G iPad 2s; the Wi-Fi–only and Wi-Fi and 4G third-gen, fourth-gen, and iPad Air iPads; the first-generation iPad mini and the iPad mini with Retina Display; version 7 of iOS (the operating system used by the iPad); and version 11 of iTunes. Apple is likely to introduce new iPad models and new versions of the iOS and iTunes between book editions. If you've bought a new iPad, and its hardware, user interface, or version of iTunes looks a little different, be sure to check out what Apple has to say at www. apple.com/ipad. You'll no doubt find updates on the company's latest releases. Also, if you don't set up iCloud to automatically update your iPad, perform updates to the operating system on a regular basis, as described in Chapter 2.

When a change is very substantial, I may add an update or bonus information that you can download at this book's companion website, www.ipadmadeclear.com.

Part I
Making the iPad Yours

Buying Your iPad

*Y*ou've read about it. You're so intrigued that you've decided to get your own iPad to have fun, explore the online world, read e-books, organize your photos, and more.

You've made a good decision, because the iPad redefines the computing experience in an exciting new way. It's also an absolutely perfect fit for many seniors.

In this chapter, you discover the different types of iPad models and their relative advantages, as well as where to buy this magical device. After you have one in your hands, I help you explore what's in the box and give you an overview of the little buttons and slots you'll encounter; luckily, the iPad has very few of them.

Discover What's New in iOS 7, iPad Air, and iPad mini with Retina Display

Apple's iPad gets its features from a combination of hardware and its software operating system (called *iOS;* the term is short for *iPhone Operating System,* in case you want to impress your friends). The current operating system is iOS 7, though small updates appear all the time, so by the time you're reading this book, you might have 7.2, 3, or 4! If you've seen the original iPad or iPad 2 in action, or if you own one, it's helpful to understand which new features the third-gen, fourth-gen, and iPad Air devices bring to the table (all of which are covered in more detail in this book). In addition to the features of previous iPads, iPad Air offers

➡ **Design:** iPad Air is lighter (1 lb.) and thinner (7.5 millimeters thick) with thinner bezels for more screen area. Both iPad Air and iPad mini with Retina Display offer awesomely crisp displays with 3.1 million pixels — which, trust me, is a lot.

➡ **An improved chip:** The 64 bit A7X processor which doubles the processor and graphics speeds accomplished by the A6X chip on the fourth-generation iPad.

➡ **Dual antennas:** Two antennae and the use of MIMO (multiple-input, multiple output) technology allows for much faster wireless connections.

➡ **M7 Motion Coprocessor:** This coprocessor processes game features like the gyroscope and accelerometer faster.

➡ **Video Recording:** Video recording quality has moved from 720p HD to 1080p HD for an improvement in quality, and 3x video zoom has been added.

 Throughout this book, I point out features that are available only on certain iPad models, so you can use this book no matter which version of the device you own.

Any iPad device from iPad 2 on can use most features of iOS 7 if you update the operating system (discussed in detail in Chapter 2); this book is based on version 7 of the iOS. This update to the operating system adds a few new features, including

➡ **A whole new look:** Apple entirely redesigned the iPad interface with iOS 7, providing flatter, more graphically bright buttons for your apps, and a simple, clean look to areas such as the Lock screen and Settings. Love it or hate it, it's an overdue face-lift for the iPad.

➡ **Control Center:** This handy group of buttons and sliders gives you access to the most commonly used settings, such as volume, playback tools for music, on/off settings for AirDrop (see next item for more about this feature), Wi-Fi, and Bluetooth, as well buttons for Flashlight, Clock, Calculator, and your Camera. Control Center appears when you flick up from the bottom of the iPad screen.

➡ **AirDrop:** Use this new feature to share pictures, videos, music, and more with somebody in your general vicinity who has an AirDrop-enabled device (iPad fourth generation and later and iPad mini).

➡ **Notification Center:** Swipe down on your iPad screen, and you reveal Notification Center. New Notification Center features in iOS 7 are the Today, All, and Missed views, which help you see useful information such as events on your Calendar, Reminders, and stock values from three perspectives.

➡ **Multitasking:** In iOS 7, Apple has made some changes in the way you work with more than one app at a time. You can press the Home button twice to get a view of all open apps to make it easier to switch among them. Also, your iPad now pays attention to the time you typically use certain apps, such as a social app or stock tracker, and updates their content at that time to make the latest content available to you faster.

➡ **Camera improvements:** Now the Camera app makes various shooting formats (still, video, panorama, and the new square format) easily accessible. In addition, Apple has provided filters so that you can add effects such as higher contrast or black-and-white to your photos with newer iPads.

➡ **Photo categories:** To help you organize your photos, iOS 7 has added Collections, Moments, and Years categories to group your images by the time and location where they were taken. In addition, you can now use iCloud to share photos with others; photos or videos are streamed to everybody's devices. Others can also post items to your stream and even make comments.

➡ **A new look for Safari:** Apple's browser, Safari, helps you get around the Internet. Now it also provides a unified search field so that you can enter a website address or search term and Safari can provide the best match for your entry. The Shared Links feature lets you view information about your Twitter time-line, and the Reading List helps you save and read articles to keep you informed. Finally, iCloud Keychain is a way to have iCloud store all your account names, passwords, and credit card numbers safely. Keychain also helps out by entering informa-tion for you when you need it.

➡ **iTunes Radio:** iTunes Radio offers you streaming music from popular radio stations, but beyond that, it learns about you as you listen. This feature allows you to build new stations, putting you in charge of how many familiar tunes are mixed with new songs to help you expand your musical vocabulary. You can also view a history of what you've heard and build a musical wish list.

➡ **Siri grows up:** Siri has jumped on the new-look bandwagon with a simpler, cleaner look in iOS 7. You can choose between a male or female Siri voice, and enjoy the fact that Siri checks even more sources for its info, including Bing, Wikipedia, and even Twitter postings related to your verbal query.

➡ **App Store apps near you:** In the App Store, you'll find two new features. You can search for apps that are popular in your area and browse the Kids category to find kid-friendly apps.

➡ **Find My iPad security features:** The Find My iPad app helps you locate a missing iPad. In iOS 7, new features help you display a message on the Lock screen stating that this device is lost and provide a phone number where someone can reach you; your iPad can't be used without your sign-in information. If you get your iPad back, you can easily deactivate the message and access your tablet again.

Choose the Right iPad for You

Though there are slight differences in thickness and weight among the different generations of the larger iPad models, if you pick up an iPad (see **Figure 1-1**), you're not likely to be able to tell one model from another at first glance, except that some models are black and some are white or silver and newer models get gradually thinner and lighter. Although the four generations have slightly different heft, and the original iPad is the only one without cameras, the differences are primarily under the hood.

If you're in the market for a new iPad, Apple currently offers iPad fourth-generation models (at a discounted price), iPad Air, and the iPad mini with Retina Display. The newest iPad mini is smaller, but its processor chip and screen resolution match those of the iPad Air. The larger iPads have three variations:

Figure 1-1

➠ Case color

➠ Amount of built-in memory

➠ Method used for connecting to the Internet: Wi-Fi
only, Wi-Fi and 3G (iPad 2), or Wi-Fi and 3G/4G
(all models after iPad 2)

Your options in the first bullet point are pretty black-and-white
(though the iPad Air added a gold color case), but if you're confused
about the other two, read on as I explain these variations in more
detail.

With the fourth-generation model Apple introduced a new kind of
connector, called a *Lightning Connector*, that has a smaller plug at the
end that slots into the iPad itself. For some, the biggest advantage
about the Lightning Connector is that it plugs into your iPad no
matter which way you hold it.

Decide How Much Memory Is Enough

Memory is a measure of how much information — for example, movies, photos, and software applications (or *apps*) — you can store on a computing device. Memory can also affect your iPad's performance when handling tasks such as streaming favorite TV shows from the World Wide Web or downloading music.

Streaming refers to watching video content from the web (or from other devices) rather than playing a file stored on your computing device. You can enjoy a lot of material online without ever downloading its full content to your hard drive — and given that every iPad model has a relatively small amount of memory, that's not a bad idea. See Chapters 11 and 13 for more about getting your music and movies online.

Your memory options with an iPad are 16, 32, 64 or 128 gigabytes (GB). You must choose the right amount of memory, because you can't open the unit and add memory, as you usually can with a desktop computer. Also, you can't insert a *flash drive* (also known as a *USB stick)* to add backup capacity, because the iPad has no USB port — or CD/DVD drive, for that matter. However, Apple has thoughtfully provided iCloud, a service you can use to save space by backing up content to the Internet (you can read more about that in Chapter 3).

With an Apple Digital AV Adapter accessory, you can plug into the Lightening Connector slot to attach an HDMI–enabled device such as an external hard drive for additional storage capacity. See Chapter 13 for more about using these AV features (some of which are just hitting the market). As of this writing, ViewSonic is offering three new HDMI projectors; DVDO is offering an HD Travel Kit for smartphones and tablets; and Belkin has introduced a new line of tools for HDTV streaming, for example.

So how much memory is enough for your iPad? Here's a rule of thumb: If you like lots of media, such as movies or TV shows, and you want to store them on your iPad (rather than experiencing or accessing this content online on sites such as Hulu or Netflix), you might need 64GB or 128GB. For most people who manage a reasonable number of photos, download some music, and watch heavy-duty media such as movies online, 32GB is probably sufficient. If you simply want to check e-mail, browse the web, read e-books, and write short notes to yourself, 16GB *might* be enough.

 Do you have a clue how big a gigabyte (GB) is? Consider this: Just about any computer you buy today comes with a minimum of 250–500GB of storage. Computers have to tackle larger tasks than iPads do, so that number makes sense. The iPad, which uses a technology called *flash* for memory storage, is meant (to a great extent) to help you experience online media and e-mail; it doesn't have to store much and in fact pulls lots of content from online. In the world of memory, 16GB for any kind of storage is puny if you keep lots of content and graphics on the device.

What's the price for more memory? For the iPad Air, a 16GB Wi-Fi unit (see the next task for more about Wi-Fi) costs $499; 32GB jumps the price to $599; and 64GB adds another $100, setting you back a whopping $699. But doubling that to 128GB adds just $100, boosting the price to $799. If you buy an iPad mini, you're looking at $399, $499, $599, and $699 for the four levels of memory it offers.

Choose Wi-Fi Only or Wi-Fi and 3G/4G

One feature that makes the iPad's price and performance variable is whether your model has Wi-Fi only or both Wi-Fi and 3G/4G. Because the iPad is great for browsing online, shopping online, e-mailing, and so on, having an Internet connection for it is important. That's where Wi-Fi and 3G/4G enter the picture. Both technologies are used to connect to the Internet. You use *Wi-Fi* to connect to a wireless network at home or at locations such as your local coffee shop, a grocery store, or an airport that offers Wi-Fi. This type of network uses short-range radio to connect to the Internet; its range is reasonably limited, so if you leave home or walk out of the coffee shop, you can't use it anymore. (These limitations are changing, however, as some towns are installing community-wide Wi-Fi networks.)

The *3G* and *4G* cellphone technologies allow an iPad to connect to the Internet via a widespread cellular-phone network. You use it in much the same way that you make calls from just about anywhere using your cellphone. 3G is available on the iPad 2. 4G is available on the third-generation iPad and later, as well as the iPad mini, but as it's the latest cellular connection technology, it may not always be available in every location. You'll still connect to the Internet when 4G service isn't available, but without the advantage of the super-fast 4G technology.

You can buy an iPad with Wi-Fi only or one with both Wi-Fi and 3G/4G capabilities. Getting a 3G or 4G iPad costs an additional $130 (see **Table 1-1**), but it also includes GPS so that you can get more accurate driving directions. You have to buy an iPad model that fits your data connection provider — either AT&T, Sprint, T-Mobile, or Verizon in the United States.

Also, to use your 3G/4G network, you have to pay Sprint, AT&T, T-Mobile, or Verizon a monthly fee. The good news is that no carrier requires a long-term contract, as you probably had to commit to with your cellphone and its data connection. You can pay for a connection during the month you visit your grandkids, for example, and get rid of it when you arrive home. Though these features and prices could change, at the time of this writing AT&T offers prepaid and postpaid options, but Verizon offers only a prepaid plan. AT&T offers plans that top out at 5GB of data connection, and Verizon offers several levels, including 3GB, 5GB, and 10GB. Note that if you intend to *stream* videos (watch them on your iPad from the Internet), you can eat through these numbers quickly.

Table 1-1	iPad Air Models and Pricing	
Memory Size	*Wi-Fi Price*	*Wi-Fi and 4G Price*
16GB	$499	$629
32GB	$599	$729
64GB	$699	$829
128GB	$799	$929

 Sprint, AT&T, T-Mobile, and Verizon could change their pricing and options at any time, of course, so go to these links for more information about iPad data plans: AT&T is at www.att.com/shop/wireless/devices/ipad.jsp; Verizon is at www.verizonwireless.com/b2c/splash/ipad.jsp; T-Mobile's address is www.t-mobile.com; and Sprint is at http://sprint.com.

So how do you choose? If you want to wander around the woods or town — or take long drives with your iPad continually connected to the Internet to get step-by-step navigation info from the newly rebuilt Maps app — get 3G and pay the price. But if you'll use your iPad mainly at home or via a Wi-Fi *hotspot* (a location where Wi-Fi access to the Internet is available, such as an Internet cafe), don't bother with 3G. Frankly, you can find *lots* of hotspots out there now, at restaurants, hotels, airports, and more.

 You can use the hotspot feature on a smartphone, which allows the iPad to use your phone's 3G or 4G connection to go online if you pay for a higher-data-use plan that supports hotspot use with your phone service carrier. Check out the features of your phone to turn on the hotspot feature.

 Because 3G and 4G iPads are also GPS devices, they know where you are and can act as a navigation system to get you from here to there. The Wi-Fi–only model uses a digital compass and triangulation method for locating your current position, which is less accurate; with no constant Internet connection, it won't help you get around town. If getting accurate directions is one iPad feature that excites you, get 3G/4G, and then see Chapter 15 for more about the Maps feature.

Understand What You Need to Use Your iPad

Before you head off to buy your iPad, you should know what other devices, connections, and accounts you'll need to work with it optimally.

At a bare minimum, you need to be able to connect to the Internet to take advantage of most iPad features. You can open an iCloud account to store and share content online, or you can use a computer to download photos, music, or applications from non-Apple online sources (such as stores, sharing sites, or your local library) and transfer them to your iPad through a process called *syncing*. You can also use a computer or iCloud to register your iPad the first time you start it, although you can have the folks at the Apple Store handle registration for you if you have an Apple Store nearby.

Can you use your iPad without owning a computer and just use public Wi-Fi hotspots to go online (or a 3G/4G connection, if you have such a model)? Yes. To go online using a Wi-Fi–only iPad and to use many of its built-in features at home, however, you need to have a home Wi-Fi network available. You also need to use iCloud or sync to your computer to get updates for the iPad operating system.

For syncing with a computer, Apple's *iPad User Guide* recommends that you have

⟹ A Mac or PC with a USB 2.0 port and one of the following operating systems:

- Mac OS X version 10.6.8 or later

- Windows 8, 7, Windows Vista, or Windows XP Home or Professional with Service Pack 3 or later

➡ iTunes 11 or later, available at www.itunes.com/
download

➡ An Apple ID and iTunes Store account

➡ Internet access

➡ An iCloud account

Apple has set up its iTunes software and the iCloud service to give you two ways to manage content for your iPad — including movies, music, or photos you've downloaded — and specify how to sync your calendar and contact information. Chapter 3 covers those settings in more detail.

Know Where to Buy Your iPad

As of this writing, you can buy an iPad at the Apple Store; at bricks-and-mortar stores such as Best Buy, Walmart, Sam's Club, and Target; and at online sites such as MacMall.com. You can also buy 3G/4G models (models that require an account with a phone service provider) from Sprint, AT&T, T-Mobile, and Verizon.

If you get your iPad from Apple, either at a retail store or online, here's the difference in the buying experience:

➡ The Apple Store advantage is that the sales staff will help you unpack your iPad and make sure that it's working properly, register the device (which you have to do before you can use it; see Chapter 2 for more about this process), and help you learn the basics. Occasional workshops are offered to help people learn about how to use the iPad. Apple employees are famous for being helpful to customers.

➡ Apple Stores aren't on every corner, so if visiting one isn't an option (or you just prefer to go it alone), you can go to the Apple Store website (http://store.apple.com/us/browse/home/shop_ipad/family/ipad) and order an iPad to be shipped to

you — and even get it engraved, if you want.
Standard shipping typically is free, and if there's a
problem, Apple's online store customer service reps
will help you solve the problem or replace your iPad.

Consider iPad Accessories

At present, Apple offers a few accessories that you may want to check
out when you purchase your iPad (or purchase down the road),
including

➡ **iPad Smart Case/Smart Cover:** Your iPad isn't cheap,
and unlike a laptop computer, it has an exposed
screen that can be damaged if you drop or scratch it.
Investing in the iPad Case or Smart Cover is a good
idea if you intend to take your iPad out of your
house — or if you have a cat or grandchildren. The
iPad Smart Cover (see **Figure 1-2**) costs about $40
for polyurethane and $70 for leather, and other cases
vary in price depending on design and material.

Figure 1-2

→ **Printers:** Apple is now offering printers from HP and Epson that support their AirPrint feature. Prices range from $129 to $399.

→ **iPad Dock:** The iPad is light and thin, which is great, but holding it all the time can get tedious. The iPad Dock lets you prop up the device so that you can view it hands-free and then charge the battery and sync to your computer. At about $30, it's a good investment for ease and comfort. Be sure to get one that matches your iPad model.

→ **Apple Digital AV Adapter:** To connect devices to output high-definition media, you can buy this adapter for about $40. More and more devices that use this technology are coming out, such as projectors and TVs. See **Figure 1-3.**

Figure 1-3

→ **Stands:** The Apple Store offers several stands, including the Incase Origami Workstation at $29.95 and the Just Mobile Upstand for iPad at $49.95. The Twelve South HoverBar Stand for iPad costs $79.95, and attaches your iPad to your computer.

Several companies produce iPad accessories, such as cases, and more will undoubtedly pop up, so feel free to do an online search for different items and prices.

Don't bother buying a wireless mouse to connect with your iPad via Bluetooth; the iPad recognizes your finger as its primary input device, and mice need not apply. However, you can use a stylus to tap your input.

Explore What's in the Box

When you fork over your hard-earned money for your iPad, you'll be left holding one box about the size of a package of copy paper. Here's a rundown of what you'll find when you take off the shrink wrap and open the box:

➡ **iPad:** Your iPad is covered in a thick plastic sleeve-thingie that you can take off and toss (unless you think there's a chance that you'll return the device, in which case you may want to keep all packaging for 14 days — Apple's standard return period).

➡ **Documentation** (and I use the term loosely): Notice, under the iPad itself, a small, white envelope about the size of a half-dozen index cards. Open it, and you'll find

- *An iPad Info sheet:* This pamphlet is essentially small print (that you mostly don't need to read) from agencies like the Federal Communications Commission (FCC).

- *A label sheet:* This sheet has two white Apple logos on it. (Apple has provided these for years with its products as a form of cheap advertising when users place stickers on places like their computers or car dashboards.)

- *A small card:* This card displays a picture of the iPad and callouts to its buttons on one side, and the other side contains brief instructions for setting it up and information about where to find out more.

➠ **Lightning to USB Cable (fourth-generation iPad and later and iPad mini first generation and the iPad mini with Retina Display) or Dock Connector to USB Cable (all earlier iPad models):** Use this cord (see **Figure 1-4**) to connect the iPad to your computer, or use it with the last item in the box: the USB Power Adapter.

➠ **10W USB Power Adapter:** The power adapter (refer to **Figure 1-4**) attaches to the Lightning to USB Cable (or the Dock Connector to USB Cable) so that you can plug it into the wall and charge the battery.

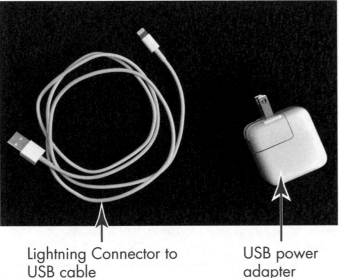

Lightning Connector to
USB cable

USB power
adapter

Figure 1-4

That's it. That's all you'll find in the box. It's kind of a study in Zen-like simplicity.

Take a First Look at the Gadget

The little card contained in the documentation (see the preceding task) gives you a picture of the iPad with callouts to the buttons you'll find on it. In this task, I give you a bit more information about those buttons and other physical features of the iPad. **Figure** 1-5 shows you where each of these items is located.

Figure 1-5

Here's the rundown on what the various hardware features are and what they do:

➡ **(The all-important) Home button:** On the iPad, press this button to go back to the Home screen to find just about anything. The Home screen displays all your installed and preinstalled apps and gives you access to your iPad settings. No matter where you are or what you're doing, press the Home button, and you're back at home base. You can also double-press the Home button to pull up a scrolling list of apps so you can quickly move from one app to another.

➠ **Sleep/Wake button:** You can use this button (whose functionality I cover in more detail in Chapter 2) to power up your iPad, put it in Sleep mode, wake it up, or power it down.

➠ **Lightning Connector slot:** Plug in the Lightning to USB Cable to charge your battery or sync your iPad with your computer (which you find out more about in Chapter 3).

➠ **Cameras:** iPads (except for the original iPad) offer front- and rear-facing cameras, which you can use to shoot photos or video. The rear one is on the top-right corner (if you're looking at the front of the iPad), and you need to be careful not to put your thumb over it when taking shots. (I have several very nice photos of my fingers already.)

➠ **Side Switch:** In case you hadn't heard, the iPad screen rotates to match the angle at which you're holding it. If you want to stick with one orientation even if you spin the iPad in circles, you can use this little switch to lock the screen, which is especially handy when you're reading an e-book. You can also customize the function of the side switch by using iPad General Settings or Control Center to make the switch lock screen rotation rather than mute sound, which it does by default (see Chapter 2 for instructions).

➠ **(Tiny, mighty) Speakers:** One nice surprise when I first got my iPad Air was hearing what a great little stereo sound system it has and how much sound can come from these tiny speakers. The speakers are located along one side of the iPad Air and iPad mini with Retina Display.

➠ **Volume:** Tap the volume switch, called a *rocker,* up for more volume and down for less. With iOS 5 and later, you can use this rocker as a camera shutter button when the camera is activated.

➡ **Headphone jack and microphone:** If you want to listen to your music in private, you can plug in a 3.5mm mini-jack headphone (including an iPhone headset, if you have one, which gives you bidirectional sound). A tiny microphone makes it possible to speak into your iPad and use the Siri personal-assistant feature to do things such as make phone calls using the Internet, use video calling services, dictate your keyboard input, or work with other apps that accept audio input.

Looking Over the Home Screen

I won't kid you: You have a slight learning curve ahead of you, because touchscreen tablets like the iPad are different from other computing devices you may have used (although if you own an iPhone or iPod touch, you've got a huge head start). That's mainly because of its Multi-Touch screen and onscreen keyboard — no mouse necessary. The iPad doesn't have a Windows or Mac operating system: It does have a modified iPhone operating system, so some of the methods you may have used on computers before (such as right-clicking) don't work in quite the same way on the touchscreen.

The good news is that getting anything done on the iPad is simple after you know the ropes. In fact, using your fingers instead of a mouse to do things onscreen is a very intuitive way to communicate with your computing device.

In this chapter, you turn on your iPad and register it and then take your first look at the Home screen. You also practice using the onscreen keyboard, see how to interact with the touchscreen in various ways, get pointers on working with cameras, and get an overview of built-in applications and the new Control Center.

Get ready to . . .

Have a soft cloth handy, like the one you might use to clean your eyeglasses. Despite a screen that's been treated to repel oils, you're about to deposit a ton of fingerprints on your iPad — one downside of a touchscreen device.

See What You Need to Use the iPad

You need to be able, at a minimum, to connect to the Internet to take advantage of most iPad features, which you can do by using a Wi-Fi network or by paying a fee and using a phone provider's network if you bought a 3G or 4G model. You may want to have a computer so that you can connect your iPad to it to download photos, videos, music, or applications and then transfer them to or from your iPad through a process called *syncing*. With iOS 5, a new Apple service called iCloud arrived; when you turn this feature on, it syncs content from all your Apple iOS devices and your Mac and/or PC wirelessly, so anything you buy on your iPhone, for example, will automatically be pushed to your iPad. In addition, you can sync without connecting a cable to a computer by using a Wi-Fi connection to your computer (a wireless network you can set up in your home).

You can register your iPad the first time you start it by using iCloud or by syncing with your computer via a cable, although you can have the folks at the Apple Store handle registration for you if you have an Apple Store nearby.

Can you use the iPad if you don't own a computer and you use public Wi-Fi hotspots to go online (or a 3G/4G connection, if you have one of those models)? Yes. However, to be able to go online using a Wi-Fi–only iPad and to use many of its built-in features at home, you need to have a Wi-Fi network available.

Apple has set up both iCloud and its iTunes software to help you manage content for your iPad — which includes the movies, TV shows, music, or photos you've downloaded — and specify where to transfer your calendar and contact information from. Chapter 3 covers these settings in more detail.

Turn On the iPad and Register It

When you're ready to get going with your new toy be sure you're within range of a Wi-Fi network that you can connect with, and then hold the iPad with one hand on either side, oriented like a pad of paper. Plug the Lightning to USB Cable (or the Dock Connector to USB Cable) that came with your device into your iPad and plug the other end into a USB port on your computer just in case you might lose your battery charge during the setup process.

Now follow these steps to set up and register your iPad:

1. Press and hold the Sleep/Wake button on the top of your iPad until the Apple logo appears.

In another moment, a screen appears with a cheery Hello on it.

2. Slide your finger to the right on the screen where it says "Slide to Set Up".

3. You next see a series of screens that involve the following settings:

- *Language:* Choose the language you prefer iPad screens to display.

- *Country or Region:* Select the place where you live.

- *Choose a Wi-Fi Network* (see **Figure 2-1**): This is where you get online so you can connect with Apple, register your iPad, and make certain settings.

- *Location Services:* You can Enable or Disable this feature which allows certain apps, such as Maps and Find My iPad to determine the physical location of your iPad.

- *Set Up iPad:* On this screen you can choose to set your device up as a new iPad, or to restore settings and content you've previously backed up to iCloud, or saved in iTunes. If you choose the latter you should have connected your iPad to the computer on which you have iTunes installed.

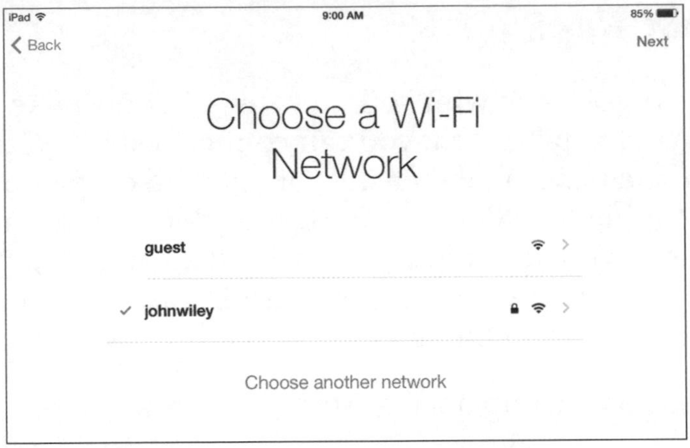

iPad 📶   9:00 AM   85% 🔋

‹ Back   Next

Choose a Wi-Fi Network

guest   📶 ›

✓ johnwiley   🔒 📶 ›

Choose another network

Figure 2-1

- *Apple ID:* Here you can sign in with an existing Apple ID, or create a new one.

- *Terms & Conditions:* Tap Agree to proceed; if you tap Disagree you can proceed. If you want a copy of the terms and conditions tap Send by Email. After you agree a screen appears saying it may take a few minutes to set up your Apple ID.

- *iCloud:* Tap Use or Don't Use depending on whether you want content automatically backed up to iCloud. (I recommend you tap Use here because iCloud backup is a handy feature).

- *Find My iPad:* If you tap Use this feature of iCloud is turned on and if you lose your iPad, it can help you locate it.

- *Create a Passcode:* If you want to require a passcode be entered to access your iPad for security reasons, enter a four digit code on this screen.

- *iCloud Keychain:* Keychain is an optional service you can use to store your passwords and credit card information in one handy and secure place. If you don't want to set this up you can tap Set Up Later.

- *Use iPad Passcode as iCloud Security Code:* By choosing Use on this screen the passcode you entered a couple of screens ago will be used to access iCloud; if you'd rather have a unique passcode, tap Create Different Code on this screen (see **Figure 2-2**).

Use iPad Passcode as iCloud Security Code?

Your iCloud Security Code can be used to set up iCloud Keychain on a new device.

Use Passcode

Create Different Code

Figure 2-2

- *Phone Number:* The phone number you enter, which must be able to receive text messages, will be used to verify your security code.

- *Siri:* Siri is a personal assistant feature that can answer questions, make appointments, create and send emails, and more. Tap Use to use the Siri feature; note that if you tap Don't Use here you can still turn Siri on later through General Settings.

- *Diagnostics:* If you don't mind if information about any errors or problems on your iPad is shared with Apple, tap Automatically Send. If you want to opt out, tap Don't Send.

- *Registration:* Tap to register your iPad with Apple, which is a good idea so they can send you information about updates and cover your device with a warranty.

4. After you deal with all the setup screens, a Welcome to iPad screen appears; tap Get Started to display the Home screen.

 You can choose to have certain items transferred to your iPad from your computer when you sync via iTunes or a wireless sync, including music, videos, downloaded apps, contacts, audiobooks, calendars, e-books, podcasts, and browser bookmarks. You can also transfer to your computer any content you download directly to your iPad by using the iTunes, iTunes U, Newsstand, iBooks, Podcasts, and App Store apps. See Chapters 8 and 9 for more about these features.

If you set up iCloud when registering or after registering (see Chapter 3), updates to your operating system will be pushed to your iPad without your having to plug it into a computer running iTunes. Apple refers to this feature as *PC Free,* simply meaning that your device has been liberated from having to use a physical connection to a computer to get upgrades.

Meet the Multi-Touch Screen

When the iPad Home screen appears (see **Figure 2-3**), you see a pretty background and two sets of icons. One set appears on the Dock, along the bottom of the screen. The *Dock* contains the Safari, Mail, Photos, and Music app icons by default, though you can add up to two other apps to it. The Dock appears on every Home screen. Another set of icons appears above the Dock, and are closer to the top of the screen. (I cover all these icons in the "Take Inventory of Built-in Apps" task, later in this chapter.) Different icons appear in this area on each Home screen. You can add new apps to populate as many as 11 additional Home screens and move apps from one Home screen to another (see Chapter 9 for more about this).

 Treat the iPad screen carefully. It's made of glass and will smudge when you touch it (and will break if you throw it at the wall).

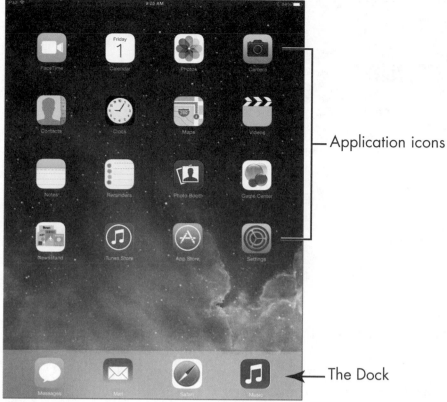

Application icons

The Dock

Figure 2-3

The iPad uses *touchscreen technology*. When you swipe your finger across the screen or tap it, you're providing input to the device just as you use a mouse or keyboard with your computer. You hear more about the touchscreen in the next task, but for now, go ahead and play with it for a few minutes; really, you can't hurt anything. Use the pads of your fingertips (not your fingernails), and follow these steps:

1. Tap the Settings icon. The various settings (which you read more about throughout this book) appear, as shown in **Figure** 2-4.

2. To return to the Home screen, press the Home button.

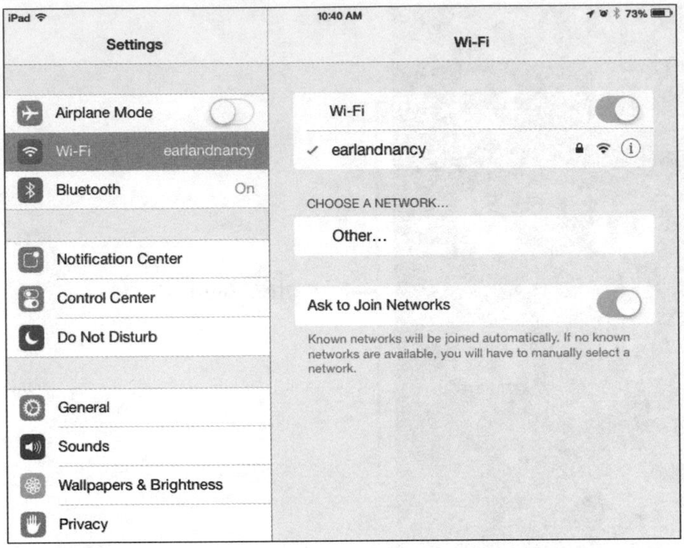

iPad 🖥	10:40 AM	◀ ✻ ✷ 73% 🔋
Settings	**Wi-Fi**	

✈ Airplane Mode ⚪

🖥 Wi-Fi   earlandnancy

✻ Bluetooth   On

📷 Notification Center

🎛 Control Center

🌙 Do Not Disturb

⚙ General

🔊 Sounds

🌼 Wallpapers & Brightness

✋ Privacy

Wi-Fi ⚫

✓ earlandnancy   🔒 🖥 ⓘ

CHOOSE A NETWORK...

Other...

Ask to Join Networks ⚫

Known networks will be joined automatically. If no known
networks are available, you will have to manually select a
network.

Figure 2-4

3. Swipe a finger or two from right to left on the screen.
If downloaded apps fill additional Home screens, this
action moves you to the next Home screen. Note that the
little dots at the bottom of the screen, above the Dock
icons, indicate which Home screen is displayed.

4. To experience the screen rotation feature, hold the iPad
firmly while turning it sideways. The screen flips to horizontal orientation. To flip the screen back, just turn the
device so it's oriented like a pad of paper again.

5. Drag your finger down from the top of the screen to
reveal Notification Center (covered in Chapter 17); drag
up from the bottom of the Home screen to display
Control Central (discussed later in this chapter).

You can customize the Home screen by changing its
wallpaper (background picture) and brightness. You
can read about making these changes in Chapter 4.

Goodbye Click-and-Drag, Hello Tap-and-Swipe

You can use several methods to get around and get things done on the iPad by using its Multi-Touch screen, including

➡ **Tap once.** To open an application on the Home screen, choose a field such as a search box, select an item in a list, select an arrow to move back or forward one screen, or follow an online link, tap the item once with your finger.

➡ **Tap twice.** Use this method to enlarge or reduce the display of a web page (see Chapter 5 for more about using the Safari web browser) or to zoom in or out in the Maps app.

➡ **Pinch.** As an alternative to the tap-twice method, you can pinch your fingers together or move them apart on the screen when you're looking at photos, maps, web pages (see **Figure 2-5**), or e-mail messages to quickly reduce or enlarge them, respectively.

You can use a three-finger tap to zoom your screen to be even larger or use multitasking gestures to swipe with four or five fingers (see the "Explore Multitasking Gestures" task later in this chapter). This method is handy if you have vision challenges. Go to Chapter 4 to discover how to turn on this feature by using Accessibility settings.

➡ **Drag to scroll (known as** *swiping)*. When you press your finger to the screen and drag to the right or left, the screen moves (see **Figure 2-6**). Swiping to the left on the Home screen, for example, moves you to the next Home screen. Swiping up while reading an online newspaper moves you down the page; swiping down moves you back up the page.

Figure 2-5

Figure 2-6

➠ **Flick.** To scroll more quickly on a page, quickly flick your finger on the screen in the direction in which you want to move.

 Notice that when you rock your iPad backward or forward, the background moves as well. This *parallax* feature is new in iOS 7. You can disable this feature if it makes you seasick. Tap Settings➪General➪ Accessibility and then tap and turn off the Reduce Motion setting.

➡ **Tap the Status bar.** To move quickly to the top of a list, web page, or e-mail message, tap the Status bar at the top of the iPad screen.

➡ **Press and hold.** If you're using Notes or Mail or any other application that lets you select text, or if you're on a web page, pressing and holding text selects a word and displays editing tools you can use to select, cut or copy, and paste the text.

Try these methods now by following these steps:

1. Tap the Safari button on the Dock at the bottom of any iPad Home screen to display the web browser. (You may be asked to enter your network password to access the network.)

2. Tap a link (typically, colored text or a button or image) to move to another page.

3. Double-tap the page to enlarge it; then pinch your fingers together onscreen to reduce it.

4. Drag one finger around the page to scroll up, down, or side to side.

5. Flick your finger quickly on the page to scroll more quickly.

6. Press and hold your finger on black text that isn't a link (links usually are blue and take you to another location on the web). The word is selected, and the Copy/Define tool is displayed, as shown in **Figure 2-7**. (You can use this tool to get a definition of a word or copy it.)

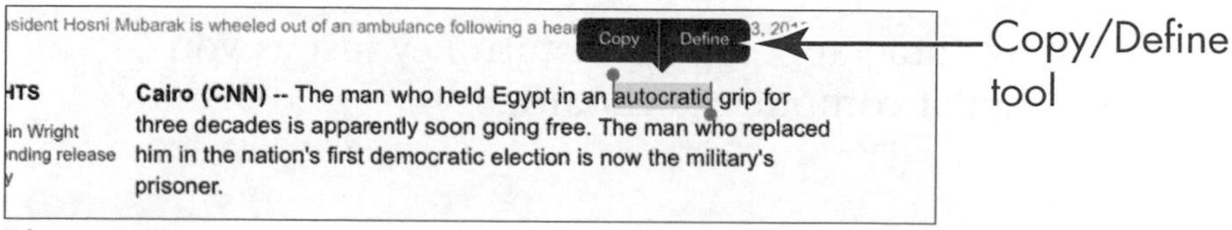

Copy/Define tool

Figure 2-7

7. Press and hold your finger on a link or an image. A menu appears, with commands you select to open the link or picture, open it in a new page, add it to your Reading List (see Chapter 5), or copy it. If you press and hold an image, the menu also offers the Save Image command.

8. Position your fingers slightly apart on the screen and then pinch your fingers together to reduce the page. With your fingers already pinched together, place them on the screen and then move them apart to enlarge the page.

9. Press the Home button to go back to the Home screen.

Display and Use the Onscreen Keyboard

1. The built-in iPad keyboard appears whenever you're in a text-entry location, such as a search field or an e-mail message. Tap the Notes icon on the Home screen to open this easy-to-use notepad and try out the keyboard.

2. Tap the note page, or if you've already entered notes, tap one to display the page; then tap anywhere on the note. The onscreen keyboard appears.

3. Type a few words, using the keyboard. To make the keyboard display as wide as possible, rotate your iPad to landscape (horizontal) orientation, as shown in **Figure 2-8**.

4. If you make a mistake while using the keyboard — and you will when you first use it — press the Delete key (it's in the top-right corner, with the little x on it) to delete text to the left of the insertion point.

5. To create a new paragraph, tap the Return key just as you would on a regular computer keyboard.

6. To type numbers and symbols, tap the number key (labeled *.?123)* on either side of the spacebar (refer to **Figure 2-8**). The characters on the keyboard change. If you type a number and then tap the spacebar, the keyboard returns to the letter keyboard automatically. To return to the letter keyboard at any time, simply tap one of the letter keys (labeled *ABC)* on either side of the spacebar.

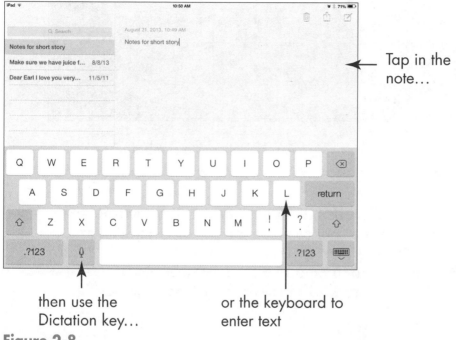

Tap in the note...

then use the Dictation key...

or the keyboard to enter text

Figure 2-8

7. Use the Shift keys (thick upward-pointing arrows in the bottom-left and bottom-right corners of the keyboard) just as you would on a regular keyboard to type upper-case letters or alternative characters. Tapping a Shift key once causes just the next letter you type to be capitalized.

8. Double-tap the Shift key to turn on the Caps Lock feature so that all letters you type are capitalized until you turn the feature off. Tap the Shift key once to turn off Caps Lock. (You have to turn this feature on by opening iPad Settings and under General settings, tapping Keyboard.)

9. To type a variation on a symbol (such as to see alternative currency symbols when you press the dollar sign on the numeric keyboard), hold down the key; a set of alternative symbols appears (see **Figure 2-9**). Note that this trick works only with certain symbols.

A set of alternate symbols

Figure 2-9

10. Tap the Dictation key (refer to **Figure 2-8**) to activate the Dictation feature (not available on the original iPad and the iPad 2), and then speak your input. Tap the Dictation key again (or tap in a note) to turn off the Dictation feature. (This feature works in several apps, such as Mail, Notes, and Maps.)

11. To hide the keyboard, tap the Keyboard key in the bottom-right corner.

12. Press the Home button to return to the Home screen.

 You can undock the keyboard to move it around the screen. To do this, press and hold the Keyboard key on the keyboard, and from the pop-up menu that appears, choose Undock. Now, by pressing the Keyboard key and swiping up or down, you can move the keyboard up and down on the screen. To dock the keyboard at the bottom of the screen again, press and hold the Keyboard key, and choose Dock from the pop-up menu.

To type a period and space, just double-tap the spacebar.

Use the Split Keyboard

1. With iOS 5 came the *split keyboard* feature, which allows you to split the keyboard so that each side appears nearer the edge of the iPad screen. For those who are into texting or typing with thumbs, this feature makes it easier to reach all the keys from the sides of the device. Open an application such as Notes where you can use the onscreen keyboard.

2. Tap in an entry field or page that displays the onscreen keyboard.

3. Place two fingers in the middle of the onscreen keyboard, and spread them left and right. The keyboard splits, as shown in **Figure 2-10.**

4. Now hold the iPad with a hand on either side and practice using your thumbs to enter text.

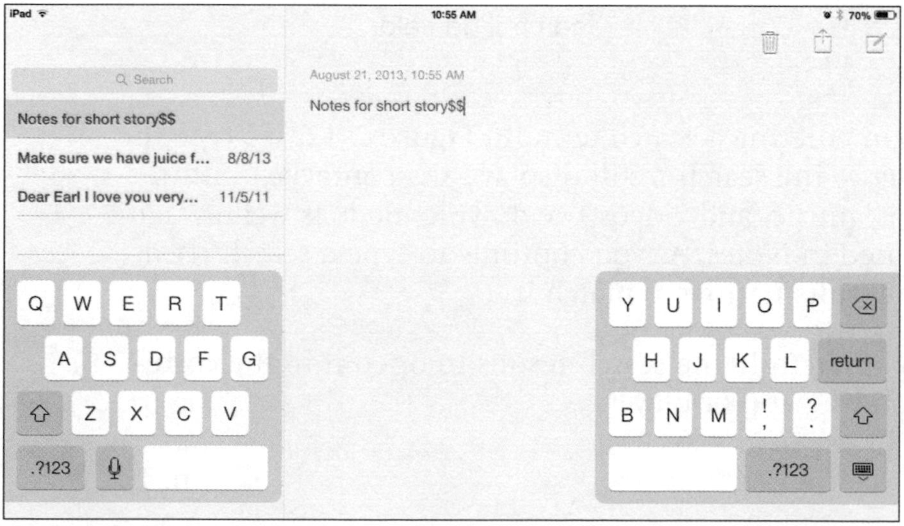

Figure 2-10

5. To rejoin the keyboard, place two fingers on each side of the keyboard and swipe to join them again.

 When the keyboard is docked and merged at the bottom of your screen, you can also simply press the Keyboard key and swipe upward simultaneously. This action undocks and splits the keyboard. To revert this action, press the Keyboard key and swipe downward. The keyboard is docked and merged.

Flick to Search

1. The search feature of the iPad helps you find photos, music, e-mails, contacts, movies, and more. Swipe down from any Home screen (but not from the top or bottom of the screen) to reveal the Search feature.

2. Tap in the Search iPad field (see **Figure 2-11**). The keyboard appears.

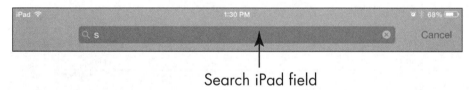

Search iPad field

Figure 2-11

3. Begin entering a search term. In **Figure 2-12,** if I type the letter *S*, the search result displays any contacts, built-in apps, music, and videos I've downloaded, as well as items created in Notes. As you continue to type a search term, the results narrow to match it.

4. Tap an item in the search results to open it in the corresponding app or player.

Figure 2-12

Update the Operating System to iOS 7

1. This book is based on the latest version of the iPad operating system at the time of writing: iOS 7. To be sure you have the latest and greatest features, update your iPad to the latest iOS now (and periodically, to receive minor upgrades to iOS 7). If you've set up an iCloud account on your iPad, updates happen automatically; otherwise, you can update over a Wi-Fi or 3G/4G connection by tapping Settings⇨General⇨Software Update. To use a physical connection to a computer to update the iOS, plug the Lightning to USB Cable (or Dock Connector to USB Cable) into your iPad, and plug the USB end into your computer's USB port.

2. When iTunes opens, click your iPad (in the top-right corner of the iTunes window or source list on the left if it's displayed) and then click the Summary tab, if it isn't already displayed (see **Figure 2-13**).

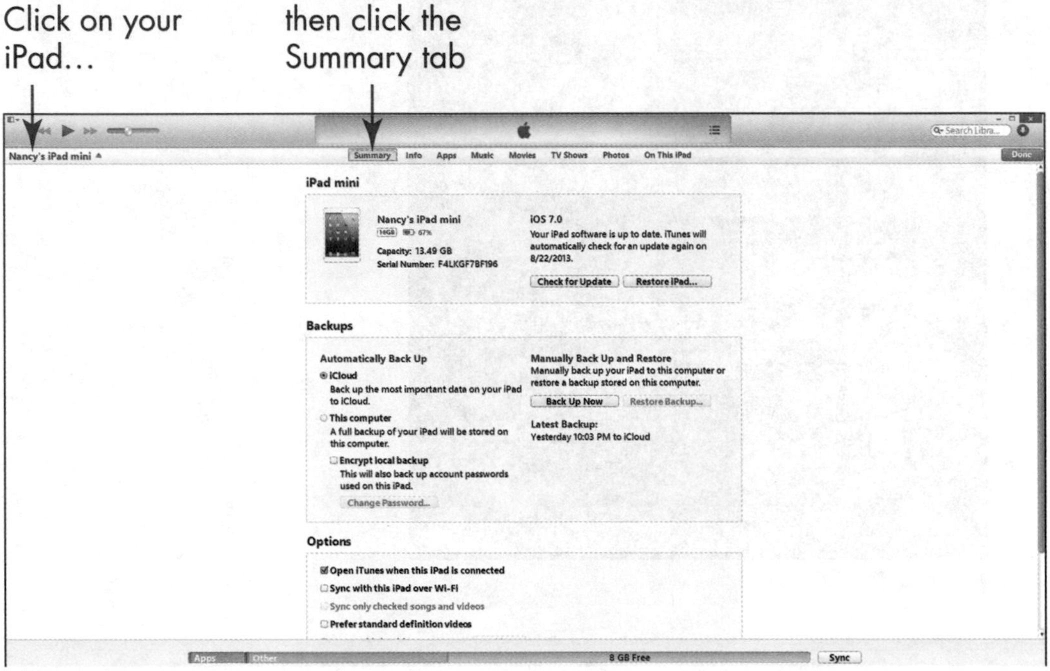

Click on your
iPad...

then click the
Summary tab

Figure 2-13

3. Read the note above the Check for Update button to see whether your iOS is up to date. If it isn't, click the Check for Update button. iTunes searches for the latest iOS version and walks you through the updating procedure.

A new iOS version may introduce new features for your iPad. If a new iOS appears after you buy this book, go to the companion website at www.ipadmadeclear.com for updates on new features introduced in major updates.

Learn Multitasking Basics

1. *Multitasking* lets you easily switch from one app to another without closing the first one and returning to the Home screen. With iOS 7, you can accomplish this task by previewing all open apps and jumping from one to another, and quit an app by simply swiping upward. First, open an app.

2. Double-press the Home button.

3. On the app preview screen that appears (see **Figure** 2-14), flick to scroll to the left or right to locate another app that you want to display.

Figure 2-14

4. Tap an app to open it.

 Press the Home button to remove the multitasking bar from the Home screen and return to the app you were working in.

Explore Multitasking Gestures

Multitasking involves jumping from one app to another. Introduced in iOS 5, the Multitasking Gestures feature allows you to use four or five fingers to multitask. You can turn on these gestures by tapping Settings on the Home screen and then, in the General Settings screen, tapping the On/Off button for Multitasking Gestures.

Here are the three multitasking gestures you can use:

➡ Swipe up with four or five fingers on any Home screen to reveal the multitasking bar.

➡ Swipe down with four or five fingers to remove the multitasking bar from the Home screen.

➡ With an app open, swipe left or right with four or five fingers to move to another app.

Examine the iPad Cameras

iPad 2 introduced front- and back-facing cameras to the iPad hardware feature list. The fourth-generation iPad and iPad mini introduced a higher-quality front-facing camera for FaceTime. You can use the cameras to take still photos (covered in detail in Chapter 12) or shoot videos (covered in Chapter 13).

There's good news and bad news. The good news is that the third- and fourth-generation iPads and the iPad Air have a super-clear Retina display and a 5-megapixel rear-facing iSight camera for viewing and taking the best iPad-generated photos and video yet. The bad news is that if you own an original iPad, you have no cameras at all.

For now, take a quick look at your camera by tapping the Camera icon on the Home screen. The Camera app opens, as shown in **Figure 2-15**.

You can use the controls on the screen to

➡ Switch between the front and rear cameras.

➡ Change from still-camera to video-camera operation by using the Camera/Video slider.

➡ Take a picture or start recording a video.

➡ Turn HDR (high dynamic range) for better contrast on or off.

➡ Open previously captured images or videos.

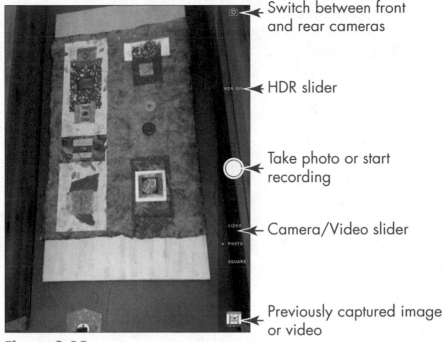

Switch between front
and rear cameras

HDR slider

Take photo or start
recording

Camera/Video slider

Previously captured image
or video

Figure 2-15

When you view a photo or video, you can share it by posting it to
Facebook or send it by using AirDrop in a tweet, message, or e-mail.
You can also print the image, use it as wallpaper (your Home- or Lock-
screen background image), assign it to a contact, run a slideshow, or
edit it. See Chapters 12 and 13 for more detail about using the iPad
cameras.

Customize the Side Switch

Starting with iOS 4.3, you can customize the Side Switch on the top-
right side of your iPad (in portrait orientation). Use these steps to set
up the switch to control screen rotation or mute the sound:

1. On the Home screen, tap the Settings icon.

2. Under General Settings, tap either the Lock Rotation or
Mute option in the Use Side Switch To section to choose
which feature you want the switch to control.

3. Press the Home button to return to the Home screen.

4. Move the Side Switch up or down to toggle between the settings you chose: lock or unlock screen rotation, or mute or unmute sound.

Explore the Status Bar

Across the top of the iPad screen is the *Status bar* (see **Figure** 2-16). Tiny icons in this area can provide useful information such as the time, battery level, and wireless-connection status. **Table** 2-1 lists some of the most common items you find on the Status bar.

iPad 🛜	2:19 PM	⦿ ☀ 65% 🔋

Figure 2-16

Table 2-1   Common Status Bar Icons

Icon	Name	What It Indicates
☀	Activity	A task is in progress — a web page is loading, for example.
🔋	Battery Life	The charge percentage remaining in the battery. The indicator changes to a lightning bolt when the battery is charging.
✳	Bluetooth	Bluetooth service is on and paired with a wireless device.
🔒	Screen Orientation Lock	The screen is locked and doesn't rotate when you turn the iPad.
12:07 PM	Time	You guessed it: You see the time.
🛜	Wi-Fi	You're connected to a Wi-Fi network.

If you have GPS, 3G, 4G, or Bluetooth service or a connection to a virtual private network (VPN), a corresponding symbol appears on the Status bar whenever one of these features is active. The GPS and 3G/4G icons appear only on 3G- or 4G-enabled iPad models. (If you can't even conceive of what a VPN is, my advice is not to worry about it.)

Take Inventory of Built-in Apps

The iPad comes with certain functionality and applications — or *apps*, for short — preinstalled. When you look at the Home screen, you see icons for each app. This task gives you an overview of what each app does. (You can find out more about every one of them as you read different chapters of this book.) From left to right, the icons on the Dock (refer to the "Meet the Multi-Touch Screen" task earlier in this chapter) are

➡ **Safari:** You use the Safari web browser (see **Figure 2-17**) to navigate on the Internet, create and save bookmarks of favorite sites, and add web clips to your Home screen so that you can quickly visit favorite sites from there. You may have used this web browser (or another such as Internet Explorer) on your desktop computer.

Figure 2-17

➡ **Mail:** You use this application to access mail accounts that you've set up for the iPad. When you do, your e-mail is displayed without your having to browse to the site or sign in. Then you can use tools to move among a few preset mail folders, read and reply to mail, and download attached photos to your iPad. Read more about e-mail accounts in Chapter 6.

➠ **Videos:** This media player is similar to Music but specializes in playing videos and offers a few features specific to this type of media, such as chapter breakdowns and information about a movie's plot and cast. From iOS 6 on, this app is placed on the Dock by default.

➠ **Music:** Music is the name of your audio media player. Though its main function is to play music, you can use it to play podcasts or audiobooks as well.

Apps with icons above the Dock and closer to the top of the Home screen include

➠ **Messages:** For those who have been waiting for instant messaging on iPad, the iMessage feature comes to the rescue. Using the Messages app, you can engage in live text- and image-based conversations with others via their phones or other devices that use messaging.

➠ **Photos:** The photo application in iPad helps you organize pictures in folders, e-mail photos to others, use a photo as your iPad wallpaper, and assign pictures to contact records. You can also run slideshows of your photos, open albums, pinch or unpinch to shrink or expand photos, and scroll photos with a simple swipe. As of iOS 6, you can use the Photo Stream feature via iCloud to share photos among your friends. In iOS 7, Photos displays images by collections, including Years and Moments, and offers filters you can apply to pictures you've taken to achieve different effects (see **Figure 2-18**).

➠ **Camera:** As you may have read earlier in this chapter, the Camera app is central control for the still and video cameras built into the iPad 2 and later. In addition the FaceTime app uses your iPad camera to make and receive FaceTime (video) calls.

Figure 2-18

⟹ **Maps:** In this cool Apple mapping program, you can view classic maps or aerial views of addresses; find directions from one place to another by car or foot; and view your maps in 3-D. You can even get your directions read out loud by a spoken narration feature.

⟹ **Clock:** This app, which appeared with iOS 6, allows you to display clocks from around the world, set alarms, and use timer and stopwatch features.

⟹ **Photo Booth:** This fun app, which has been supplied with Mac computers for some time, lets you add effects to photos you take with your iPad camera in weird and wonderful ways.

⟹ **Calendar:** Use this handy onscreen daybook to set up appointments and send alerts to remind you about them.

⟹ **Contacts:** In this address-book feature (see **Figure 2-19**), you can enter contact information (including photos, if you like, from your Photos or Cameras app) and share contact information by e-mail. You can also use the search feature to find your contacts easily.

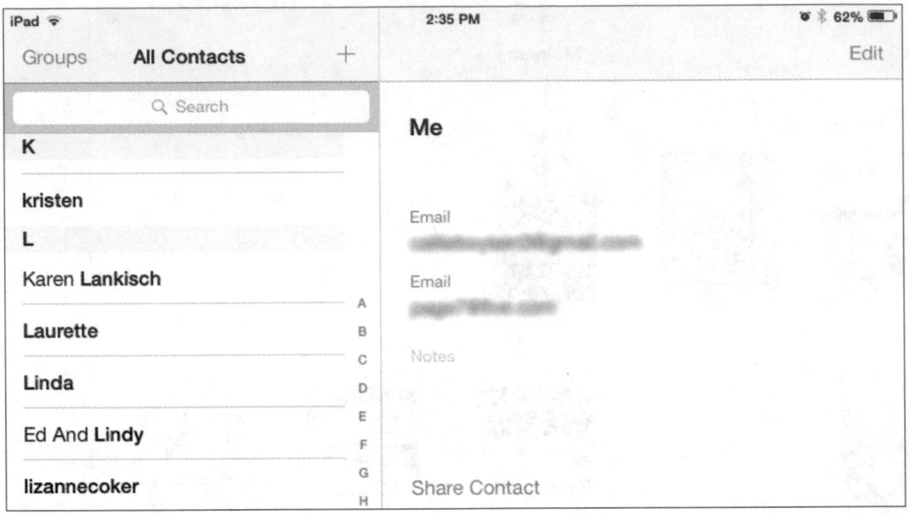

Figure 2-19

➠ **Notes:** Enter text or cut and paste text from a website into this simple notepad app. You can't do much except save notes or e-mail them; the app has no features for formatting text or inserting objects. You'll find Notes handy, though, for taking simple notes on the fly.

➠ **Reminders:** This useful app centralizes all your calendar entries and alerts to keep you on schedule, and also allows you to create to-do lists.

➠ **Newsstand:** Similar to an e-reader for books, Newsstand is a handy reader app for subscribing to and reading magazines, newspapers, and other periodicals.

➠ **iTunes Store:** Tapping this icon takes you to the iTunes Store, where you can shop 'til you drop (or until your iPad battery runs out of juice) for music, movies, TV shows, audiobooks, and podcasts and then download them directly to your iPad. (See Chapter 8 for more about how iTunes works.)

➠ **App Store:** At the online App Store, you can buy and download applications that enable you to do everything from playing games to building business presentations. Some of these apps are even free!

⟼ **Game Center:** The Game Center app helps you browse games in the App Store and track scores when you play games with other people online. You can add friends and challenge one another to beat best scores. See Chapter 14 for more about Game Center.

⟼ **Settings:** Settings isn't exactly an app, but it's an icon you should know about, anyway: It's the central location on the iPad where you can specify settings for various functions and perform administrative tasks such as set up e-mail accounts or create a password.

⟼ **FaceTime:** The FaceTime video-calling app lets you use the iPad cameras (not present on the original iPad) to talk face-to-face with someone who has an iPad 2; third- or fourth generation iPad; iPad Air; iPad mini or iPad mini with Retina Display; Mac (running OS X 10.6.6 or later); fourth-generation iPod touch or later; or iPhone 4 or later. Chapter 7 fills you in on FaceTime features.

The iBooks application isn't bundled with the iPad out of the box. Though iBooks is free, you have to download it from the App Store. Because the iPad has been touted as an outstanding *e-reader* — a device that enables you to read books on an electronic device, similar to the Amazon Kindle — you should definitely consider downloading the app as soon as possible. For more about downloading applications for your iPad, see Chapter 9. To work with the iBooks e-reader application itself, go to Chapter 10.

Discover Control Center

1. With iOS 7 comes Control Center, a one-stop screen for common features and settings, such as connecting to a network, increasing screen brightness or volume, and using the Calculator or Camera. To display Control Center, swipe up from the bottom of the screen.

2. At the bottom of the screen that appears, tap a button or slider to access or adjust a setting (see **Figure 2-20**).

3. Swipe the top of Control Center down to hide it.

Figure 2-20

Lock the iPad, Turn It Off, and Unlock It

Earlier in this chapter, I mention how simple it is to turn on the power to your iPad. Now it's time to put it to *sleep* (a state in which the screen goes black, though you can quickly wake up the iPad) or to turn off the power to give your new toy a rest. Here are the procedures you can use:

➡ **Press the Sleep/Wake button.** The iPad goes to sleep: The screen goes black and is locked.

➡ **Press the Home button.** The iPad wakes up. Swipe the onscreen arrow on the Slide to Unlock bar at the bottom of the screen to unlock the iPad.

➡ **On any app or Home screen, press and hold the Sleep/Wake button until the Slide to Power Off bar appears at the top of the screen; then swipe the bar.** You've just turned off your iPad.

 The iPad automatically enters sleep mode after a few minutes of inactivity. You can change the time interval at which it sleeps by adjusting the Auto-Lock feature in Settings. See this book's companion Cheat Sheet at www.dummies.com/cheatsheet/ipadforseniors to review tables of various settings.

Getting Going

Your first step in getting to work with the iPad is making sure that its battery is charged. Next, if you want to find free or paid content for your iPad from Apple, from movies to music to e-books to audiobooks, you may want to open an iTunes account.

After you have an iTunes account and the latest iTunes software on your computer, you can connect your iPad to your computer and sync them to exchange content between them (for example, to transfer your saved photos or music to the iPad). You can also use the wireless sync feature to exchange content over a wireless network.

If you prefer, you can take advantage of the iCloud service from Apple to store and *push* (send or share) all kinds of content and data to all your Apple devices —wirelessly.

This chapter also introduces you to the *iPad User Guide*, which you access using the Safari browser on your iPad. The guide essentially serves as your iPad Help system to provide advice and information about your magical new device.

Charge the Battery

1. My iPad showed up in the box almost fully charged, and let's hope yours did, too. Because all batteries run down

Get ready to...

eventually, one of your first priorities is to know how to recharge your iPad battery. Go get your iPad and its Lightning to USB Cable (iPad fourth generation and later) and the Apple USB power adapter.

2. Gently plug the USB end of the Lightning to USB Cable (or the Dock Connector to USB Cable) into the USB Power Adapter.

3. Plug the other end of the cord (see **Figure 3-1**) into the Lightning Connector (or Dock Connector) slot on the iPad.

Attach the USB Connector
to the power adapter

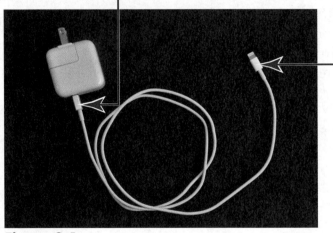

Plug this end
into the iPad

Figure 3-1

4. Unfold the two metal prongs on the power adapter (refer to **Figure 3-1**) so that they extend from it at a 90-degree angle; then plug the adapter into an electrical outlet.

 If you buy the iPad Dock accessory ($29), you can charge your iPad while it's resting on the Dock. Just plug the larger connector into the back of the Dock instead of at the bottom of the iPad.

Power adapters for earlier versions of the iPad or other Apple devices (such as the iPhone and iPod) no longer work with your fourth-generation iPad or iPad Air. Adapters are available from Apple and other companies, however.

Make iPad Settings Using iTunes

1. Before you can use iTunes to manage your iPad, you have to download the latest version of iTunes by going to www.apple.com/itunes. You should also create an iTunes account, providing a payment method so that you can use iTunes on your computer or the iTunes app on your iPad to purchase apps and content.

2. Next, open your iTunes software on your computer. (On a Windows 7 computer, choose Start➪All Programs➪iTunes; on a Windows 8 or 8.1 computer, begin typing iTunes on the Start screen and then click iTunes on the search results; on a Mac, click the iTunes icon on the Dock or Launchpad.) iTunes opens, and if you've connected it to your computer using the Lightning to USB Cable (or Dock Connector to USB Cable), your iPad is listed near the top-right corner, as shown in **Figure** 3-2.

Figure 3-2

3. Click your iPad, and a series of tabs displays. The tabs offer information about your iPad and settings to determine how to download music, movies, or podcasts, for example. (**Figure 3-3** shows the settings on the Summary tab that control backups and updating of the iOS.) The settings on the various tabs relate to the kind of content you want to download and whether you want to download it automatically (when you sync) or manually. See **Table 3-1** for an overview of the settings that are available on each tab.

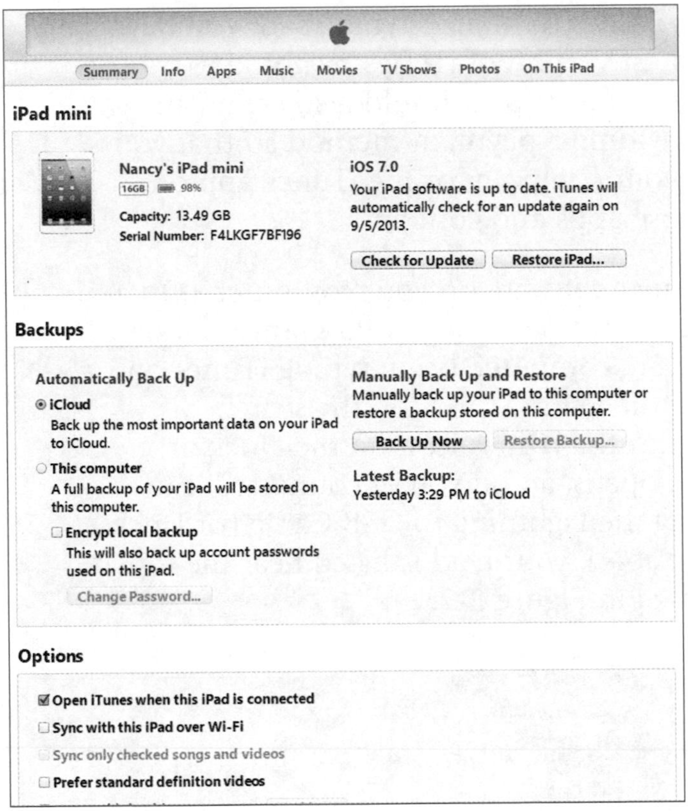

iPad mini

Nancy's iPad mini
16GB 98%
Capacity: 13.49 GB
Serial Number: F4LKGF7BF196

iOS 7.0
Your iPad software is up to date. iTunes will automatically check for an update again on 9/5/2013.

Check for Update   Restore iPad...

Backups

Automatically Back Up

◉ iCloud
Back up the most important data on your iPad to iCloud.

○ This computer
A full backup of your iPad will be stored on this computer.

☐ Encrypt local backup
This will also back up account passwords used on this iPad.

Change Password...

Manually Back Up and Restore
Manually back up your iPad to this computer or restore a backup stored on this computer.

Back Up Now   Restore Backup...

Latest Backup:
Yesterday 3:29 PM to iCloud

Options

☑ Open iTunes when this iPad is connected
☐ Sync with this iPad over Wi-Fi
☐ Sync only checked songs and videos
☐ Prefer standard definition videos

Figure 3-3

4. Make all settings for the types of content you plan to obtain on your computer. **Table 3-1** provides information about the settings on the different tabs.

Table 3-1	iPad Settings in iTunes
Tab Name	**What You Can Do with the Settings on the Tab**
Summary	Perform updates to the iPad software and set general backup and syncing options.
Info	Specify which information to sync: Contacts, Calendars, e-mail accounts, Bookmarks, or Notes. Perform an advanced replacement of info on the iPad with info from the computer.
Apps	Sync with the iPad the apps you've downloaded to your computer, and manage the locations of those apps and folders. Choose whether to install new apps automatically.
Tones	Sync ringtones and sound effects from the iTunes Tones Store.
Music	Choose which music to download to your iPad when you sync.
Movies	Specify whether to download movies automatically.
TV Shows	Choose shows and episodes to sync automatically.
Photos	Choose the folders from which you want to download photos or albums.
On This iPad	Select content on the iPad to copy to iTunes.

 If you've downloaded certain Apple apps, such as iTunes U or Podcasts, settings for them may appear here as well.

Sync the iPad to Your Computer Using iTunes

1. After you specify which content to download in iTunes (see the preceding task), you can use the Lightning to USB Cable (or Dock Connector to USB Cable) to connect your iPad and computer at any time and sync files, contacts, calendar settings, and more. After iTunes is downloaded to your computer and your iTunes account is set up, plug the smaller end of your Lightning to USB Cable into your iPad, and plug the other end of the cord into a USB port on your computer. iTunes opens and shows an icon for your iPad near the top-right corner.

2. Click the Sync button in the bottom-right corner (refer to **Figure 3-3**). Your iPad screen shows the phrase *Sync in Progress.* When the syncing is complete, the Lock screen returns on the iPad.

3. Disconnect the cable. Any media you chose to transfer in your iTunes settings, and any new photos in the photos folder on your computer, have been transferred to your iPad.

Sync Wirelessly

1. You can use the iTunes Wi-Fi Sync setting to allow cordless syncing if you're within range of a Wi-Fi network that has a computer connected to it with iTunes installed. Tap Settings➪General➪iTunes Wi-Fi Sync.

2. In the dialog shown in **Figure 3-4**, tap Sync Now to sync with a computer connected to the same Wi-Fi network.

iPad 🔋		10:14 AM		🔋 Not Charging 🔋
	Settings	❮ General	**iTunes Wi-Fi Sync**	

To enable Wi-Fi syncing with iTunes, connect to iTunes on your computer using a cable and click "Sync with this iPad over Wi-Fi".

- ✈ Airplane Mode ⬜
- 📶 Wi-Fi   earlandnancy
- ⓑ Bluetooth   On

Sync Now

FLIP

Last Sync: Today at 9:59 AM

- ⊡ Notification Center

Figure 3-4

 If you have your iPad set up to sync wirelessly to your Mac or PC, and both devices are within range of the same Wi-Fi network, the iPad appears in your iTunes Source list. Selecting iPad on your Source list allows you to sync and manage syncing from within iTunes.

Understand iCloud

There's an alternative to syncing content with iTunes. When iOS 5 launched in fall 2011, it introduced iCloud, a service that allows you to back up all your content and certain settings (such as bookmarks) to online storage. That content and those settings are pushed automatically to all your Apple devices through a wireless connection.

All you need to do is get an iCloud account, which is free, and then make settings on your devices to specify which types of content you want pushed to each device. After you've done that, any content you create (except video) or purchase on one device — such as music, apps, books, and TV shows, as well as documents created in Apple's iWork apps, photos, and so on — can be synced among your devices automatically.

When you get an iCloud account, you get 5GB of free storage. Content that you purchase through Apple (such as apps, books, music, and TV shows) won't be counted against your storage. If you want additional storage, you can buy an upgrade from one of your devices. 10GB costs $20 per year, 20GB is $40 per year, and 50GB is $100 a year. Most people do just fine with the free 5GB of storage.

To upgrade your storage, tap Settings➪iCloud➪Storage & Backup➪ Manage Storage. In the dialog that appears, tap Buy More Storage. Tap the amount you need and then tap Buy.

 You can make settings for backing up your content to iCloud in the iCloud section of the Settings screen. You can back up content automatically or manually.

 If you pay $24.99 a year for the iTunes Match service, you can sync almost any amount of content in your iTunes library to your devices, which may be a less expensive way to go than paying for added iCloud storage. Tap Match in iTunes or visit www.apple. com/itunes/itunes-match for more information.

Get an iCloud Account

Before you can use iCloud, you need an iCloud account, which is tied to the Apple ID you probably already have. You can turn on iCloud when you first set up your iPad, or you can use the Settings app on your iPad to sign up with your Apple ID.

1. When you first set up your iPad (except for an original iPad), in the sequence of screens that appears, tap Use iCloud.

2. In the next dialog, tap Back Up to iCloud. In the next screen, shown in **Figure** 3-5, enter your Apple ID and password.

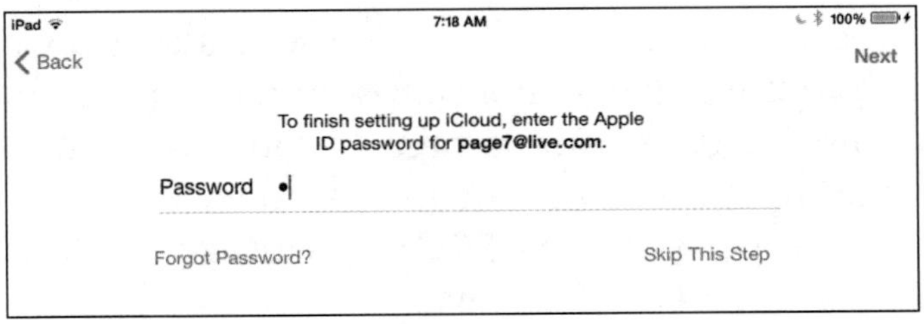

iPad 🛜	7:18 AM	⌁ ⌁ 100% 🔋⚡
‹ Back		Next

To finish setting up iCloud, enter the Apple ID password for **page7@live.com**.

Password •|

Forgot Password?   Skip This Step

Figure 3-5

Your account is now set up based on the Apple ID you entered earlier in the setup sequence.

Here are the steps for setting up iCloud on your iPad if you didn't do so when first setting up iPad:

1. Tap Settings⇨Mail, Contacts, Calendars⇨Accounts⇨iCloud.

2. Scroll to the bottom of the next screen, tap Storage and Backup and then tap the On/Off button to turn on iCloud Backup (see **Figure** 3-6).

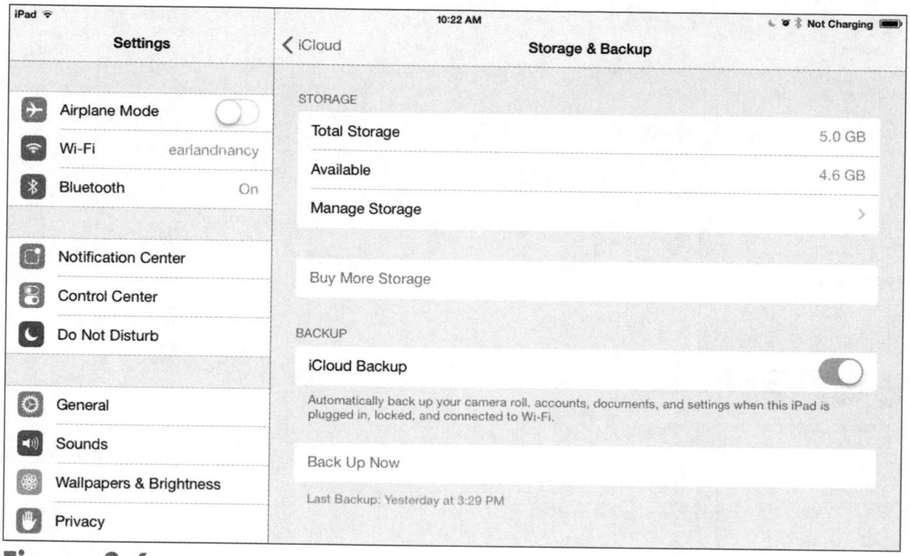
iPad
10:22 AM
Not Charging
Settings
iCloud
Storage & Backup
Airplane Mode
Wi-Fi
earlandnancy
Bluetooth
On
Notification Center
Control Center
Do Not Disturb
General
Sounds
Wallpapers & Brightness
Privacy
STORAGE
Total Storage
5.0 GB
Available
4.6 GB
Manage Storage
Buy More Storage
BACKUP
iCloud Backup
Automatically back up your camera roll, accounts, documents, and settings when this iPad is plugged in, locked, and connected to Wi-Fi.
Back Up Now
Last Backup: Yesterday at 3:29 PM

Figure 3-6

3. When a message appears that your computer will no longer back up to your computer when you sync with a cable, click OK.

4. A dialog may appear, asking whether you want to allow iCloud to use the location of your iPad. Tap OK. Your account is now set up.

Make iCloud Sync Settings

When you have an iCloud account up and running (see the preceding task), you have to specify which types of content should be synced with your iPad via iCloud. Note that the content you purchase and download will be synced among your devices automatically via iCloud.

1. Tap Settings➪iCloud.

2. In the iCloud Settings screen, shown in **Figure 3-7**, tap the On/Off button for any item that's turned off that you want to turn on (or vice versa). You can sync Mail, Contacts, Calendars, Reminders, Safari Bookmarks, and Notes.

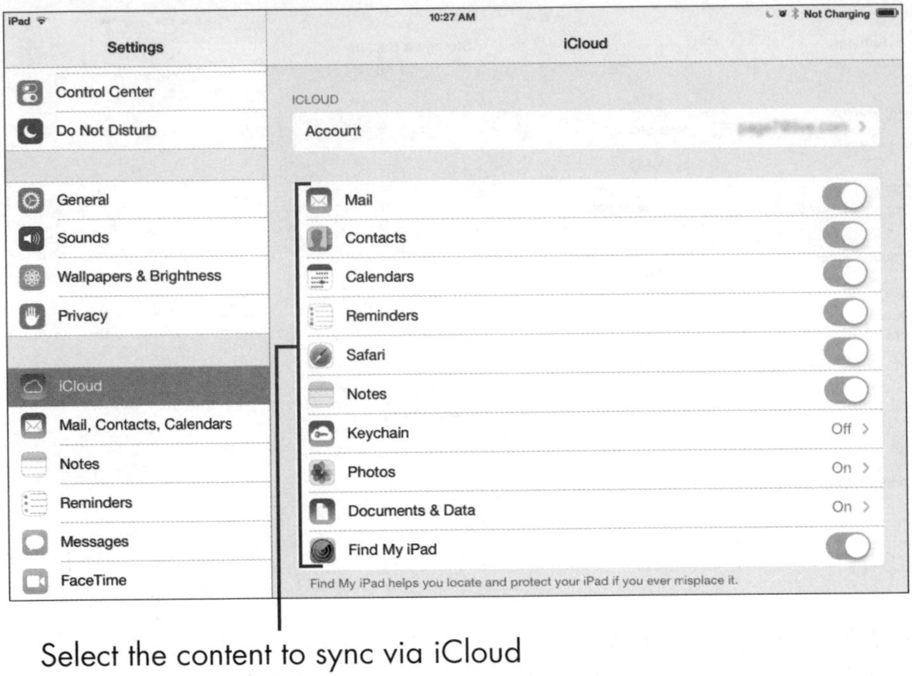

iPad ⚡	10:27 AM	⚡ ⚡ ⚡ Not Charging ▬
Settings	**iCloud**	

📦 Control Center	ICLOUD
🌙 Do Not Disturb	Account page7@live.com >
⚙ General	✉ Mail ⬤
🔊 Sounds	👤 Contacts ⬤
🌐 Wallpapers & Brightness	📅 Calendars ⬤
✋ Privacy	▤ Reminders ⬤
	🧭 Safari ⬤
☁ iCloud	▭ Notes ⬤
✉ Mail, Contacts, Calendars	🔑 Keychain Off >
▭ Notes	🌸 Photos On >
▤ Reminders	▢ Documents & Data On >
◯ Messages	◉ Find My iPad ⬤
▢ FaceTime	Find My iPad helps you locate and protect your iPad if you ever misplace it.

Select the content to sync via iCloud

Figure 3-7

3. To enable automatic downloads of music, apps, and books, tap iTunes & App Store in the Settings pane (see **Figure 3-8**).

4. Tap the On/Off button for Music, Apps, or Books to set up automatic downloads of any of this content to your iPad via iCloud.

 If you want to allow iCloud to provide a service for locating a lost or stolen iPad, tap the On/Off button in the Find My iPad field (refer to **Figure 3-7**) to activate it. This service helps you locate, send a message to, or delete content from your iPad if it falls into other hands.

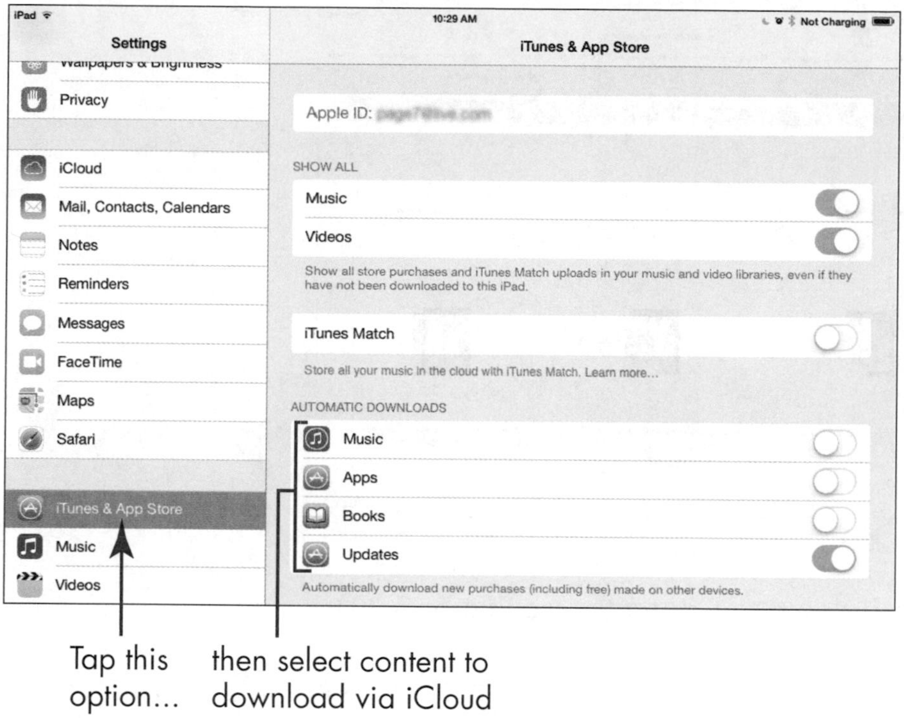

Tap this   then select content to
option...   download via iCloud

Figure 3-8

View the iPad User Guide

1. The *iPad User Guide* is equivalent to the Help system you may have used on a Windows or Mac computer. You access the guide online using the Safari browser. From the iPad Home screen, tap the Safari icon.

2. Go to `http://support.apple.com/manuals/` `#iPad` and on the screen that appears (see **Figure 3-9**), tap iPad and iPad mini User Guide (For iOS 7 Software). The User Guide downloads and opens.

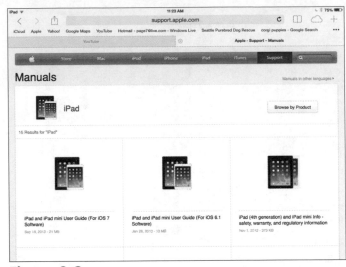

Figure 3-9

3. Scroll down to Contents (see **Figure 3-10**).

Figure 3-10

4. Tap a subtopic to display information about it, as shown in **Figure 3-11**.

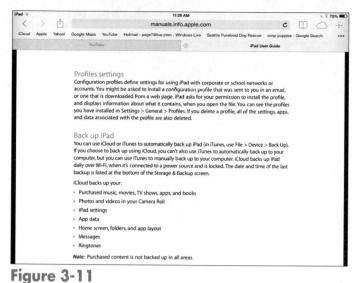

Figure 3-11

5. Tap any link in the subtopic information to access additional topics.

6. Press the Home button to close the browser.

 To save the User Guide to your iPad so you can use it when you don't have an Internet connection, with the User Guide open tap in the middle of the screen and then tap the Open in "iBooks" link in the top-right corner. The User Guide is now saved in iBooks.

Making Your iPad More Accessible

*i*Pad users are all different; some face visual, motor, or hearing challenges. If you're one of these folks, you'll be glad to hear that the iPad offers some handy accessibility features, with iOS 7 adding a few more.

To make your screen easier to read, you can adjust the brightness or change wallpaper. You can also set up the VoiceOver feature to read onscreen elements out loud. Then there are a slew of features you can turn on or off, including Zoom, Invert Colors, Speak Selection, and Large Type.

If hearing is your challenge, you can do the obvious thing and adjust the system volume. The iPad also has settings for mono audio (useful when you're wearing headphones) and a setting to use Speak Auto-text. Features that help you deal with physical and motor challenges include AssistiveTouch for those who have difficulty using the iPad touchscreen, Switch Control for working with adaptive accessories, and the new Home Click Speed settings that allow you to adjust how quickly you have to tap the iPad screen to work with features.

Get ready to . . .

Finally, the Guided Access feature, introduced with iOS 6, provides help for those who have difficulty focusing on one task. It also provides a handy mode for showing presentations of content in settings where you don't want users to flit off to other apps, as in school or a public kiosk.

Set Brightness

1. Especially when you're using the iPad as an e-reader, you may find that a slightly less-bright screen reduces strain on your eyes. To adjust screen brightness, tap the Settings icon on the Home screen.

2. In the Settings dialog, tap Wallpapers & Brightness.

3. To control brightness manually, tap the Auto-Brightness On/Off button (see **Figure 4-1**) to turn off this feature.

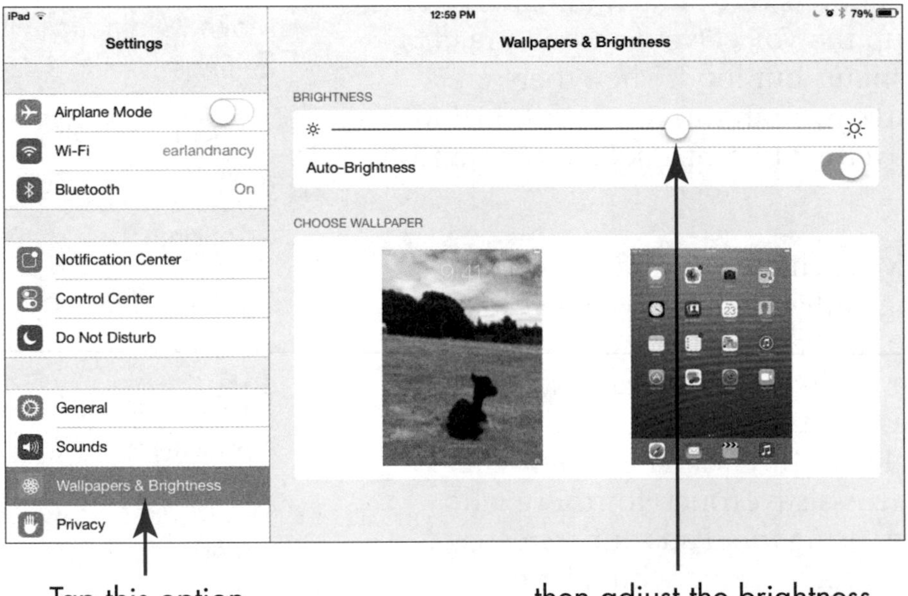

Tap this option…   …then adjust the brightness

Figure 4-1

4. Tap and drag the Brightness slider (refer to **Figure 4-1**) to the right to make the screen brighter or to the left to make it dimmer.

5. Press the Home button to close the Settings dialog.

 If glare from the screen is a problem for you, consider getting a *screen protector*. This thin film not only protects your screen from damage, but also reduces glare.

 In the iBooks e-reader app, you can set a sepia tone for the page, which might be easier on your eyes. See Chapter 10 for more about using iBooks.

Change the Wallpaper

1. The picture of rippling water — the default iPad background image — may be pretty, but it may not be the one that works best for you. Choosing different wallpaper may help you see all the icons on your Home screen. Start by tapping the Settings icon on the Home screen.

2. In the Settings dialog, tap Wallpapers & Brightness and then tap a wallpaper sample.

3. In the Wallpaper settings that appear, tap a wallpaper category such as Dynamic, shown in **Figure 4-2**, to view your choices, and tap a sample to select it. Alternatively, on the initial wallpaper screen, tap an album in the Photos section, locate a picture to use as your wallpaper, and tap it.

4. In the preview that appears (see **Figure 4-3**), use your finger to move and shrink or expand the image to manage exactly what portion of the image will be used.

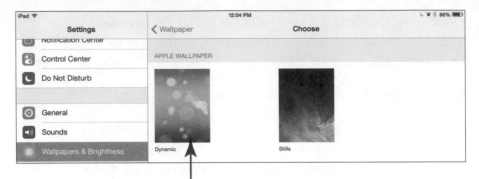

Tap a wallpaper sample

Figure 4-2

Tap to set one or both screens

Figure 4-3

5. At the bottom of the preview, tap Set Lock Screen, Set Home Screen, or Set Both depending on which screen or screens you want to use the new wallpaper.

6. Press the Home button to return to your Home screen, where the new wallpaper is set as the background.

Set Up VoiceOver

1. VoiceOver reads the names of screen elements and settings to you, but it also changes the way you provide input to the iPad. In Notes, for example, you can have VoiceOver read the name of the Notes buttons to you, and when you enter notes, it reads words or characters you've entered. It can also tell you whether features such as Auto-Correction are on. To turn on this feature, tap the Settings icon on the Home screen. Tap General; then scroll down and tap Accessibility.

2. In the Accessibility pane, shown in **Figure** 4-4, tap the VoiceOver On/Off button to display the VoiceOver pane.

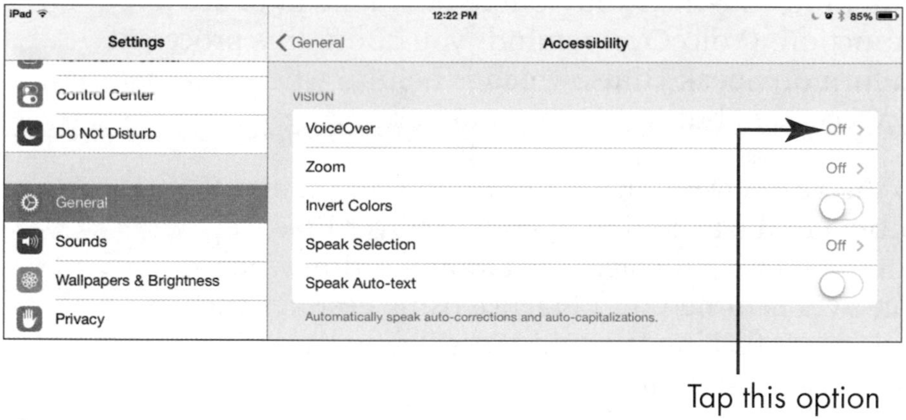

Tap this option

Figure 4-4

3. In the VoiceOver pane, shown in **Figure** 4-5, tap the VoiceOver On/Off button to turn on this feature.

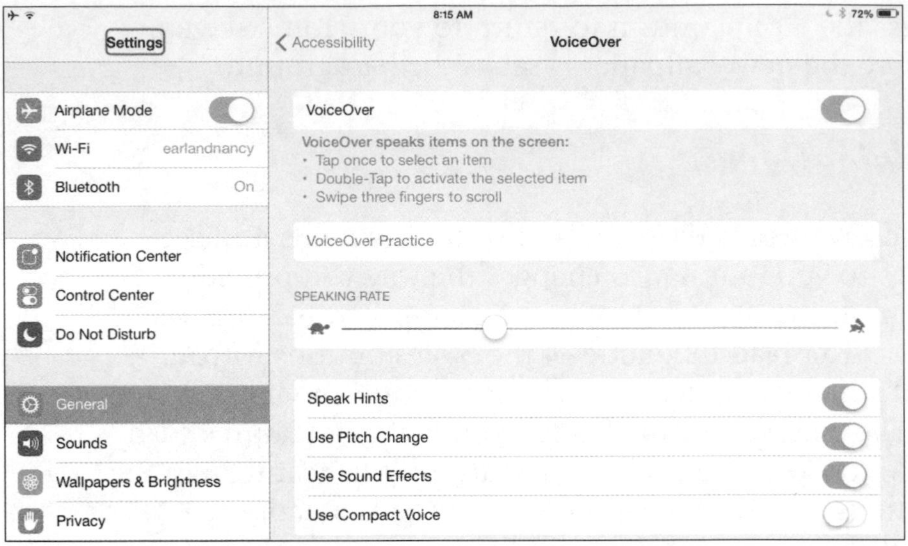

Figure 4-5

When VoiceOver is on, you first tap to select an item such as a button, which causes VoiceOver to read the name of the item to you; then you double-tap the item to activate its function. (VoiceOver reminds you about this process if you turn on Speak Hints, which is helpful when you first use VoiceOver, but it soon becomes annoying.)

4. Tap the VoiceOver Practice button to select it and then double-tap the button to open VoiceOver Practice. (Double-tapping replaces the tapping action when VoiceOver is turned on.) Practice using gestures such as pinching or flicking left, and VoiceOver tells you what action each gesture initiates.

5. Tap the Done button and then double-tap it to return to the VoiceOver dialog.

6. Tap the Speak Hints field. VoiceOver speaks the name of each tapped item.

7. Double-tap the On/Off slider to turn off Speak Hints.

8. If you want VoiceOver to read words or characters to you (in the Notes app, for example), scroll down and tap and then double-tap Typing Feedback.

9. In the Typing Feedback dialog, tap and then double-tap to select the option you prefer. The Words option causes VoiceOver to read words to you but not characters, such as the dollar sign ($). The Characters and Words option causes VoiceOver to read both, and so on.

10. Press the Home button to return to the Home screen. Read the next task to find out how to navigate your iPad after you've turned on VoiceOver.

 You can change the language that VoiceOver speaks. In the General Settings screen, choose International and then Language, and select another language. This action, however, also changes the language used for labels on Home-screen icons and various settings and fields on the iPad.

 You can use the Accessibility Shortcut setting to toggle the VoiceOver, Zoom, Switch Control, AssistiveTouch, and Invert Colors features rapidly. In the Accessibility dialog, tap Accessibility Shortcut. In the dialog that appears, choose what you want a triple press of the Home button to activate. Now a triple press of the Home button opens the option you selected in this dialog (such as Zoom or Invert Colors, for example) wherever you go in iPad.

Use VoiceOver

After VoiceOver is turned on, you need to figure out how to use it. I won't kid you — using it is awkward at first, but you'll get the hang of it! Here are the main onscreen gestures you should know how to use:

➠ **Tap an item to select it.** VoiceOver speaks the item's name.

➠ **Double-tap the selected item.** This action activates the item.

➠ **Flick three fingers.** It takes three fingers to scroll around a page when VoiceOver is turned on.

Table 4-1 provides additional gestures that help you use VoiceOver. I suggest that if you want to use this feature often, you read the VoiceOver section of the *iPad User Guide* (see Chapter 3), which goes into a great deal of detail about the ins and outs of using VoiceOver. You'll find the *iPad User Guide* in the Bookmarks section of the Safari browser.

Table 4-1	VoiceOver Gestures
Gesture	*Effect*
Flick right or left.	Select the next or preceding item.
Tap with two fingers.	Stop speaking the current item.
Flick two fingers up.	Read everything from the top of the screen.
Flick two fingers down.	Read everything from the current position.
Flick three fingers up or down.	Scroll one page at a time.
Flick three fingers right or left.	Go to the next or preceding page.
Tap three fingers.	Speak the scroll status (for example, line 20 of 100).
Flick four fingers up or down.	Go to the first or last element on a page.
Flick four fingers right or left.	Go to the next or preceding section (as on a web page).

 If tapping with two or three fingers is difficult for you, try tapping with one finger of one hand and one or two fingers of the other hand. When you're double- or triple-tapping, you have to perform these gestures as quickly as you can to make them work.

Check out some of the settings for VoiceOver, including Braille, Language Rotor (for making language choices), a setting for navigating images, and a setting that directs the iPad to read notifications to you.

Make Additional Vision Settings

Several vision features are simple on/off settings, so rather than give you the steps to get to those settings repeatedly, I provide this useful bullet list of additional features you can turn on or off after you tap Settings➪General➪Accessibility:

➡ **Zoom:** The Zoom feature enlarges the contents displayed on the iPad's screen when you double-tap the screen with three fingers. The Zoom feature works almost everywhere on the iPad: in Photos, on web pages, on your Home screens, in Mail, in Music, and in Videos. Give it a try!

➡ **Invert Colors:** The Invert Colors setting reverses colors on your screen so that white backgrounds are black and black text is white.

 The Invert Colors feature works well in some places and not so well in others. In the Photos app, for example, pictures appear almost like photo negatives. Your Home-screen image will likewise look a bit strange. And don't even think of playing a video with this feature turned on! However, if you need help reading text, White on Black can be useful in several apps.

➡ **Turn On Larger Type:** If having larger text in apps such as Contacts, Mail, and Notes would be helpful to you, you can turn on the Larger Type feature and choose the text size that works best for you.

➡ **Bold Text:** Turning on this setting first restarts your iPad (after asking you for permission to do so) and then causes text in various apps and in Settings to be bold. This setting is a handy one, as text in the iOS 7 redesign was simplified (meaning thinner!).

➠ **Increase Contrast:** Use this setting to add greater contrast to backgrounds in some areas of the iPad and apps, which should improve visibility.

➠ **Reduce Motion:** Tap this accessibility feature and then tap the On/Off button to turn off the parallax effect (new with iOS 7), which causes the backgrounds of your Home screens to appear to float as you move the iPad around.

➠ **Manage On/Off Labels:** If you have trouble making out colors, and so have trouble telling when an On/Off button is On (green) or Off (white), use the Manage On/Off Labels setting to add a circle to the right of a setting when it's off and a white vertical line to a setting when it's on (see **Figure 4-6**).

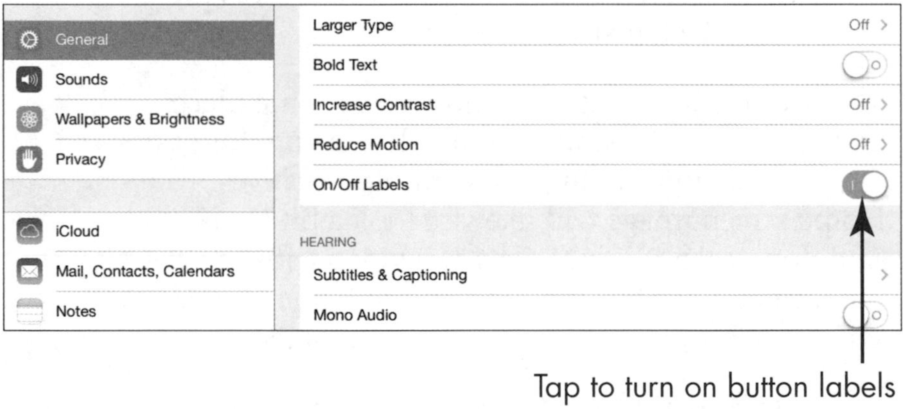

Tap to turn on button labels

Figure 4-6

Adjust the Volume

1. Though individual apps such as Music and Video have their own volume settings, you can set your iPad system volume for your ringer and alerts as well to help you better hear what's going on. To start, tap Settings⇨Sounds.

2. In the Sounds pane that appears (see **Figure** 4-7), tap and drag the Ringer and Alerts slider to the right to increase the volume of these audible attention-grabbers or to the left to lower the volume.

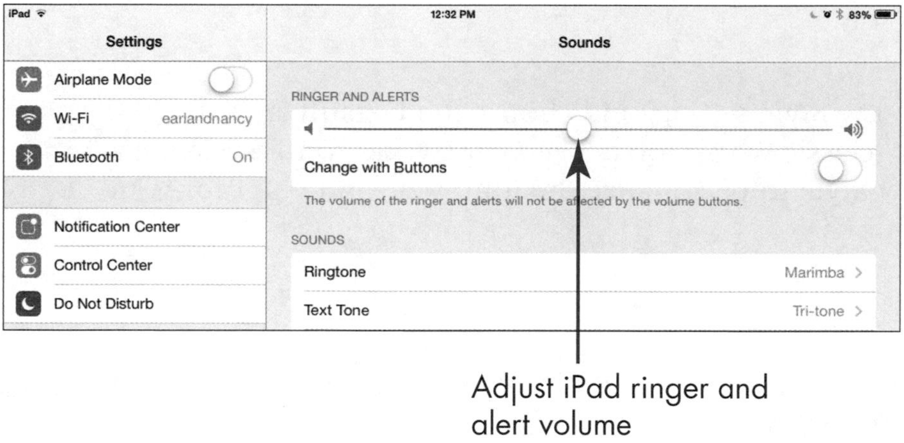

iPad 🛜	12:32 PM	📶 🔋 💲 83% ▰
Settings	**Sounds**	

Airplane Mode

Wi-Fi   earlandnancy

Bluetooth   On

Notification Center

Control Center

Do Not Disturb

RINGER AND ALERTS

Change with Buttons

The volume of the ringer and alerts will not be affected by the volume buttons.

SOUNDS

Ringtone   Marimba >

Text Tone   Tri-tone >

Adjust iPad ringer and alert volume

Figure 4-7

3. Press the Home button to close Settings.

 In the Sounds pane, you can turn on or off the sounds that the iPad makes when certain events occur (such as new mail or Calendar alerts). These sounds are turned on by default.

Set Up Subtitles and Captioning

1. Closed captioning and subtitles help folks with hearing challenges enjoy entertainment and educational content. On the Accessibility Settings screen (refer to **Figure** 4-6), tap Subtitles and Captioning.

2. On the Subtitles & Captioning screen, shown in **Figure** 4-8, tap the On/Off button to turn on Closed Captions and SDH (Subtitles for the Deaf and Hard of Hearing).

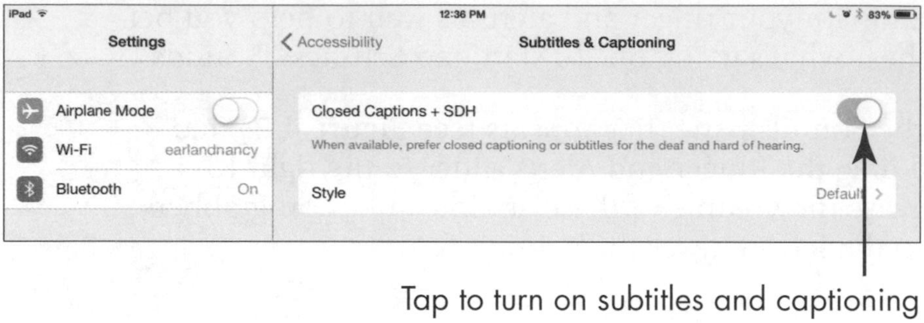

Tap to turn on subtitles and captioning

Figure 4-8

3. Tap the Style setting, and choose the Default style, large
text, classic which looks like a typewriter font, or Create a
New Style to personalize the font, size, and color for your
captions.

Manage Other Hearing Settings

A couple of hearing accessibility settings are simple on/off settings,
including these:

➡ **Use Mono Audio:** Using the stereo effect in headphones or a headset breaks up sounds so that you
hear a portion in one ear and a portion in the other
ear, simulating the way that your ears process
sounds. If there's only one channel of sound, that
sound is sent to both ears. If you're hard of hearing
or deaf in one ear, however, you're picking up only a
portion of the sound in your hearing ear, which can
be frustrating. If you have such hearing challenges
and want to use the iPad with a headset connected,
you should turn on Mono Audio. When that setting
is turned on, all sound is combined and distributed
to both ears.

➡ **Have iPad Speak Auto-text:** The Speak Auto-text feature speaks autocorrections and autocapitalizations.
(You can turn on both these features on the

Keyboard Settings screen.) When you enter text in an app such as Notes or Mail, the app makes either type of change, while Speak Auto-text lets you know what change was made.

 Why would you want the iPad to tell you whenever an autocorrection has been made? If you have vision challenges, and you know that you typed *ain't* when writing dialogue for a character in your novel, but the iPad corrected that word to *isn't,* you want to know. Similarly, if your grandson's girlfriend's name is SUNshine (don't worry, he'll break up with her soon), and autocapitalization corrects it (incorrectly), you need to know immediately so that you can change it back.

Turn On and Work with AssistiveTouch

1. The AssistiveTouch Control Panel helps those who have challenges working with a touchscreen or who have to use some kind of assistive device for providing input. To turn on AssistiveTouch, tap Settings on the Home screen; then tap General⇨Accessibility.

2. In the Accessibility pane, scroll down to tap AssistiveTouch.

3. In the pane that appears, tap the On/Off button for AssistiveTouch to turn it on (see **Figure 4-9**). A gray square, called the AssistiveTouch Control Panel, appears on the right side of the pane. This square now appears in the same location in whatever apps you display on your iPad.

4. Tap the AssistiveTouch Control Panel to display its options, shown in **Figure 4-10**. You can tap Favorites or Device on the panel to see additional choices, tap Siri to activate the personal-assistant feature, or tap Home to go directly to the Home screen.

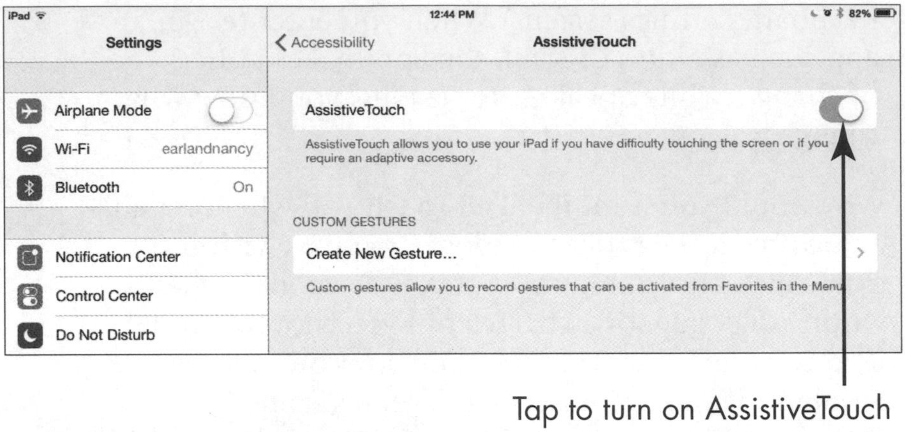

Tap to turn on AssistiveTouch

Figure 4-9

Figure 4-10

5. When you've chosen an option, tap the Back arrow to go back to the main panel.

Table 4-2 shows the major options available in the AssistiveTouch Control Panel and their purposes.

 In addition to using Siri, don't forget about using the Dictation key on the onscreen keyboard to speak text entries and basic keyboard commands.

Table 4-2	AssistiveTouch Controls
Control	**Purpose**
Siri	Activates the Siri feature, which allows you to speak questions and make requests of your iPad.
Favorites	Displays a set of gestures with only the Pinch gesture preset; you can tap any of the other blank squares to add your own favorite gestures.
Device	Allows you to rotate the screen, lock the screen, turn the volume up or down, mute or unmute sound, or shake the iPad to undo an action by using the presets in this option.
Home	Sends you to the Home screen.

Manage Home Click Speed

Sometimes, if you have dexterity challenges, it's hard to double-press or triple-press the Home button fast enough to make an effect. Choose the Slow or Slowest setting when you tap this setting to allow you a bit more time to make that second or third tap. Follow these steps:

1. Tap Settings⇨General⇨Accessibility.

2. Scroll down, and tap Home Click Speed.

3. Tap the Slow or Slowest setting to change how rapidly you have to double-press or triple-press the Home button to initiate an action.

 If you have certain adaptive accessories, you can use head gestures to control your iPad, highlighting features in sequence and then selecting one. Use the Switch Control feature in the Accessibility Settings screen to turn this mode on and configure settings.

Focus Learning with Guided Access

1. Guided Access arrived with iOS 6. You can use this feature to limit a user's access to the iPad to a single app and even limit access to that app to certain features. This feature is useful in several settings, ranging from a classroom to use by someone with attention deficit disorder and even to a public setting (such as a kiosk) where you don't want users to be able to open other apps. To activate it, start by tapping Settings⇨General⇨Accessibility⇨Guided Access.

2. On the screen that appears (see **Figure 4-11**), tap the Guided Access On/Off button to turn the feature on.

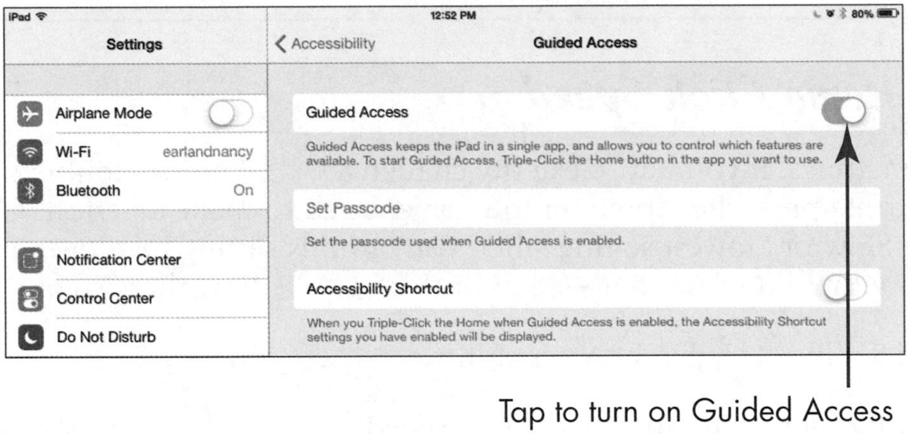

iPad 🔋		12:52 PM		⚡ ☀ ⅛ 80% 🔋
Settings	❮ Accessibility	**Guided Access**		
✈ Airplane Mode ⬜	**Guided Access**			⬜
🔗 Wi-Fi earlandnancy	Guided Access keeps the iPad in a single app, and allows you to control which features are available. To start Guided Access, Triple-Click the Home button in the app you want to use.			
✶ Bluetooth On				
	Set Passcode			
🔲 Notification Center	Set the passcode used when Guided Access is enabled.			
🔲 Control Center	**Accessibility Shortcut**			⬜
🌙 Do Not Disturb	When you Triple-Click the Home when Guided Access is enabled, the Accessibility Shortcut settings you have enabled will be displayed.			

Tap to turn on Guided Access

Figure 4-11

3. Tap Set Passcode to activate a passcode so that those using an app can't return to the Home screen to access other apps. In the Set Passcode dialog that appears (see **Figure 4-12**), enter a passcode, using the numeric pad. Enter the number again when you're prompted.

4. Press the Home button to return to the Home screen.

5. Tap an app to open it.

6. Triple-press the Home button. An Option button appears at the bottom of the screen.

Set Passcode   Cancel

Enter a passcode

— — — —

1	2 ABC	3 DEF
4 GHI	5 JKL	6 MNO
7 PQRS	8 TUV	9 WXYZ
	0	⊗

Figure 4-12

7. Tap the Option button to display two options:

- **Sleep/Wake Button:** You can put your iPad to sleep or wake it up with a triple press of the Home button.

- **Volume Buttons:** Tap Always On or Always Off. If you don't want users to be able to adjust volume by using the volume toggle on the side of the iPad, for example, use the Volume Buttons setting.

8. At this point, you can also use your finger to circle areas of the screen that you want to disable, such as a Store button in the Music app.

9. Triple-press the Home button and then enter your passcode (if you set one in Step 3) to return to the Home screen.

Part II
Taking the Leap Online

Visit www.dummies.com/extras/ipadforseniors for a listing of free iPad apps in a variety of categories to get you going with your iPad experience.

Browsing the Internet with Safari

*G*etting on the Internet with your iPad is easy thanks to its Wi-Fi, 3G, or 4G capabilities. After you're online, the preinstalled browser (software that helps you navigate the Internet's contents), *Safari,* is your ticket to a wide world of information, entertainment, education, and more. Safari will look familiar to you if you've used it on a PC or Mac device before, though the way you move around it on the iPad touchscreen may be new to you. If you've never used Safari, this chapter takes you by the hand and shows you all its ins and outs.

In this chapter, you discover how to connect your iPad to the Internet, navigate among web pages, and use iCloud tabs to share your browsing among devices. Along the way, you see how to place a bookmark for a favorite site or place a web clip on your Home screen. You can also view your browsing history, save online images to your photo library, post photos to certain sites from within Safari, or e-mail or tweet a hotlink to a friend. You explore the Safari Reader and Safari Reading List features, and see how to keep yourself safer while you're online by using Private Browsing. Finally, you review the simple steps involved in printing what you find online.

Connect to the Internet

How you connect to the Internet depends on which iPad model you own:

➥ The Wi-Fi–only iPad connects to the Internet only via a Wi-Fi network, logically enough. You can set up this type of network in your own home by using your computer and some equipment from your Internet service provider. You can also connect over public Wi-Fi networks, referred to as *hotspots*. You'll probably be surprised to discover how many hotspots your town or city has: Look for Internet cafes, coffee shops, hotels, libraries, and transportation centers such as airports or bus stations, for example. Many of these businesses display signs alerting you to their free Wi-Fi.

➥ If you own a Wi-Fi+3G or Wi-Fi+4G–enabled iPad, you can still use a Wi-Fi connection (in fact, when one is available, the iPad defaults to using Wi-Fi to save money), but you can also use the paid data network provided by AT&T, Verizon, or Sprint to connect from just about anywhere you can get cellphone coverage via a cellular network.

If you have a 3G or 4G model, you don't have to do anything; with a contract for coverage, the connection is made automatically wherever cellular service is available, just as it is on your cellphone. To connect to a Wi-Fi network, you have to complete a few steps:

1. Tap the Settings icon on the Home screen and then tap Wi-Fi.

2. Make sure that Wi-Fi is set to On (see **Figure 5-1**), and choose a network to connect to. Network names should appear automatically when you're in range of networks. When you're in range of a public hotspot, if access to several nearby networks is available, you may see a message asking you to tap a network name to select it.

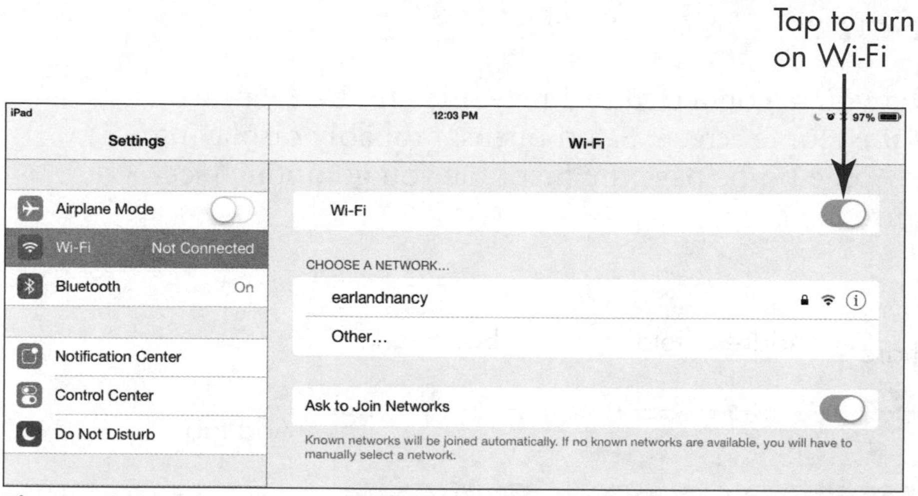

Tap to turn
on Wi-Fi

iPad	12:03 PM	97%
Settings		**Wi-Fi**

Airplane Mode

Wi-Fi   Not Connected

Bluetooth   On

Notification Center

Control Center

Do Not Disturb

Wi-Fi

CHOOSE A NETWORK...

earlandnancy

Other...

Ask to Join Networks

Known networks will be joined automatically. If no known networks are available, you will have to manually select a network.

Figure 5-1

3. After you select a network (or if only one network is available), you may see a message asking for your password. Ask the owner of the hotspot (such as a hotel desk clerk or business owner) for this password, or enter your home network password.

4. Tap the Join button, and you're connected.

 See Chapter 1 for more about the capabilities of different iPad models and the costs associated with 3G and 4G.

 Free public Wi-Fi networks typically don't require a password, or the password is posted prominently for all to see. These networks are *unsecured*, however, so it's possible for someone else to track your online activities over these networks. Avoid accessing financial accounts or sending e-mails that contain sensitive information when you're connected to a public hotspot.

Explore Safari

1. After you're connected to a network, tap the Safari icon on the Home screen. Safari opens, probably displaying the Apple home page the first time you go online (see **Figure 5-2**).

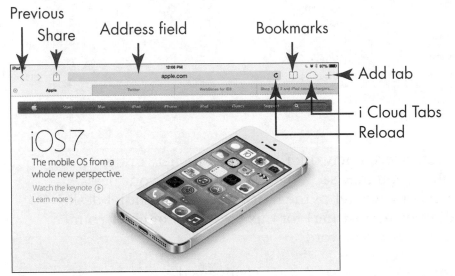

Figure 5-2

2. Put two fingers together on the screen and swipe them outward to enlarge the view, as shown in **Figure 5-3**. Double-tap the screen with a single finger to restore the default screen size.

3. Put your finger on the screen and flick upward to scroll the page contents and view additional contents lower on the page.

4. To return to the top of the web page, put your finger on the screen and drag downward, or tap the Status bar at the top of the screen.

Figure 5-3

 Using the pinch method to enlarge a web page on your screen allows you to view what's displayed at various sizes, giving you more flexibility than the double-tap method.

 When you enlarge the display, you gain more control using two fingers to drag the screen from left to right or from top to bottom. On a reduced display, one finger works fine for making these gestures.

Navigate among Web Pages

1. With Safari open, tap the Address field below the Status bar. The onscreen keyboard appears (see **Figure 5-4**).

2. To clear the Address field, if necessary, tap the Delete key on the keyboard.

3. Enter a web address. You can enter this book's companion website: www.ipadmadeclear.com.

4. Tap the Go key on the keyboard (see **Figure 5-4**). The website you entered appears.

Delete key

Go key

Figure 5-4

↻ • If for some reason the page doesn't appear, tap the Reload icon at the right end of the Address field.

✕ • If Safari is loading a web page, and you change your mind about viewing the page, you can tap the Stop icon (the X), which appears at the right end of the Address field during this process, to stop loading the page.

‹ **5.** Tap the Previous arrow to go backward to the last page you displayed.

› **6.** Tap the Next arrow to go forward to the page you just came from.

7. To follow a link to another web page (links typically are colored text or graphics), tap the link with your finger. To view the destination web address of the link before you tap it, just touch and hold the link. A menu appears, displaying the address at the top, as shown in **Figure 5-5.**

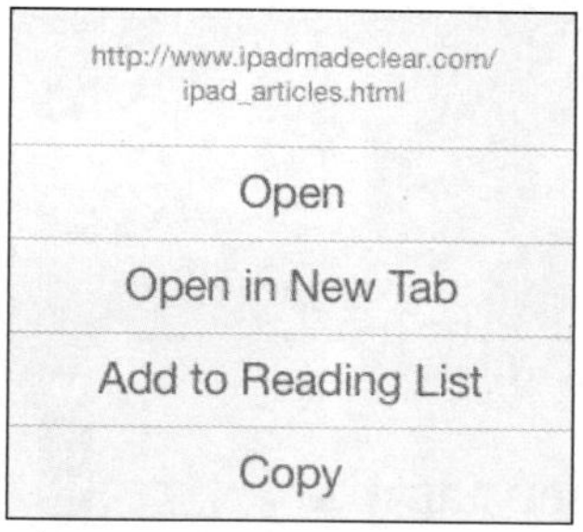

http://www.ipadmadeclear.com/ipad_articles.html
Open
Open in New Tab
Add to Reading List
Copy

Figure 5-5

 By default, AutoFill is turned on, causing entries that you make in fields such as Address to display possible matching entries automatically. You can turn off AutoFill by tapping Settings⇨Safari⇨Passwords & Autofill.

Use Tabbed Browsing

1. Safari includes a feature called *tabbed browsing*, which allows you to have several websites open at the same time on separate tabs so that you can move among those sites easily. To add a tab, tap the Add Tab button near the top-right corner of the screen (refer to **Figure 5-2**). A new tab appears.

2. To add a new page (meaning that you're opening a new website), tap one of the frequently used sites displayed onscreen (see **Figure 5-6**), or tap the address bar that appears. (Note you can get to the same new page simply by tapping the address bar on any site.)

Figure 5-6

3. Switch among open sites by tapping another tab.

4. To close a tab, scroll to locate the tab and then tap the Close button in the top-left corner of the tab.

 When you're using tabbed browsing, you can place not only a site on a tab, but also a search results screen. If you recently searched for something, those search results are in your Recent Searches list. Also, if you're displaying a search results page when you tap the plus sign to add a tab, the first ten suggested sites in the results are listed for you to choose among.

View Browsing History

1. As you move around the web, your browser keeps a record of your browsing history. This record can be handy when you want to visit a site that you viewed previously but have forgotten its address. With Safari open, tap the Bookmarks icon. The Bookmarks menu, shown in **Figure 5-7**, appears.

2. On the Bookmarks menu, tap History.

3. In the History list that appears, tap a date, if one is available, and then tap a site to navigate to it (see **Figure 5-8**).

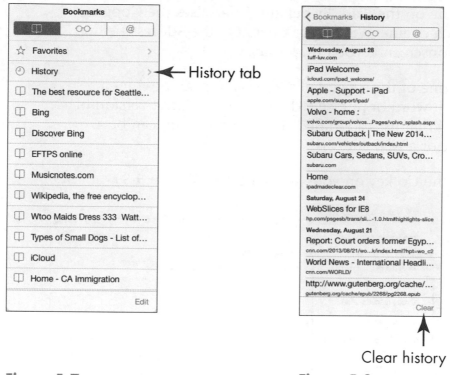

Figure 5-7

Figure 5-8

 To clear the history, tap the Clear button in the bottom-right corner of the History list (refer to **Figure 5-8**). This button is useful when you don't want your spouse or grandchildren to see where you've been browsing for birthday or holiday presents!

 You can tap and hold the Previous button to quickly display your browsing history.

Search the Web

1. If you don't know the address of the site you want to visit (or if you want to research a topic and find other information online), get acquainted with Safari's Search feature on the iPad. By default, Safari uses the Google search engine. With Safari open, tap the Address field. The onscreen keyboard appears.

2. Tap one of the suggested sites that appear, or enter a search word or phrase (which, with the latest version of Safari that uses a Unified smart search field, can be a topic or a web address).

3. Tap the Go key on your keyboard (see **Figure 5-9**).

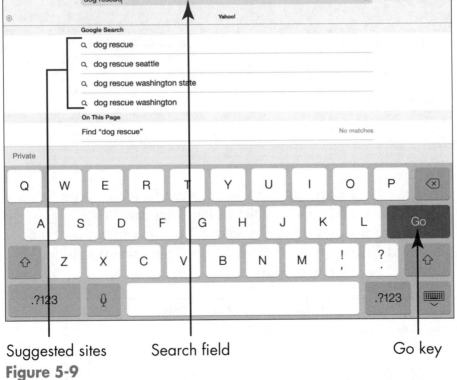

Suggested sites   Search field   Go key

Figure 5-9

4. In the search results, tap a link to visit that site.

 To change your default search engine from Google to Yahoo! or Bing, tap Safari in the iPad Settings screen and then tap Search Engine. Tap Yahoo! or Bing, and your default search engine changes.

You can browse for specific items such as images, videos, or news by tapping the corresponding link at the top of the Google results screen. Also, tap the More button in this list to see additional options to narrow your results, such as searching for books or shopping sources related to the subject.

Add and Use Bookmarks

1. Bookmarks enable you to save favorite sites so you can easily visit them again. With a site that you want to bookmark displayed, tap the Share icon in the top left of the screen.

2. On the menu that appears (see **Figure 5-10**), tap Bookmark. The Add Bookmark dialog appears.

3. In the Add Bookmark dialog, shown in **Figure 5-11,** edit the name of the bookmark, if you want to. To do so, tap the name of the site and then use the onscreen keyboard to edit its name.

Tap this option

Figure 5-10

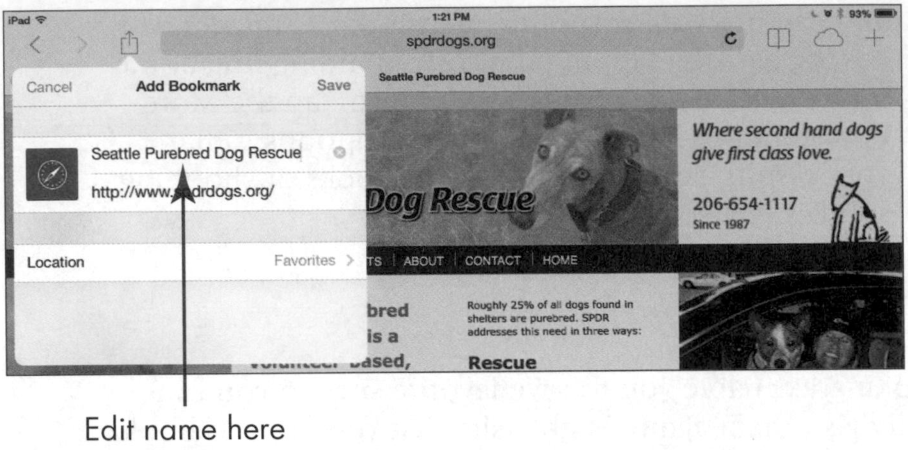

Edit name here

Figure 5-11

> To set your default location for saved bookmarks, tap Location and then tap Bookmarks. Tapping Favorites adds saved bookmarks to the Favorites list.

4. Tap the Save button.

5. To go to the bookmark, tap the Bookmarks icon near the top right of the screen (shaped like a little book).

6. On the Bookmarks menu that appears (see **Figure 5-12**), tap the bookmarked site that you want to visit.

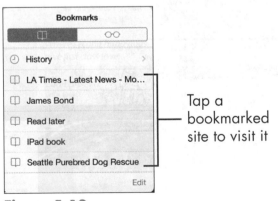

Tap a bookmarked site to visit it

Figure 5-12

If you want to sync your bookmarks on your iPad browser with those on your computer, connect your iPad to your computer, and make sure that the Sync Safari Bookmarks setting on the Info tab of iTunes is activated.

 When you tap the Bookmarks icon, you can tap Edit on the Bookmarks tab and then use the New Folder option to create folders to organize your bookmarks. When you next add a bookmark, you can choose the folder to which you want to add the new bookmark.

Save Links and Web Pages to the Safari Reading List

The Safari Reading List provides a way to save web pages with content you want to read later so that you can easily visit those saved pages again. You can save not only links to sites, but also the sites themselves, so you can read the content even when you're offline. Where a bookmark takes you to a live, updated page, adding an item to the Reading List simply saves a static copy of the item when you added it to the Reading List. In the latest version of Safari, you can scroll from one item to the next easily.

1. With a site you want to add to your Reading List displayed, tap the Share icon.

2. On the menu that appears, tap Add to Reading List.

3. To view your Reading List, tap the Bookmarks icon and then tap the Reading List tab (which looks like a pair of reading glasses).

4. On the Reading List that appears (see **Figure 5-13**), tap the content you want to revisit and resume reading.

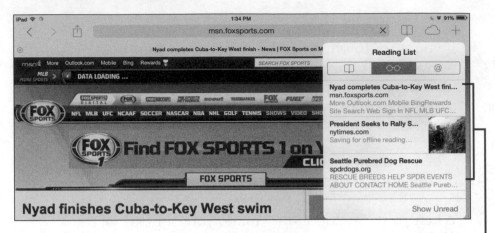

Tap an item to
resume reading

Figure 5-13

 If you want to see both the Reading List material that you've read and material that you haven't read, tap Show unread near the bottom of the Reading List (refer to **Figure 5-13**). To see only the material that you haven't read, tap the Show Unread tab.

 To save an image to your Reading List, tap and hold the image until a menu appears; then tap Add to Reading List. To delete an item, with the Reading List displayed, swipe left or right over the item; a Delete button appears. Tap this button to delete the item from the Reading List.

Enjoy Reading with Safari Reader

The Safari Reader feature gives you an e-reader type of experience right within your browser, removing other stories and links as well as those distracting advertisements. When you're on a website, reading content, such as an article, Safari displays a Reader button at the left end of the Address field.

1. Tap the Reader button (see **Figure 5-14**). The content appears in Reader format (see **Figure 5-15**).

Reader button

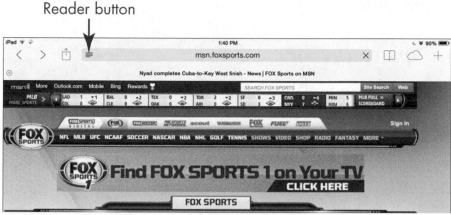

Figure 5-14

Figure 5-15

2. Scroll down the page. The entire content is contained in one long page.

3. When you finish reading the material, just tap the Reader button in the Address field again to return to the material's source.

> If you're holding the iPad in landscape orientation, the Reader window doesn't fill the screen, and you can tap either side of the window to go back to the source material.

Add Web Clips to the Home Screen

1. The *Web Clips* feature allows you to save a website as an icon on your Home screen so that you can go to the site at any time with one tap. With Safari open and displaying the site you want to add, tap the Share icon.

2. On the menu that appears (refer to **Figure 5-10**), tap Add to Home Screen.

3. In the Add to Home dialog that appears (see **Figure 5-16**), you can edit the name of the site to be more descriptive, if you like. To do so, tap the name of the site and use the onscreen keyboard to edit its name.

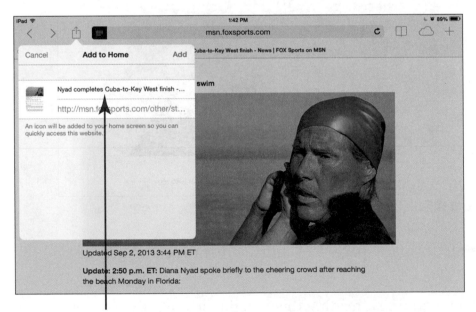

Edit the name here

Figure 5-16

4. Tap the Add button. The site is added to your Home screen.

 You can have several Home screens on your iPad to accommodate all the web clips and apps you download (though as of iOS 7 you can save an unlimited number of apps within folders). If you want to delete an item from your Home screen for any reason, press and hold the icon on the Home screen until all items on the screen start to jiggle and Delete icons appear on all items except the preinstalled apps. Tap the Delete icon on each item you want to delete, and it's gone. (To get rid of the jiggle, press the Home button.)

Save an Image to Your Photo Library

1. Display a web page that contains an image you want to copy.

2. Press and hold the image. The menu shown in **Figure 5-17** appears.

3. Tap the Save Image option (refer to **Figure 5-17**). The image is saved to your Camera Roll.

 Be careful about copying images from the Internet and using them for business or promotional activities. Most images are copyrighted, and you may violate the copyright even if you simply use an image in, say, a brochure for your association or a flyer for your community group. Note that some search engines' advanced search settings offer the option of browsing only for images that aren't copyrighted.

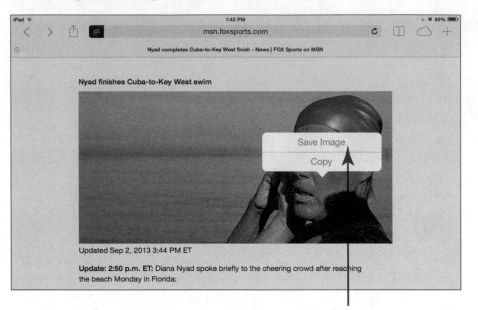

Tap this option

Figure 5-17

Post Photos from Safari

1. Before iOS 6, you had to post photos from within apps such as Photos. Now you can post photos to sites such as eBay, craigslist, and Facebook from within Safari, rather than go through Photos or Videos. For this example, go to Facebook, and sign in. (To follow this example, you have to have downloaded the Facebook for iPad app and created a Facebook account.)

2. Tap Add Photos/Video or a link similar to the one shown in **Figure 5-18.** (On Facebook, you might have to verify that you wish to upload a photo or video rather than create a photo album.)

3. Tap the appropriate source for the image, such as your Camera Roll.

4. Tap a photo on your iPad (see **Figure 5-19**).

5. Tap Done to post the photo or video.

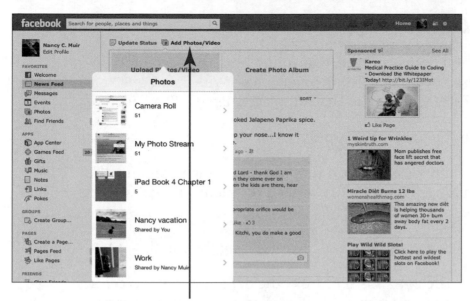

Tap the Add Photos/Video link

Figure 5-18

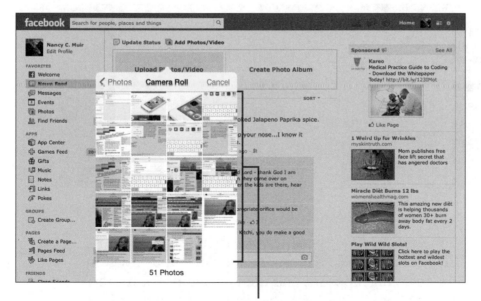

Tap a photo to upload

Figure 5-19

Send a Link

1. If you find a great site that you want to share, you can do so easily by sending a link in an e-mail. With Safari open and the site you want to share displayed, tap the Share icon.

2. On the menu that appears (refer to **Figure 5-10**), tap Mail.

3. On the message form that appears, which contains the link (see **Figure 5-20**), enter a recipient's e-mail address, a subject, and your message.

4. Tap Send, and the e-mail containing the link is sent.

The e-mail is sent from the default e-mail account you set up on your iPad. For more about setting up an e-mail account, see Chapter 6.

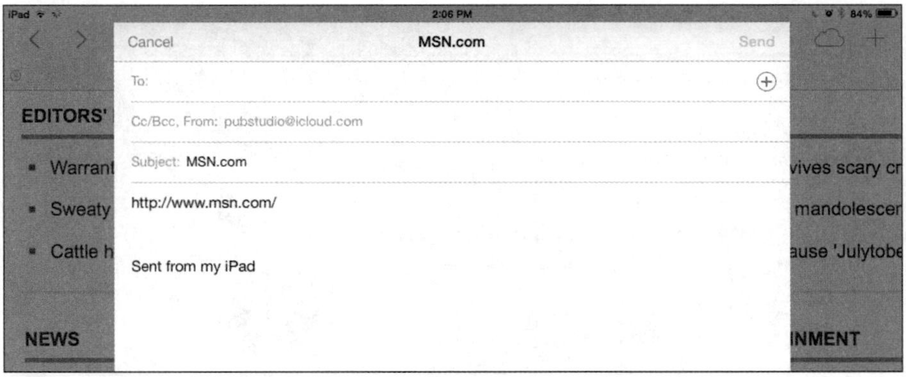

iPad 📶
2:06 PM
84%

Cancel   **MSN.com**   Send

To: ⊕

Cc/Bcc, From: pubstudio@icloud.com

Subject: MSN.com

http://www.msn.com/

Sent from my iPad

Figure 5-20

To tweet the link by using your Twitter account, in Step 2 of this task, choose Twitter, enter your tweet in the form that appears, and then tap Send. For more about using Twitter with the iPad, see Chapter 7. You can also choose AirDrop (4th generation iPad and later) from the same menu to share with someone in your immediate vicinity who has an AirDrop-enabled device.

Make Private Browsing and Cookie Settings

Apple has provided some privacy settings for Safari that you should consider using. *Private Browsing* automatically removes items from the download list, stops Safari from letting AutoFill save information used to complete your entries in the search or address fields as you type, and doesn't save some browsing history information. These features can keep your online activities more private. The *Accept Cookies* setting allows you to stop the downloading of *cookies* (small files that document your browsing history so that you can be recognized by a site the next time you go to or move within that site) to your iPad.

You can control both settings by tapping Safari in the Settings screen. In the Privacy & Security section, tap Do Not Track to turn that feature on or off (see **Figure 5-21**). Tap the arrow next to Block Cookies, and choose to never save cookies, always save cookies, or save only cookies from visited third-party and advertiser sites.

Settings	Safari	
Sounds	GENERAL	
Wallpapers & Brightness	Search Engine	Google >
Privacy	Passwords & AutoFill	>
	Favorites	Favorites >
iCloud	Open New Tabs in Background	
Mail, Contacts, Calendars	Show Favorites Bar	
Notes	Block Pop-ups	
Reminders	PRIVACY & SECURITY	
Messages	Do Not Track	
FaceTime	Block Cookies	From third parties and advertisers >
Maps	Smart Search Field	>
Safari	Fraudulent Website Warning	

Tap to turn on these privacy settings

Figure 5-21

 You can also tap the Clear History and the Clear Cookies and Data settings (refer to **Figure 5-21**) to clear your browsing history, saved cookies, and other data manually.

Print a Web Page

 1. If you have a wireless printer that supports Apple's AirPrint technology (a few manufacturers, such as Canon, Epson, and Hewlett-Packard, include AirPrint printers in their product lines), you can print web content via a wireless connection. With Safari open and the site you want to print displayed, tap the Share icon.

> The Mac applications Printopia and handyPrint make any shared or network printer on your home network visible to your iPad. Printopia has more features but costs you, whereas handyPrint is free.

2. On the menu that appears, tap Print.

3. In the Printer Options dialog that appears (see **Figure** 5-22), tap Select Printer. Then, in the list of printers that appears, tap the name of your wireless printer.

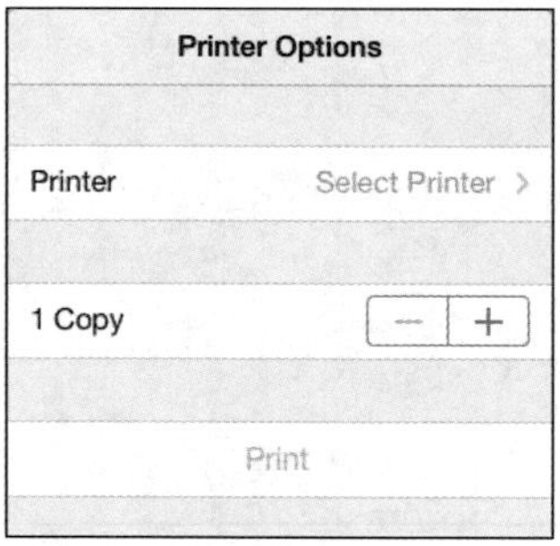

Printer Options	
Printer	Select Printer >
1 Copy	− +
	Print

Figure 5-22

4. Tap the plus or minus button in the Copy field to adjust the number of copies to print.

5. Tap Print to print the displayed page.

 If you don't have an AirPrint-compatible wireless printer or don't want to use an app to print wirelessly, just e-mail a link to the web page to yourself, open the link on your computer, and print the page from there.

Understand iCloud Tabs

The iCloud Tabs feature was new with iOS 6. This feature allows you to access the browsing histories on all your devices that use iCloud-compatible browsers from any of those devices. Here's how iCloud Tabs could come in handy. Suppose that you begin to research a topic on your iPad before you leave home. Later, while sitting in a waiting room with your iPhone, you can pick up where you left off.

1. First, check to make sure that the devices are using the same iCloud account by tapping Settings⇨iCloud and verifying the account name is the same.

2. Open Safari on your iPad, and tap the iCloud Tabs button, shown in **Figure 5-23**. All items in your other devices' browsing history are displayed. (In **Figure 5-23**, the history is for my iPhone.)

Figure 5-23

Working with E-mail in Mail

Staying in touch with others by using e-mail is a great way to use your iPad. You can access an existing account by using the handy Mail app supplied with your iPad or sign in to your e-mail account by using the Safari browser (see Chapter 5). Using Mail involves adding one or more existing e-mail accounts by way of iPad Settings. Then you can use Mail to write, format, retrieve, and forward messages from one or more accounts.

Mail offers the capability to mark the messages you've read, delete messages, organize your messages in folders, and use the handy search feature. New with iOS 6 was the ability to create a VIP list so that you're notified when that special person sends you an e-mail. In this chapter, you read all about Mail and its various features.

Add an iCloud, Gmail, Yahoo!, AOL, or Microsoft Outlook.com Account

1. You can add one or more e-mail accounts, including the e-mail account associated with your iCloud account, by using iPad Settings. If you have an account with iCloud, Gmail, Yahoo!,

AOL, or Outlook.com (this includes Microsoft accounts from Live, Hotmail, and so on), iPad pretty much automates setup. To set up the iPad to retrieve messages from your e-mail account at one of these popular providers, tap Settings⇨Mail, Contacts, Calendars. The settings shown in **Figure 6-1** appear.

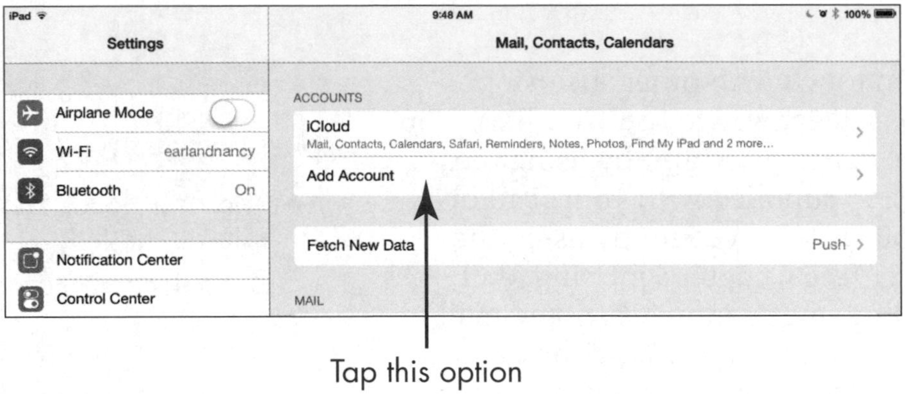

Tap this option

Figure 6-1

2. Tap Add Account. The options shown in **Figure 6-2** appear.

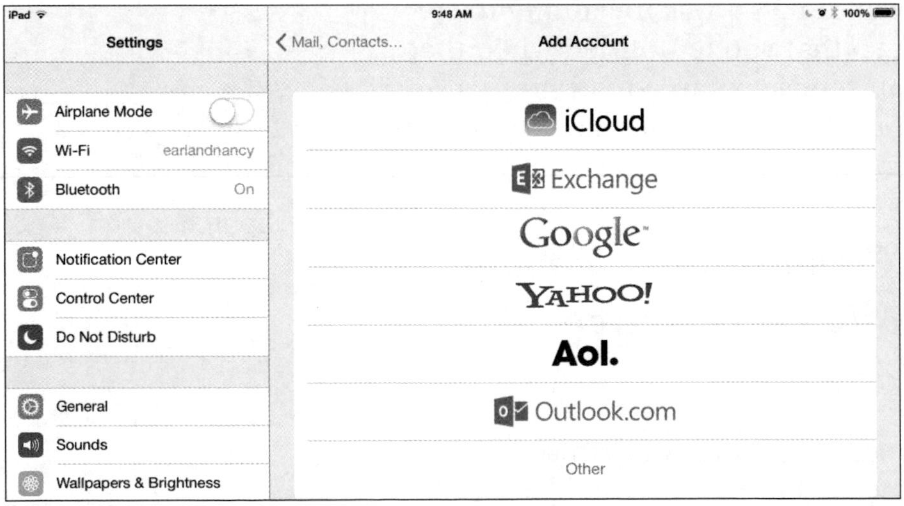

Figure 6-2

3. Tap iCloud, Google, Yahoo!, AOL, or Outlook.com.

4. Enter your account information in the form that appears (see **Figure 6-3**), and tap Next.

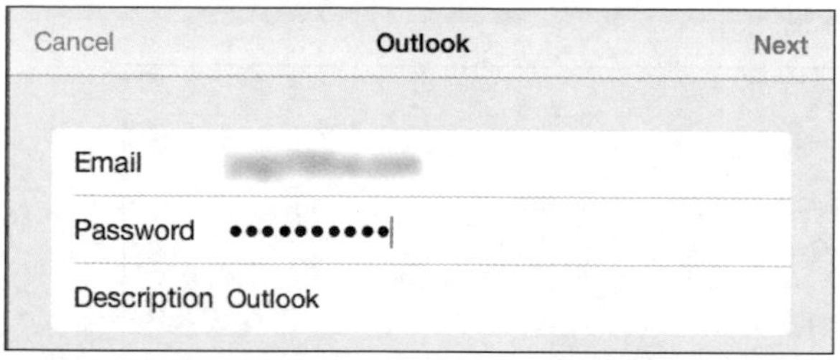

Cancel	**Outlook**	Next
Email		
Password	•••••••••	
Description	Outlook	

Figure 6-3

5. After the iPad takes a moment to verify your account information, tap any On/Off button to have Mail, Contacts, Calendars, or Reminders from that account synced with the iPad.

6. When you're done, tap Save. The account is saved, and you can now open it by using Mail.

Set Up a POP3 E-mail Account

1. You can also set up most popular e-mail accounts, such as those available through EarthLink or a cable provider's service, by obtaining the host name from the provider. To set up an existing account with a provider other than iCloud, Gmail, Outlook.com, Yahoo!, or AOL, you have to enter the account settings yourself. First, tap Settings⇨Mail, Contacts, Calendars.

2. Tap the Add Account button in the top-right corner of the screen that appears.

3. On the screen that appears (refer to **Figure** 6-2), tap Other.

4. On the screen shown in **Figure** 6-4, tap Add Mail Account.

iPad 🔋	9:51 AM	⬆ ❤ ⚡ 100% 🔋
Settings	‹ Add Account **Other**	

MAIL

Add Mail Account   ›

CONTACTS

Add LDAP Account   ›

Add CardDAV Account   ›

Settings column:
- ✈ Airplane Mode ⬭
- 📶 Wi-Fi   earlandnancy
- ᳵ Bluetooth   On
- 🔲 Notification Center

Figure 6-4

5. In the next form, enter your name and an account address, password, and description; then tap Next. The iPad takes a moment to verify your account and then returns you to the Mail, Contacts, Calendars page, where your new account is displayed.

 If you have a less-mainstream e-mail service, you may have to enter the mail server protocol (POP3 or IMAP; ask your e-mail provider for this information) and your password. The iPad probably will add the outgoing mail server (SMTP) information for you, but if it doesn't, you may have to enter it yourself. Your Internet service provider (ISP) can provide this information as well.

6. To make sure that the Account field is set to On for receiving e-mail, tap the account name on the Mail, Contacts, Calendars pane of the Settings screen (refer to **Figure** 6-1). In the dialog that appears, tap the On/Off button for the Mail field and then tap Done to save the setting. Now you can access the account through Mail.

If you turn on Calendars in the Mail account settings, any information you've put in your calendar in that e-mail account will be brought over into the Calendar app on your iPad and reflected in Notification Center (discussed in more detail in Chapter 17).

Open Mail and Read Messages

1. Tap the Mail app icon, located on the Dock on the Home screen (see **Figure 6-5**). A circled red number on the icon indicates the number of unread e-mails in your Inbox.

Figure 6-5

2. In the Mail app, if the Inbox you want isn't displayed, tap Mailboxes in the top-left corner (see **Figure 6-6**) to display your list of inboxes. Then tap the inbox whose contents you want to display.

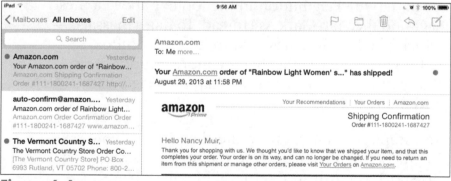

Figure 6-6

3. Tap a message to read it. It opens (see **Figure 6-7**).

4. If you need to scroll to see the entire message, just place your finger on the screen and flick upward to scroll down.

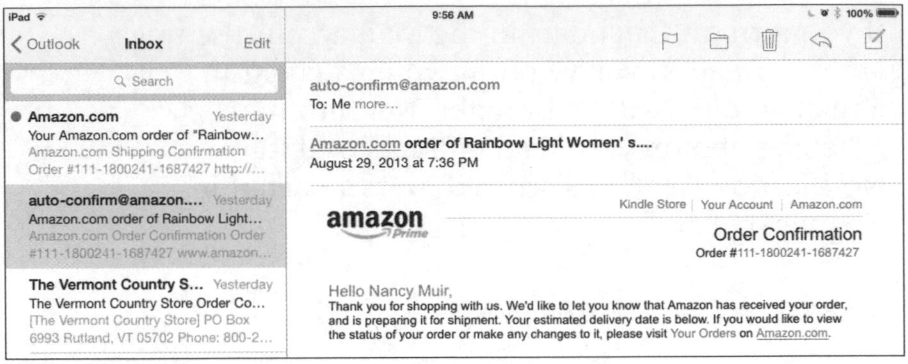

Figure 6-7

 You can swipe right while reading a message in portrait orientation to open the Inbox list of messages and then swipe left to hide the list.

 You can tap the Next or Previous button (top-left corner of the message in portrait orientation) to move to the next or previous message.

 E-mail messages that you haven't read are marked with a blue circle in your Inbox (refer to **Figure 6-6**). After you read a message, the blue circle disappears. You can mark a read message as unread to help remind you to read it again later. With a message open, tap the Flag button in the toolbar above a message and then tap Mark As Unread. To flag a message — which places a little flag next to it in your inbox, helping you spot items that are more important or that you want to read again — tap the Flag button and then tap Flag.

 To escape your e-mail now and then (or to avoid having messages retrieved while you're at a public Wi-Fi hotspot), you can stop retrieval of e-mail by using the Manual setting for the Fetch New Data control in the Mail, Contacts, Calendars pane of iPad Settings.

Reply To or Forward E-mail

1. With an e-mail message open (see the preceding task), tap the Reply/Forward button, which looks like a left-facing arrow (refer to **Figure 6-7**).

2. Tap Reply, Reply All (if the e-mail has multiple recipients), or Forward in the menu that appears (see **Figure 6-8**).

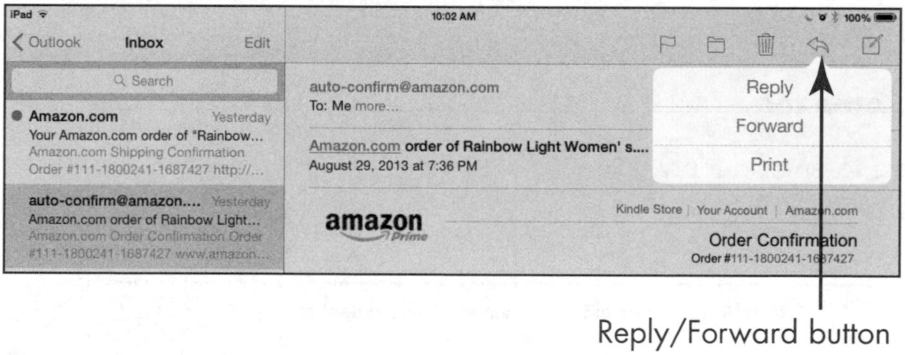

Reply/Forward button

Figure 6-8

3. Take one of the following actions:

- Tap Reply to respond to the sender of the message, or if the message had other recipients, tap Reply All to respond to the sender and to all recipients. The Reply Message form, shown in **Figure 6-9**, appears. Tap in the message body, and enter a message.

- Tap Forward to send the message to somebody else. The form shown in **Figure 6-10** appears. Enter a recipient in the To: field, tap in the message body, and enter a message.

Cancel
Re: Amazon.com order of Rainbow Light Women' s....
Send
To: auto-confirm@amazon.com
Cc/Bcc, From:
Subject: Re: Amazon.com order of Rainbow Light Women' s....
Sent from my iPad
On Aug 29, 2013, at 7:36 PM, "auto-confirm@amazon.com" <auto-confirm@amazon.com> wrote:
Kindle Store | Your Account | Amazon.com

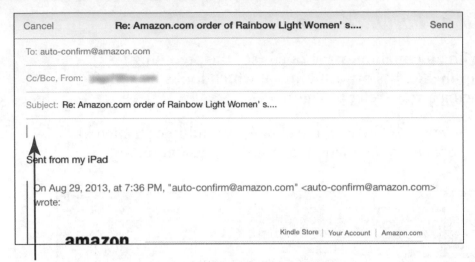

Tap here to enter a reply

Figure 6-9

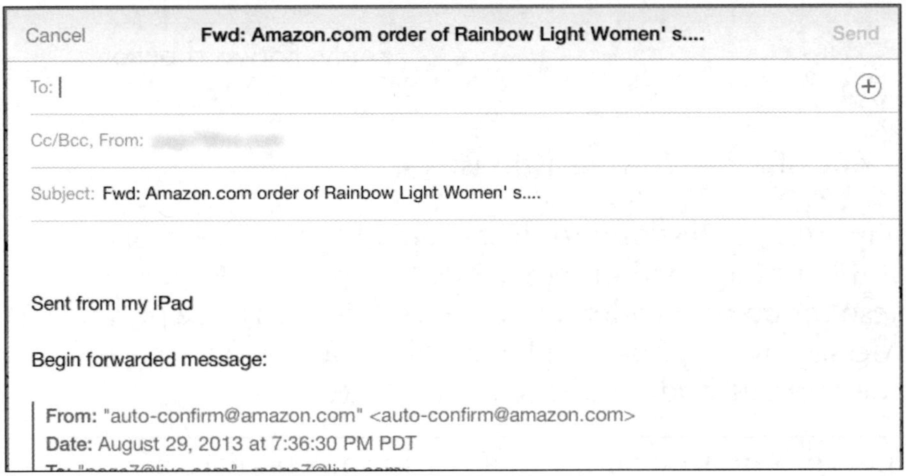

Cancel
Fwd: Amazon.com order of Rainbow Light Women' s....
Send
To:
Cc/Bcc, From:
Subject: Fwd: Amazon.com order of Rainbow Light Women' s....
Sent from my iPad
Begin forwarded message:
From: "auto-confirm@amazon.com" <auto-confirm@amazon.com>
Date: August 29, 2013 at 7:36:30 PM PDT

Figure 6-10

4. Tap Send. The message goes on its way.

If you want to copy an address from the To: field to the Cc or Bcc field, tap and hold the address, and drag it to the other field.

If you tap Forward to send the message to somebody else, and the original message had an attachment, you're offered the option of including or not including the attachment when forwarding.

Create and Send a New Message

1. With Mail open, tap the New Message icon. A blank message form appears (see **Figure 6-11**).

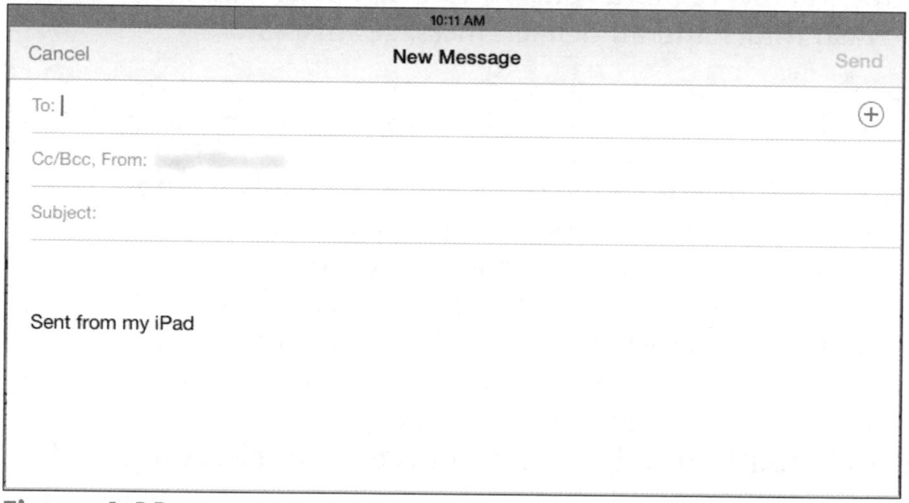

10:11 AM		
Cancel	**New Message**	Send

To: | ⊕

Cc/Bcc, From:

Subject:

Sent from my iPad

Figure 6-11

2. Enter a recipient's address in the To: field either by typing or by tapping the Dictation key on the onscreen keyboard and speaking the address. If you have saved addresses in Contacts, tap the plus sign (+) in the Address field to choose an addressee from the Contacts list that appears.

3. If you want to send a copy of the message to other people, enter their addresses in the Cc/Bcc field. If you want to send both carbon copies and *blind* carbon copies (copies that you don't want other recipients to be aware of), note that when you tap the Cc/Bcc field, two fields are displayed; use the Bcc field to specify recipients of blind carbon copies.

4. Enter the subject of the message in the Subject field.

5. Tap in the message body, and type your message.

6. Tap Send.

 Mail keeps a copy of all deleted messages in the Trash folder for a time. To view deleted messages, tap the Mailboxes button; then, in the dialog that appears, tap the account name in the Accounts list of the Mailboxes pane. A list of folders opens. Tap the Trash folder and all deleted messages display.

Format E-mail

1. A feature that arrived with iOS 5 was the capability to apply formatting to e-mail text. You can use character formats (bold, underline, and italic) and indent text by using the Quote Level feature. To use it, tap the text in a new message, and choose Select or Select All in the pop-up menu to select a single word or all the words in the e-mail. Note that if you select a single word, handles appear; you can drag the handles to add adjacent words to your selection.

2. To apply bold, italic, or underline formatting, tap the B*I*U button (see **Figure 6-12**).

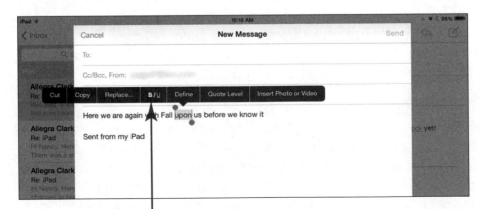

Tap to add text formatting

Figure 6-12

3. In the pop-up menu that appears (see **Figure 6-13**), tap Bold, Italics, or Underline to apply the respective formatting.

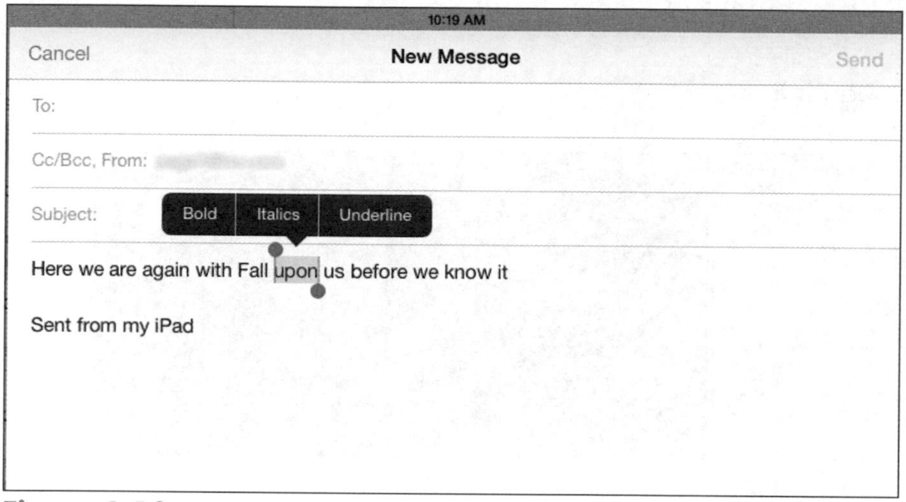

	10:19 AM	
Cancel	**New Message**	Send
To:		
Cc/Bcc, From:		
Subject:	Bold | Italics | Underline	

Here we are again with Fall upon us before we know it

Sent from my iPad

Figure 6-13

4. To change the indent level, tap and hold at the beginning of a line, and then in the toolbar that appears, tap Quote Level.

5. Tap Increase to indent the text or Decrease to move indented text farther toward the left margin.

 To use the Quote Level feature, make sure that it's on. Tap Settings⇨Mail, Contacts, Calendars and then tap the Increase Quote Level On/Off button.

Search E-mail

1. What if you want to find all messages that are from a certain person or that contain a certain word in the Subject field? You can use Mail's handy Search feature to find these e-mails. With Mail open, tap an account to display its inbox.

2. In the Inbox, tap in the Search field. The onscreen keyboard appears.

3. Enter a search term or name, as shown in **Figure 6-14**. Matching e-mails are listed in the results.

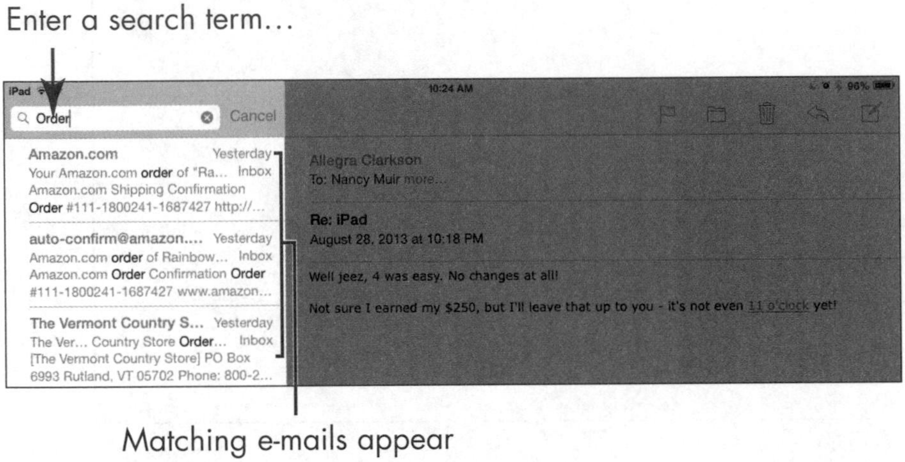

Enter a search term...

Matching e-mails appear

Figure 6-14

To start a new search or go back to the full Inbox, tap the Delete key in the top-right corner of the onscreen keyboard to delete the term, or just tap the Cancel button.

Delete E-mail

1. When you no longer want an e-mail cluttering your Inbox, you can delete it. With the Inbox displayed, tap the Edit button. A circular check box displays to the left of each message (see **Figure 6-15**).

Check marks indicate selected messages

Tap to select a message

Figure 6-15

2. Tap the circle next to the message you want to delete. (You can tap multiple items if you have several e-mails to delete.) A message marked for deletion has a check mark in its circular check box (refer to **Figure 6-15**).

3. Tap Trash at the bottom of the Inbox. The message is moved to the Trash folder.

 You can also delete an open e-mail by tapping the Trash icon on the toolbar that runs across the top of Mail or by swiping left over a message displayed in the Inbox and then tapping Trash.

Organize E-mail

1. You can move messages into any of several predefined folders in Mail. (These folders will vary, depending on your e-mail provider and the folders you've created on its server.) After displaying the folder containing the message you want to move (for example, Archive, Trash, or Inbox), tap the Edit button. A circular check box is displayed to the left of each message (refer to **Figure 6-15**).

2. Tap the circle next to the message you want to move. A check mark appears in its circular check box.

3. Tap the Move button.

4. In the Mailboxes list that appears on the left side of the screen (see **Figure 6-16**), tap the folder where you want to store the message. The message is moved.

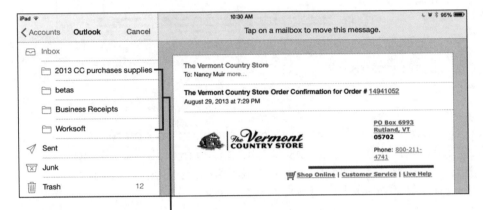

Tap a folder to move an e-mail into it

Figure 6-16

 If you receive a junk e-mail, you may want to move it to the Spam or Junk folder, if your e-mail account provides one. Then any future mail from the same sender is automatically placed in that folder.

 If you have an e-mail open, you can move it to a folder by tapping the Folder icon on the toolbar at the top of the screen. The Mailboxes list appears (refer to **Figure 6-16**). Tap a folder to move the message.

Create a VIP List

1. iOS 6 brought Mail a new feature called VIP List. This feature is a way to create a list of senders. When any of these senders sends you an e-mail, you're notified through the iPad's Notifications feature. In the Mailboxes list in Mail (refer to **Figure 6-16**), tap the Information button to the right of VIP (see **Figure 6-17**).

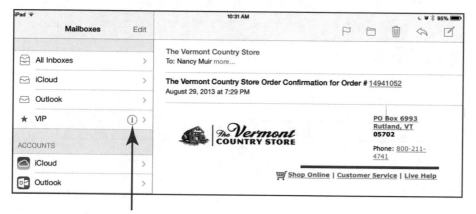

Information button

Figure 6-17

2. Tap Add VIP. Your Contacts list appears (see **Figure 6-18**).

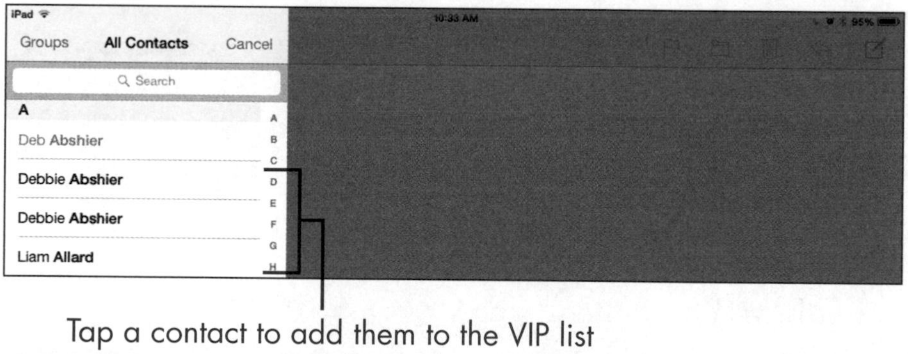

Tap a contact to add them to the VIP list

Figure 6-18

3. Tap a contact to add them person to your VIP list.

4. Press the Home button.

5. Tap Settings⇨Notification Center⇨Mail.

6. In the screen that appears, shown in **Figure 6-19**, tap VIP.

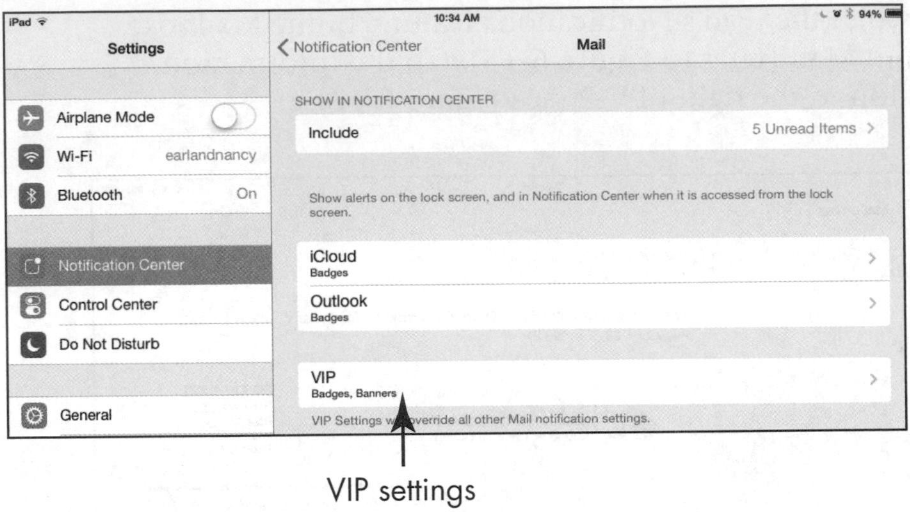

VIP settings

Figure 6-19

7. Tap the Show in Notification Center On/Off button to turn on notifications for VIP mail.

8. Tap an alert style, and specify whether the iPad should use a badge icon or sound to alert you. You can also choose to display VIP alerts on your Lock screen (see **Figure 6-20**).

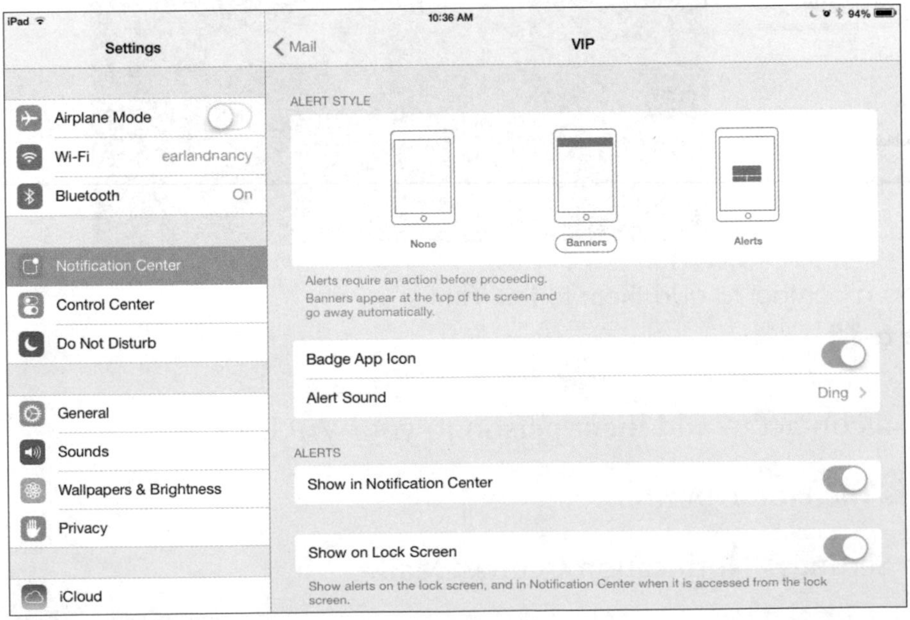

Figure 6-20

9. Press the Home button to close Settings. New mail from your VIPs should now appear in Notification Center when you swipe down from the top of the screen. Depending on the settings you chose in Step 8, the iPad may play a sound, display a note on your Lock screen, or display a blue star icon to the left of these messages in your Mail Inbox.

Getting Social with FaceTime, Twitter, and iMessage

FaceTime is an excellent video-calling app that's been available on the iPhone since the release of the iPhone 4 in mid-2010; then it came to the iPad and iPod touch lines and to the Mac. The app lets you use either a phone number or an e-mail address to call people who have FaceTime on their devices. You and your friend, colleague, or family member can see each other as you talk, which makes for a much more personal calling experience.

Twitter is a social networking service referred to as a *microblog* because it involves only short posted messages. Twitter has been incorporated into iOS 7 in a more integrated way that allows you to "tweet" people from within Safari, Photos, Camera, YouTube, Maps, and many other apps. You can also download the free Twitter app and use it to post tweets whenever you like.

Finally, iMessage is an instant messaging (IM) feature available through the preinstalled

Messages app. IM involves sending a text message to somebody's iPhone (using their phone number) or iPod touch or iPad (using their e-mail address) to carry on an instant conversation.

In this chapter, I introduce you to FaceTime, Twitter, and iMessage, and review their simple controls. In no time, you'll be socializing with all and sundry.

Understand Who Can Use FaceTime

Here's a quick rundown of what device and what information you need to use FaceTime's various features:

➡ FaceTime is available on all iPads except the original iPad.

➡ You can use FaceTime to call people who have the iPhone 4 or later, the iPad 2 or later, the iPad mini, a fourth-generation or later iPod touch, or a Mac running Mac OS X 10.6.6 or later.

➡ You can use a phone number to connect with an iPhone 4 or later.

➡ You can connect via e-mail address with a Mac, iPod touch, or iPad 2 or later.

Get an Overview of FaceTime

The FaceTime app works with the cameras built into the iPad 2 or later and lets you call other folks who have a device that supports FaceTime (see the previous task for compatibility). You can use FaceTime to chat while sharing video images with another person. This preinstalled app is useful for seniors who want to keep up with distant family members and friends and to see (as well as hear) the latest-and-greatest news.

You can make and receive calls with FaceTime by using a phone number (iPhone 4 or later) or an e-mail account (iPad 2 or later, iPod touch, or Mac) and show the person on the other end what's going on around you. Just remember that you can't adjust audio volume from within the app or record a video call. Nevertheless, on the positive side, even though its features are limited, this app is straightforward to use.

You can use your Apple ID and e-mail address to access FaceTime, so it works pretty much right away after you install it. See Chapter 3 for more about getting an Apple ID.

 If you're having trouble using FaceTime, make sure that the FaceTime feature is turned on. That's quick to do: Tap Settings on the Home screen; tap FaceTime; and then tap the On/Off button to turn the feature on, if necessary. On this Settings page, you can also select the e-mail and phone account that others can use to call you.

Make a FaceTime Call with Wi-Fi or 3G/4G

1. If you know that the person you're calling has FaceTime on an iPhone 4 or later, an iPad 2 or later, a fourth-generation or later iPod touch, or a Mac running OS X 10.6.6 or later, first be sure that you've added that person to your iPad Contacts. (See Chapter 18 for details on how to do this.)

2. Tap the FaceTime app icon on the Home screen. The first time you use the app, you may be asked to select the phone number and e-mail accounts you want to use for FaceTime calls, and then to tap Next. On the screen that appears, tap the Contacts button in the bottom-right corner.

3. Scroll to locate a contact, and tap the contact's name to display his or her information (see **Figure 7-1**).

Figure 7-1

4. In the contact's information, tap a stored phone number that's FaceTime-capable or an e-mail address that the contact has associated with FaceTime, and then tap the FaceTime button (shaped like a video camera). You've just placed a FaceTime call!

 You have to use the appropriate method to place a FaceTime call, depending on the kind of device the person you're calling has. If you're calling someone who has an iPhone 4 or later, you should use a phone number the first time you call; thereafter, you can use the phone number or e-mail address. If you're calling an iPad 2 or later, an iPod touch, or a FaceTime for Mac user, you have to make the call by using that person's e-mail address.

 When you use an e-mail address to call somebody, that person must be signed in to his or her Apple ID account and must have verified that the address can be used for FaceTime calls. iPad 2 or later and iPod touch (fourth-generation and later) users can make this setting by tapping Settings⇨FaceTime and signing in with an Apple ID.

5. When the person accepts the call, you see the recipient's image and a small draggable box containing your image, referred to as a Picture in Picture (PiP) (see **Figure 7-2**).

Figure 7-2

 You can also simply go to the Contacts app, find a contact, tap the FaceTime icon in that person's record, and then tap the phone number or e-mail address in the pop-up that appears to make a FaceTime call.

 To view recent calls, tap the Recents button in Step 2. Tap a recent call to call that person back.

 If you have iOS 6 or 7, you can use FaceTime over both a Wi-Fi network and your iPad's 3G or 4G connection. However, remember that if you use FaceTime over a phone connection, you may incur costly data usage fees.

 New with iOS 7, you can make audio only FaceTime calls which cuts down on the data streaming that can cost you when you share video. In Step 4 above simply tap the Call button (shaped like a phone handset) instead of the FaceTime button to initiate your audio only call.

Accept and End a FaceTime Call

1. If you're on the receiving end of a FaceTime call, accepting the call is about as easy as it gets. When the call comes in, tap the Answer button to take the call, or tap the Decline button to reject it (see **Figure 7-3**).

Figure 7-3

2. Chat away with your friend, tapping the FaceTime button if you want to view video images.

3. To end the call, tap the End button (see **Figure 7-4**).

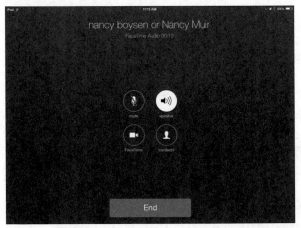

Figure 7-4

To mute sound during a call, tap the Mute button, which looks like a microphone with a line through it (refer to **Figure** 7-4). Tap the button again to unmute your iPad.

 To add a caller to your Favorites list, with FaceTime open, tap the Favorites button, tap the plus sign (+), and select a name from the Contacts list. Then you can locate the person you want to call by tapping Favorites and choosing that person from a short list rather than scrolling through all your contacts.

 If you'd rather not be available for calls, tap Settings⇨ Do Not Disturb. This feature stops any incoming calls or notifications. After you turn on Do Not Disturb, you can schedule when it's active, allow calls from certain people, or accept a second call from the same person after a three-minute interval by using the Do Not Disturb Repeated Calls setting.

Switch Views

1. When you're on a FaceTime call, you may want to use the iPad's built-in camera to show the person you're talking to what's going on around you. Tap the Switch Camera button to switch from the front-facing camera that's displaying your image to the back-facing camera that captures whatever you're looking at (see **Figure** 7-5).

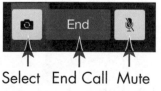

Select   End Call   Mute
camera

Figure 7-5

2. Tap the Switch Camera button again to switch back to the front camera, which displays your image.

Experience Twitter on the iPad

Twitter is a social networking service for *microblogging*, which involves posting very short messages (limited to 140 characters), called *tweets*, so that your friends can see what you're up to. As of iOS 5 for the iPad, the capability to tweet became integrated into several apps. You can post tweets by tapping the Share icon within Safari, Photos, Camera, YouTube, and Maps. First, tap Settings⇨ Twitter. Then tap the Install button and add your account information. After you have an account, you can post tweets, have people follow your tweets, and follow the tweets that other people post.

Now when you're using Safari, Photos, Camera, YouTube, or Maps, you can choose Twitter in the screen that appears when you tap the Share icon. A form like the one shown in **Figure 7-6** appears. Just write your message in the form and then tap Post.

Cancel	**Twitter**	Post
Jane Arnold		31st St
97		
Location		None >

Figure 7-6

 See Chapters 5, 12, and 13 for more about tweeting from the Safari, Photos, and YouTube apps, respectively.

Set Up an iMessage Account

1. iMessage is a feature that was new in iOS 5 (available through the preinstalled Messages app) that allows you to send and receive instant messages (IMs) to others using an Apple iOS device or suitably configured Mac. Instant messaging differs from e-mail or tweeting in an important way. Whereas you might e-mail somebody and wait days or weeks before that person responds, or you might post a tweet that could sit there a while before anybody views it, with instant messaging, the message is sent. You send an IM, and it appears on the recipient's Apple device right away. Assuming that the person wants to participate, a live conversation begins, allowing a back-and-forth dialogue in real time. To set up iMessage, tap Settings on the Home screen.

2. Tap Messages. The settings shown in **Figure** 7-7 appear.

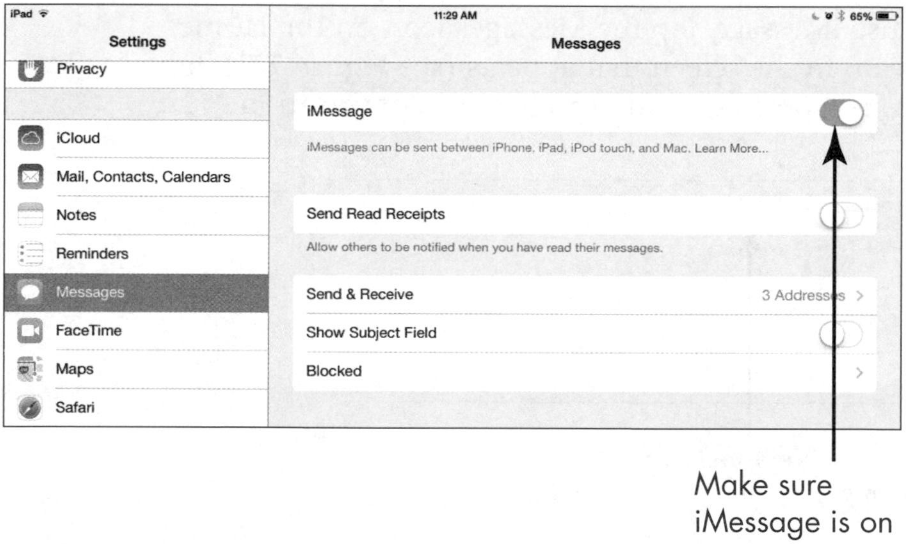

Make sure
iMessage is on

Figure 7-7

3. If iMessage isn't set to On (refer to **Figure** 7-7), tap the On/Off button to turn it on.

4. Check the Send & Receive setting to be sure the phone and/or e-mail account associated with your iPad are correct (should be set up automatically based on your Apple ID).

5. To allow a notice to be sent when you've read somebody's messages, tap the On/Off button for Send Read Receipts. You can also choose to show a Subject field in your messages.

6. Press the Home button to leave the settings or to add people that you want to block from sending you messages.

 To change the e-mail account that iMessage uses, tap Send & Receive, tap Add Another Email, and then follow the directions to add another e-mail account. To delete an account, tap the Information button to the right of it and then tap Remove This Email.

Use iMessage to Address, Create, and Send Messages

1. To use iMessage, tap the Messages icon on the Home screen. In the screen that appears (see **Figure 7-8**), tap the New Message button to begin a conversation.

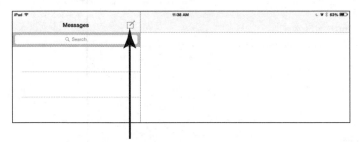

New message

Figure 7-8

2. You can address a message in a couple of ways:

- Begin to type an address in the To: field, and tap the recipient in the list of matching contacts that appears. Or tap the Dictation key on the onscreen keyboard and speak the address.

- Tap the plus icon to the right of the address field, and the All Contacts list appears, as shown in **Figure 7-9**. Tap the contact to whom you want to send the message.

| iPad 📶 | | 11:38 AM | 🔋 63% ▰ |
| Messages 📝 | | New Message | Cancel |

To: field   Plus icon

Figure 7-9

3. If the contact has both an e-mail address and phone number stored, the Info dialog appears, allowing you to tap either the e-mail address or phone number to use for sending the message.

4. To create a message, simply tap the message field near the bottom of the screen and then type or dictate your message.

5. To send the message, tap the Send button. When your recipient responds, you see the conversation displayed on the right side of the screen, as shown in **Figure 7-10**.

6. Tap the message field to respond to the last comment.

 You can address a message to more than one person simply by choosing more recipients in Step 2.

 If you want to include a photo or video with your message, tap the Camera button to the left of the message field (see **Figure 7-10**). Tap Take Photo or Video, or Choose Existing, and then tap Use to attach a photo or video. When you send your message, the photo or video goes along with your text.

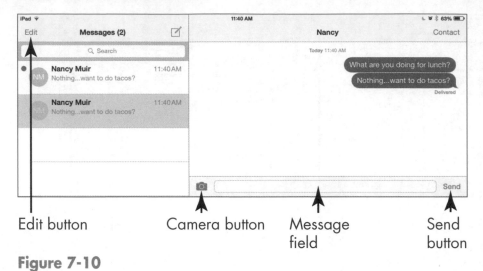

Edit button   Camera button   Message field   Send button

Figure 7-10

Clear a Conversation

1. When you're done chatting, you may want to clear a conversation to remove the clutter before you start a new one. With Messages open, tap the Edit button (refer to **Figure 7-10**).

2. Tap the round red Delete button next to any item you want to clear and then tap the square Delete button to complete the deletion (see **Figure 7-11**).

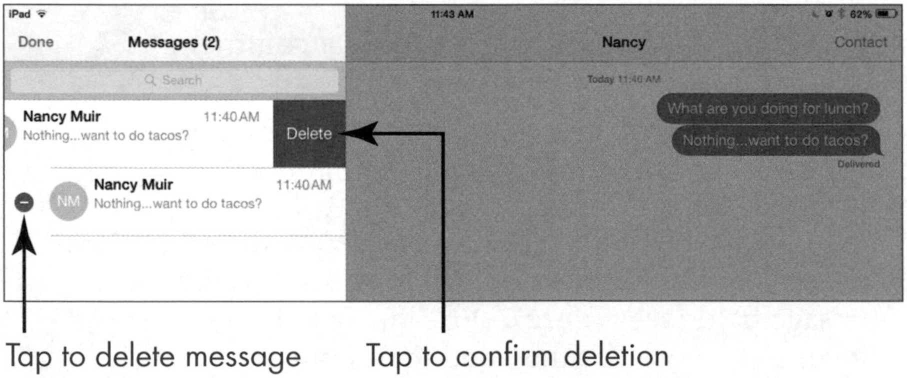

Tap to delete message   Tap to confirm deletion

Figure 7-11

From the Edit screen you can press and hold a message in a conversation and then tap More in the menu that appears. You can tap the check boxes to the left of individual comments of a particular conversation, and then tap the Delete button around the middle of the bottom of the screen, or the Forward button in the bottom right of the screen to enter a recipient's information and forward the conversation's contents to somebody.

Shopping the iTunes Store

*T*he iTunes Store app that comes preinstalled on iPad lets you easily shop for music, movies, TV shows, and audiobooks at Apple's iTunes Store.

In this chapter, you discover how to find content in the iTunes Store. The content can be downloaded directly to your iPad or to another device and then synced to your iPad. In addition, I cover a few options for buying content from other online stores.

Note that I cover opening an iTunes account and downloading iTunes software to your computer in Chapter 3. If you need to, refer to Chapter 3 to see how to handle these two tasks before digging into this chapter.

Explore the iTunes Store

1. Visiting the iTunes Store from your iPad is easy with the built-in iTunes Store app. Tap the iTunes Store icon on the Home screen.

2. If you're not already signed in to iTunes, the dialog shown in **Figure 8-1** appears, asking for your iTunes password. Enter your password and tap OK.

Tap here and enter your password

Figure 8-1

3. Tap the Music button in the row of buttons at the bottom of the screen, if it's not already selected, to view selections as shown in **Figure 8-2**.

See All link

Music button

Figure 8-2

4. Tap the See All link (refer to **Figure 8-2**) in any category of music to display more music selections.

5. Tap the button in the top-left corner labeled Music to go back to the featured Music selections; then tap the More button at the top of the screen. This step displays a list of music categories you can choose among. Tap one category. Items in the category are organized by criteria such as New and Noteworthy Albums and What We're Listening To.

6. Tap a genre tab at the top of the screen (such as Pop, Rock, or Hip-Hop) to narrow your selection.

7. Tap any listed item to see more details about it, as shown in **Figure 8-3**.

American Blues Brilliance				⬆
Various Artists				
Blues				
24 Songs				
Released Jun 25, 2013				
No Ratings				
$7.99				

	Songs	Reviews	Related		
	Name		Time	Popularity	Price
1	**Black Satin** Katie Webster		3:48	‖‖‖‖‖‖‖	$0.99
2	**War** JJ Grey & Mofro		3:27	‖‖‖‖‖‖‖	$0.99
3	**Third Degree** Johnny Winter		6:35	‖‖‖‖‖‖‖	$0.99
4	**Give Me My Blues** Albert Collins		4:14	‖‖‖‖‖‖‖	$0.99
5	**Pop's Recipe** Mavis Staples		5:26	‖‖‖‖‖‖‖	$0.99
6	**Darkness At the Bottom** Anders Osborne		6:00	‖‖‖‖‖‖‖	$0.99
7	**Greedy Man** Koko Taylor		3:30	‖‖‖‖‖‖‖	$0.99
8	**Story of My Life**		3:13	‖‖‖‖‖‖‖	$0.99

Figure 8-3

 The navigation techniques in these steps work essentially the same way in any of the content categories (the buttons at the bottom of the screen), which include Music, Movies, and TV Shows. Just tap one to explore it.

Podcasts and iTunes U (courses) used to be accessible through the iTunes Store, but now you have to install separate apps for them. Go to the App Store on your iPad, search for Podcasts or iTunes U, and install these free apps to get access to this additional content.

If you want to use the Genius playlist feature, which recommends additional purchases based on the contents of your library, in the iTunes app on your iPad, tap the Genius button at the bottom of the screen. If you've made enough purchases in iTunes, song and album recommendations appear based on those purchases as well as on the content in your iTunes Match library, if you have one.

Find a Selection

You can look for a selection in the iTunes Store in several ways. You can use the Search Store feature, search by genre or category, or view artists' pages. Here's how these methods work:

➡ Tap the Search Store field shown in **Figure 8-4**, and enter a search term with the onscreen keyboard. If a suggestion in the list of search results appeals to you, just tap it, or tap Search on the keyboard.

➡ Tap a category button at the top of the screen, or tap the More button. A list of genres or categories like the one shown in **Figure 8-5** appears.

➡ On the description page that appears when you tap a selection, you can find more offerings by the people involved by tapping the Related tab, as shown in **Figure 8-6**.

Figure 8-4

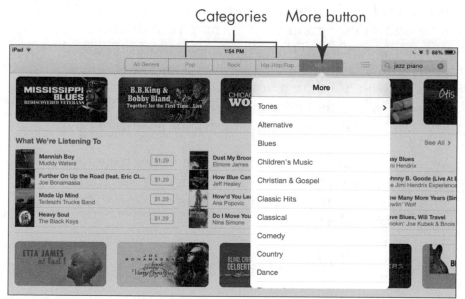

Figure 8-5

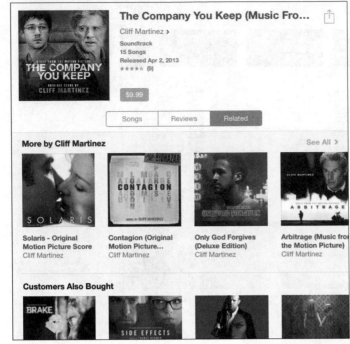

Figure 8-6

 If you find a selection that you like, tap the Share icon on its description page to share your discovery with a friend via AirDrop (fourth generation iPad and later), Mail, Twitter, or Facebook. A message form appears with a link that your friend can click or tap to view the selection. Enter an address in the To: field, and tap Send or Post. Now your friend is in the know.

 When you're displaying items on the home page for any type of content, tap the See All link to see all featured selections rather than only the top New and Noteworthy selections.

Preview Music, a Movie, or an Audiobook

1. If you've already set up an iTunes account (if you haven't done so yet, see Chapter 3), when you choose to buy an item, it's automatically charged to the credit card or

PayPal account you have on record or against any allowance you have outstanding on an iTunes gift card or
allowance. You may want to preview an item before you
buy it. If you like it, buying and downloading are easy and
quick. Open iTunes Store, and use any method outlined
in earlier tasks to locate a selection you may want to buy.

2. Tap the item to see detailed information about it, as
shown in **Figure 8-7**.

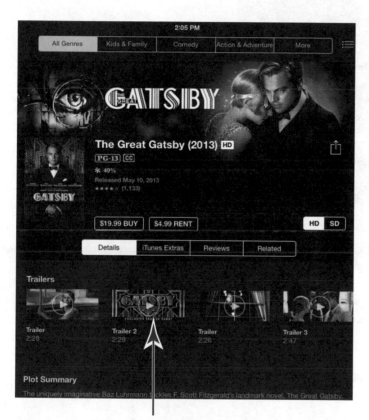

Tap a trailer to
preview the item

Figure 8-7

3. For a movie selection, tap the Trailer button (refer to
Figure 8-7) to view the theatrical trailer if one's available
(for audiobooks, tap the Preview button to play a preview).

For a TV show, tap an episode to get further information. If you want to listen to a sample of a music selection, tap the track number (see **Figure 8-8**) or the name of a selection with a Preview button to the right of it (see **Figure 8-9**).

Album price

Song price

Tap a track number or name to hear a preview

Figure 8-8

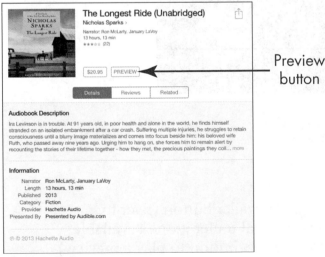

Preview button

Figure 8-9

Buy a Selection

1. When you find an item that you want to buy, tap the button that shows the price (if the selection is available for purchase) or the button with the word *Free* on it (if the selection is available for free). The button label changes to Buy *X*, where *X* is the type of content you're buying, such as a song or album.

2. Tap the Buy *X* button (see **Figure 8-10**). The iTunes Password dialog appears (refer to **Figure 8-1**).

Buy the album

Figure 8-10

3. Enter your password, and tap OK. The item begins downloading, and the cost is automatically charged against your account. When the download finishes, you can view the content in the Music or Video app, depending on the type of content.

If you want to buy music, you can open the description page for an album and tap the album price, or buy individual songs rather than the entire album. Tap the price for a song and then proceed to purchase it.

 Notice the Redeem button on many iTunes Store screens. Tap this button to redeem any iTunes gift certificates you may have received from your generous friends (or from yourself).

 If you don't want to allow purchases from within apps (such as Music or Videos) and want to allow purchases only through the iTunes Store, tap Settings⇨General⇨Restrictions⇨Enable Restrictions, and enter a passcode. After you've set a passcode, you can tap individual apps to turn on restrictions for them, as well as for actions such as deleting apps, sharing via AirDrop, or using Siri.

 If you have a 3G or 4G iPad model, you can allow content to be downloaded over your cellular network. Be aware that you could incur hefty data charges from your provider for these downloads. If you aren't near a Wi-Fi hotspot, however, cellular downloading may be your only option. To activate this feature, tap Settings⇨iTunes & App Store, and tap the On/Off button for the Cellular setting.

Rent a Movie

1. In the case of movies, you can either rent or buy content. If you rent, which is less expensive than buying but makes the content yours for only a short time, you have 30 days from the time you rent the item to begin watching it. After you've begun to watch it, you have 24 hours remaining to watch it on the same device as many times

as you like. With the iTunes Store open, tap the Movies button.

2. Locate the movie you want to rent, and tap the Rent button, shown in **Figure 8-11.** The Rent button changes to a Rent Movie button.

Rent button

Figure 8-11

3. Tap Rent Movie (see **Figure 8-12**) to confirm the rental. The movie begins to download to your iPad immediately, and the rental fee is charged to your account. To check the status of your download, tap the Downloads button. The progress of your download is displayed.

4. When the download is complete, use either the Music or Videos app to watch it. (See Chapters 11 and 13, respectively, to read about how these apps work.)

Tap to rent the movie

Figure 8-12

 Some movies are offered in high-definition (HD) versions. These HD movies look great on that crisp, colorful iPad screen, especially if you have a third-generation or later iPad with Retina display.

 You can also download content to your computer and sync it to your iPad. See Chapter 3 for more about this process.

Shop Anywhere Else

One feature that's missing from the iPad is support for Adobe Flash. *Flash* is a video-playback format that many video-on-demand services use. Many online stores that sell content such as movies and music are hurriedly adding iPad-friendly videos to their collections, so you do have alternatives to iTunes for movies and TV shows. You can also shop for music from sources other than iTunes, such as Amazon.com.

You can open accounts at one of these stores by using your computer's web browser or your iPad's Safari browser and then following the store's instructions to purchase and download content.

These content providers offer iPad-compatible video content, and more are opening all the time:

➡ **ABC:** http://abc.go.com

➡ **CBS News:** www.cbsnews.com

➡ **TV.com:** www.tv.com

➡ **Netflix:** www.netflix.com

➡ **Ustream:** www.ustream.tv

➡ **iMP4Movies:** http://imp4movies.com

 For non–iPad-friendly formats, you can download the content on your computer and stream it to your iPad by using Air Video ($2.99) on the iPad or Air Video Server (which is free) on your Mac or Windows computer. For more information, go to www.inmethod.com/air-video/index.html. Another free utility for Mac and Windows that converts most video to an iPad-friendly format is HandBrake. Go to http://handbrake.fr for more information.

Enable Autodownloads of Purchases from Other Devices

1. With iCloud, you can make a purchase or download free content on any of your Apple devices and have those purchases automatically copied to all your Apple devices. To enable this autodownload feature on iPad, start by tapping Settings on the Home screen.

To use iCloud, first set up an iCloud account. See Chapter 3 for detailed coverage of iCloud, including setting up your account.

2. Tap iTunes & App Store.

3. In the options that appear, tap the On/Off button to turn on any category of purchases you want to autodownload to your iPad from other Apple devices (see **Figure 8-13**).

Settings	iTunes & App Store
iCloud	Apple ID: page7@live.com
Mail, Contacts, Calendars	
Notes	SHOW ALL
Reminders	Music
Messages	Videos
FaceTime	Show all store purchases and iTunes Match uploads in your music and video libraries, even if they have not been downloaded to this iPad.
Maps	
Safari	iTunes Match
	Store all your music in the cloud with iTunes Match. Learn more...
iTunes & App Store	AUTOMATIC DOWNLOADS
Music	Music
Videos	Apps
Photos & Camera	Books
iBooks	Updates
	Automatically download new purchases (including free) made on other devices.

Turn on to
autodownload
this content

Figure 8-13

At this point, Apple doesn't offer an option to autodownload video content by using these settings because video is such a memory and bandwidth hog. You can always download video directly to your iPad through the iTunes Store, Podcasts, or iTunes U (for educational content) apps or sync to your computer via iTunes to get the content.

Expanding Your iPad Horizons with Apps

Some *apps* (short for *applications*) come pre-installed on your iPad, such as Contacts and Videos. But there's a world of other apps out there that you can get for your iPad, some for free (such as iBooks) and some for a price (typically, from $0.99 to about $10, though some can top out at $90 or more).

Apps range from games to financial tools such as loan calculators to productivity applications, including the iPad version of Pages, the Apple software for word processing and page layout.

In this chapter, I suggest some apps you may want to check out and explain how to use the iPad's App Store feature to find, purchase, and download apps.

Explore Senior-Recommended Apps

As I write this book, apps are being created for the iPad at a furious pace, so many more apps that could fit your needs will be available by the time you have this book in your hands.

Still, to get you exploring what's available, I want to provide a quick list of apps that may whet your appetite.

Access the App Store by tapping the App Store icon on the Home screen. Then check out an app by typing its name in the Search Store box and tapping the Search key on the onscreen keyboard. Here are some interesting apps to explore:

➡ **Sudoku 2 (free):** If you like this mental logic puzzle in print, try it out on your iPad (see **Figure 9-1**). It has three lessons and several levels ranging from easiest to nightmare, making it a great way to make time fly by in the doctor's or dentist's waiting room.

Figure 9-1

➡ **Real-Time Stocks (free):** Keep track of your investments on your iPad with this app. You can use the app to create a watch list and record your stocks' performance.

➡ **DealCatcher iPad Edition (free):** Use this app to find low prices on just about everything local to your area. Read product reviews, and compare list prices.

➡ **Flickr (free):** If you use the Flickr photo-sharing service on your computer, why not bring the same features to your iPad? This app is useful for sharing images with family members and friends.

➡ **Paint Studio ($3.99):** Get creative! You can use this powerful app to draw, add color, and even create special effects. If you prefer a free paint program, try iPaint Studio.

➡ **GarageBand ($4.99):** If you love to make music, you'll love this app, which has been part of the Mac stable for several years. Play piano, guitar, or a variety of other virtual musical instruments.

➡ **Mediquations Medical Calculator ($4.99):** Use this handy utility to help calculate medications with built-in formulas and read scores for various medications. Check with your physician before using!

➡ **iPhoto ($4.99):** This Apple app provides all kinds of tools for editing those great photos you can grab with the iPad's cool iSight rear-facing camera (not available on the original iPad).

➡ **Travelzoo (free):** Get great deals on hotels, airfare, rental cars, entertainment, and more. This app also offers tips from travel experts.

 iBooks is the outstanding, free e-reader app that opens up a world of reading on your iPad. See Chapter 10 for details about using iBooks.

 Most iPhone apps work on your iPad, so if you own the mobile phone and have favorite apps on it, sync them to your iPad!

Be aware that apps that haven't been optimized for the third- or fourth-generation iPad's or iPad Air's 2048 x 1536 Retina display won't look super-crisp. In fact, they may look worse than they do on an iPad 2. When the third-generation iPad came out, only a few apps were optimized, but developers the world over have been producing optimized apps at a rapid clip. Check to see whether an app has been optimized for the Retina display before you buy it. Apple offers a list of some of these apps at www.apple.com/ipad/ from-the-app-store.

Search the App Store

1. Tap the App Store icon on the Home screen. The site shown in **Figure 9-2** appears.

Figure 9-2

2. At this point, you have several options for finding apps:

- Tap the Search Store field, enter a search term, and then tap the Search button on the onscreen keyboard to see results.

- Swipe the screen downward to scroll down, or swipe to the right to see more selections.

- Tap the All Categories, Games, Newsstand, Education, or More tab at the top of the screen to see that category of apps.

- Tap the Top Charts button at the bottom of the screen to see which free and paid apps other people are downloading most.

- The Near Me option at the bottom of the screen, new in iOS 7, displays apps that are popular among people in or near your location. (This may or may not produce useful results. depending on where you are!)

- Tap the Purchased button at the bottom of the screen to view apps you've already purchased, as shown in **Figure 9-3**.

Get Applications from the App Store

1. Getting free apps or buying apps requires an iTunes account, which I cover in Chapter 3. After you have an account, you can use your saved payment information to buy apps or download free apps in a few simple steps. I strongly recommend that you install the free iBooks app (which I walk you through using in Chapter 10), so in this task, I give you the steps for getting it. With the App Store open, tap the Search field, enter *iBooks*, and then tap Search on the onscreen keyboard.

Figure 9-3

2. Tap the Free button for iBooks in the results that appear. (To get a *paid* app, you'd tap the same button, which would be labeled with a price.) The Free button changes to Install (or, in the case of a paid app, to Buy).

3. Tap the Install button.

4. You may be asked to enter your iTunes password. If so, tap the OK button to proceed. The app downloads and appears on a Home screen (probably your second Home screen, if you haven't downloaded many apps yet), as shown in **Figure** 9-4. If you purchase an app that isn't free, at this point, your credit card or gift card allowance is charged for the purchase price.

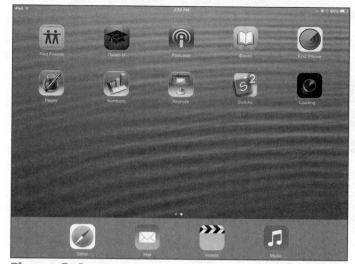

Figure 9-4

 Out of the box, only preinstalled apps are located on the first iPad Home screen. Apps that you download are placed on additional Home screens, and you have to scroll to view and use them. See the next task for help in finding your newly downloaded apps on multiple Home screens.

 If you've opened an iCloud account, anything you purchase on your iPad can be set up to be pushed to other Apple iOS devices automatically. See Chapter 3 for more about iCloud.

Organize Your Applications on Home Screens

1. The iPad can display several Home screens. By default, the first contains preinstalled apps; other screens are created to contain any apps you download or sync to your iPad. At the bottom of any iPad Home screen (just above the Dock), dots indicate the number of Home screens, and a solid dot specifies the Home screen you're on, as shown in **Figure 9-5.** Press the Home button to open the last displayed Home screen.

2. Flick your finger from right to left to move to the next Home screen. To move back, flick from left to right.

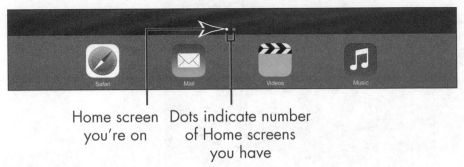

Home screen   Dots indicate number
you're on   of Home screens
               you have

Figure 9-5

3. To reorganize apps on a Home screen, press and hold any app on that screen. The app icons begin to jiggle (see **Figure 9-6**), and any apps you've installed sport a Delete button (a black circle with a white *X* on it). Pre-installed apps cannot be deleted and so have no Delete button on them.

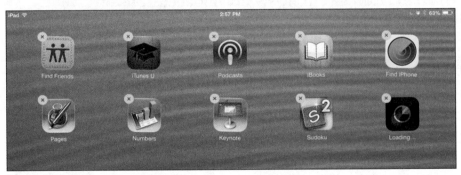

Figure 9-6

4. Press, hold, and drag an app icon to another location on the screen to move it.

5. Press the Home button to stop all those icons from jiggling!

To move an app from one page to another, while the apps are jiggling, you can press, hold, and drag an app to the left or right to move it to the next Home screen. You can also use iTunes to manage what app resides on what Home screen and in which folder when you've connected the iPad to iTunes via a cable or wireless sync. This process may be easier for some people and allows you to reorder Home screens which you can't do from the iPad.

With iOS 7 come some new multitasking features for switching between apps easily. Press the Home button twice, and you get a preview of open apps. Scroll among them, and tap the one you want to go to. Swipe an app upward from this preview list to close it.

Organize Apps in Folders

Like the iPhone, the iPad lets you organize apps in folders so that you can find them more easily. With iOS 7 there is now no limit on the number of apps you can store in a folder. The process is simple:

1. Tap and hold an app until all apps do their jiggle dance.

2. Drag an app on top of another app. The two apps appear in a box with a placeholder name in a strip above them (see **Figure 9-7**).

3. To change the folder name, tap the bar above the box. The keyboard appears.

4. Tap the Delete key to delete the placeholder name, and type one of your own.

5. Tap anywhere outside the bar to save the name.

Figure 9-7

6. Press the Home button to stop the icons from dancing around. Your folder appears on the Home screen where you began this process.

Delete Applications You No Longer Need

1. When you no longer need an app that you installed, it's time to get rid of it. (You can't delete apps that are prein- stalled on the iPad, such as Notes, Calendar, and Photos.) If you use iCloud to push content across all Apple iOS devices, note that deleting an app on your iPad won't affect that app on other devices. Display the Home screen that contains the app you want to delete.

2. Press and hold the app until all apps begin to jiggle.

3. Tap the Delete button for the app you want to delete (see **Figure 9-8**). A confirmation message like the one shown in **Figure 9-9** appears.

4. Tap Delete to proceed with the deletion.

Delete button

Figure 9-8

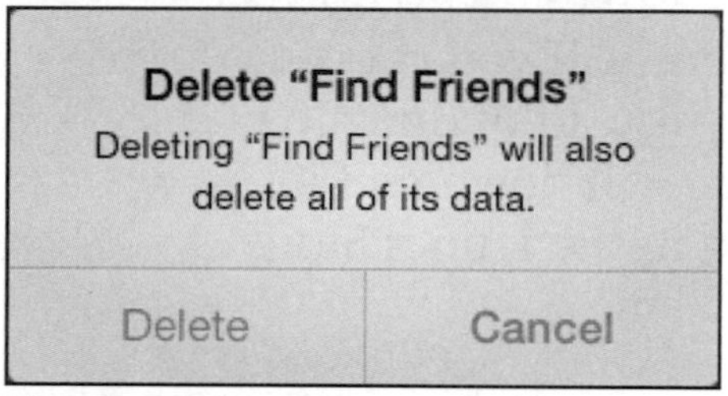

Delete "Find Friends"

Deleting "Find Friends" will also
delete all of its data.

Delete   Cancel

Figure 9-9

 Don't worry about wiping out several apps at once by
deleting a folder. When you delete a folder, the apps
that were contained within the folder are placed back
on Home screens.

 If you have several apps to delete, you can delete
them by using iTunes connected to your iPad, making the process a bit more streamlined.

Update Apps

1. App developers update their apps all the time to fix problems or add new features, so you may want to check for
those updates. The App Store icon on the Home screen
displays the number of available updates in a red circle.
Tap the App Store icon.

2. Tap the Updates button to access the Updates screen and
   then tap any item you want to update. To update all apps
   that have updates, tap the Update All button.

3. On the screen that appears, tap Update. You may be
   asked to confirm that you want to update or to enter
   your Apple ID Password; tap OK to proceed. You may
   also be asked to confirm that you're over a certain age or
   agree to terms and conditions; if so, scroll down the
   terms dialog (reading the terms as you go, of course),
   and at the bottom, tap Agree.

In iOS 5, Apple introduced the capability to download multiple apps simultaneously. If you choose
more than one app to update, instead of downloading them sequentially, all items will download in
parallel. You can keep working in the iTunes Store
while you're downloading an item.

If you have an iCloud account that you've made
active on various devices, when you update an app
on your iPad, it also updates automatically on any
other Apple iOS devices you have (and vice versa).

Part III
Having Fun and Consuming Media

Visit www.dummies.com/extras/ipadforseniors for more ideas about how to use iTunes Radio custom channels.

Using Your iPad as an E-Reader

A traditional *e-reader* is a device that's used primarily to read the electronic versions of books, magazines, and newspapers. Apple has touted the iPad as a great e-reader, so although it isn't a traditional e-reader device like the Barnes & Noble Nook, you won't want to miss out on this cool functionality.

Apple's free, downloadable app that turns your iPad into an e-reader is *iBooks*, which enables you to buy and download books from Apple's iBookstore. You can also use one of several other free e-reader apps — for example, Kindle or Stanza, or Bluefire Reader — to download books to your iPad from a variety of online sources, such as Amazon and Google, so you can read to your heart's content.

An app that arrived with iOS 5 was Newsstand. It has a similar look and feel to iBooks, but its focus is on subscribing to and reading magazines, newspapers, and other periodicals. With iOS 7 comes a dramatic revision to the appearance of Newsstand, which now boasts a contemporary background replacing the wooden-shelf look of yore.

In this chapter, you discover the options available for reading material and how to buy books

Get ready to...

and subscribe to publications. You also learn how to get around electronic publications: how to navigate an e-book, interactive book, or periodical; adjust brightness and type; search books; and organize your iBooks and Newsstand libraries.

Discover How the iPad Differs from Other E-Readers

An e-reader is any electronic device that enables you to download and read books, magazines, PDF files, or newspapers. These devices typically are portable and dedicated only to reading the electronic version of published materials. Most e-readers use E Ink technology to create a paper-like reading experience.

The iPad is a bit different: It isn't only for reading books, and you have to download an app to enable it as an e-reader (although almost all the apps are free). Also, the iPad doesn't offer a paper-like reading experience; you read from a computer screen (though you can adjust the brightness and background color of the screen).

When you buy a book or magazine online (or get one of many free publications), it downloads to your iPad in a few seconds over a Wi-Fi or 3G/4G connection. The iPad offers several navigation tools that let move around a book, which you explore in this chapter.

 iBooks version 2.0 introduced tools for reading and interacting with book content. You can even create and publish your own interactive books by using a free app called iBooks Author.

Find Books with iBooks

1. In Chapter 9, I walk you through the process of downloading the iBooks application, so you should do that now if you haven't already. To shop with iBooks, tap the iBooks application icon to open it. (It's probably on your second Home screen, so you may have to swipe your finger to the left on the Home screen to locate it, or consider placing iBooks on the iPad Dock by pressing and holding its icon until it jiggles and then dragging the icon to the Dock or first Home screen.)

2. In the iBooks library that opens (see **Figure 10-1**), you see a bookshelf; yours probably has only one free book already downloaded to it. (If you don't see the bookshelf, tap the Library button to go there. If no Library button is onscreen, tap the Bookshelf button in the top-right corner of the screen.) Tap the Store button, and the shelf pivots 180 degrees.

Figure 10-1

3. In the iBooks Store, shown in **Figure 10-2**, featured titles are shown by default. Try any of the following methods to find a book:

- Tap the Search Store field at the top of the screen and then use the onscreen keyboard to type a search word or phrase.

- Tap the More button at the top of the screen and scroll down to browse categories, with links to popular categories of books, as shown in **Figure 10-3**.

- Tap Purchased at the bottom of the screen to see any books you've bought on devices signed in with the same Apple ID. You can tap the All tab to show content from all devices or tap the Not on This iPad tab to see only content purchased on other devices.

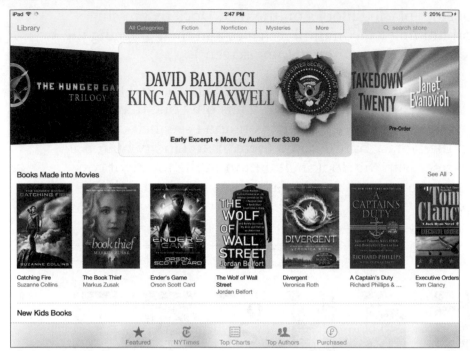

Figure 10-2

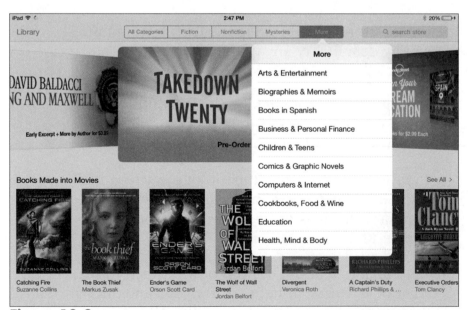

Figure 10-3

- Tap the appropriate button at the bottom of the screen to view particular categories: Books to see featured books, NYTimes to display *The New York Times* best-seller list, Top Charts for books listed on top charts, and Top Authors.

 Scroll to the bottom of many screens to access Quick Links, which includes shortcuts to Best of the Month, Free Books, and Award Winners.

- Tap a suggested selection or featured book to open more information about it.

 Download a free sample before you buy. You get to read several pages of the book to see whether it appeals to you, and it doesn't cost you a dime! Look for the Get Sample button when you view details about a book. If you like the book, you can buy it from within the iBooks app by tapping the sample and then tapping Buy.

Explore Other E-Book Sources

The iPad is capable of using other e-reader apps to display book content from other bookstores. To do so, first download another e-reader application, such as the Kindle from Amazon, from the App Store. (See Chapter 9 for details on how to download apps.) You can also download a non-vendor-specific app, such as Bluefire Reader, that handles ePub and PDF format, as well as the format that most public libraries use. Then use the app's features to search for, purchase, and download content.

The Kindle e-reader application is shown in **Figure 10**-4. After downloading the free app from the App Store, you just enter the e-mail address associated with your Amazon account and password. Any content you've already bought from Amazon is archived online (tap the Cloud tab to see these titles) and can be downloaded to your iPad for you to read any time you like. Use features to enhance your reading experience, such as changing the background to a sepia tone or changing the font. Tap the Device tab to see titles stored on the iPad. To delete a book from this reader, press the title with your finger; the Remove from Device button appears.

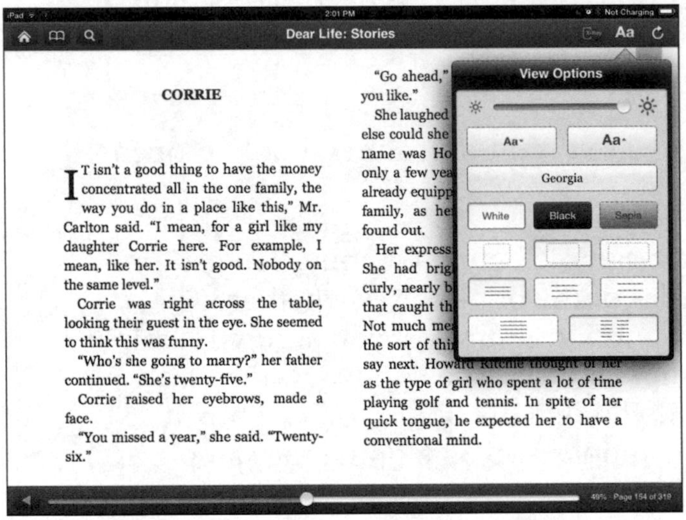

Figure 10-4

Electronic books are everywhere! You can also get content from a variety of other sources: Project Gutenberg (www.gutenberg.org), Google, publishers such as Baen (www.baen.com), and so on. Get the content on your computer, add it to Books in iTunes, and sync with your iPad. Many public library systems allow you to "borrow" e-book versions of books and sync them to your iPad.

Buy Books

1. If you've set up an account in the iTunes Store, you can use the iBooks app to buy books at the iBook Store. (See Chapter 3 for more about iTunes.) Open iBooks, and tap Store. When you find a book in the iBooks Store that you want to buy, tap it and then tap the button that shows the price (see **Figure 10-5**). The button changes to the Buy Book button (see **Figure 10-6**). (If the book is free, these buttons are labeled Free and Get Book, respectively.)

Figure 10-5

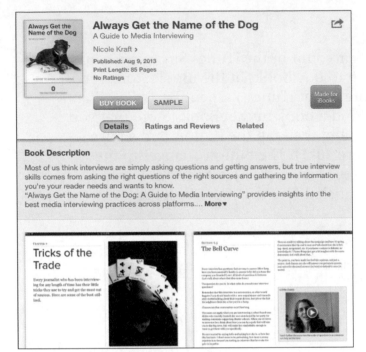

Figure 10-6

2. Tap the Buy Book or Get Book button. If you haven't already signed in, the iTunes Password dialog appears.

 If you have signed in, your purchase is accepted immediately.

3. Enter your password, and tap OK. The book appears on your bookshelf, and the cost is charged to whichever credit card you specified when you opened your iTunes account.

 You can also sync books you've downloaded to your computer to your iPad by using the data-connection cord and your iTunes account, or by setting up iCloud and choosing to automatically download books by tapping Settings⇨iTunes & App Store.

You can also sync wirelessly from your computer to your iPad. See Chapter 3 for more about syncing and iCloud.

Navigate a Book

1. Tap iBooks, and if your library (the bookshelf) isn't already displayed, tap the Library button.

2. Tap a book to open it. The book opens, as shown in **Figure 10-7.** (If you hold your iPad in portrait orientation, it shows one page; in landscape orientation, it shows two.)

Table of Contents button

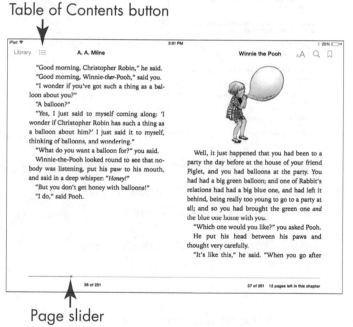

Page slider

Figure 10-7

3. Perform any of these actions to navigate the book:

- **To go to the book's table of contents:** Tap the Table of Contents button near the top-left corner (it looks like a little bulleted list) and then tap the name of a chapter to go to it (see **Figure 10-8**).

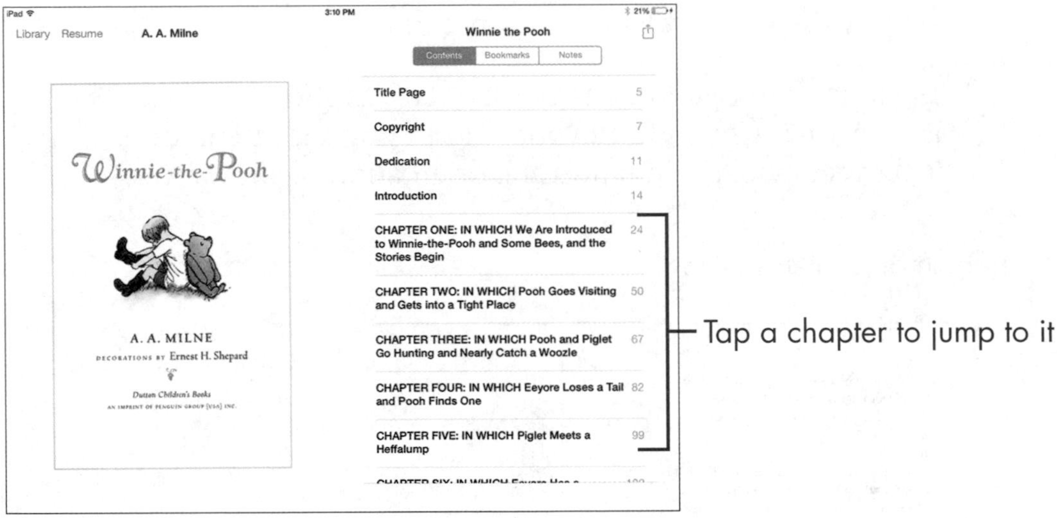

Figure 10-8

- **To turn to the next page:** Place your finger anywhere on the right edge of a page and flick to the left.

- **To turn to the preceding page:** Place your finger anywhere on the left edge of a page and flick to the right.

- **To move to another page in the book:** Tap and drag the slider at the bottom of the page to the right or left.

To return to the Library to view another book at any time, tap the Library button. If the button isn't visible, tap anywhere on the page, and the tool appears.

Adjust Brightness

1. iBooks offers an adjustable brightness setting that you can use to make reading book pages more comfortable for you. With a book open, tap the Font button, shown in **Figure 10-9.**

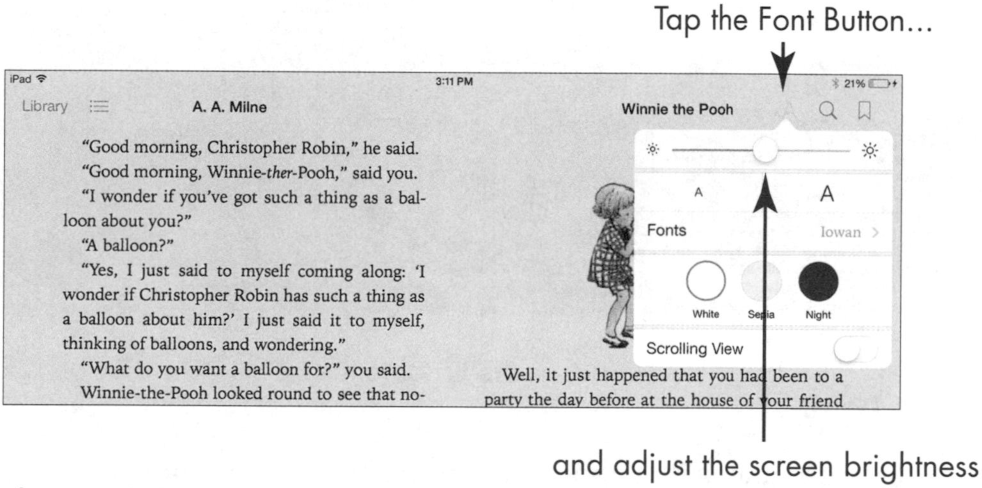

Tap the Font Button...

and adjust the screen brightness

Figure 10-9

2. In the Font dialog that appears (refer to **Figure 10-9**), tap and drag the Brightness slider to the right to make the screen brighter, or tap and drag the slider to the left to dim the screen.

3. Tap anywhere in the book to close the Brightness dialog.

 Try tapping the Themes button in the Font dialog to choose a different-color background, which is covered in the next task.

 Bright-white screens are commonly thought to be hard on the eyes, so setting the brightness halfway relative to its default setting or less is probably a good idea (and saves battery life). Sepia mutes the background to a soft beige that may work better for some people.

Change the Font Size and Type

1. If the type on your screen is a bit small for your taste, you can change to a larger font size or choose a different font for readability. With a book open, tap the Font button (it sports a small letter *A* and a large *A,* as shown in **Figure 10-10**).

Tap the Font button...

to change the font size

or see the list of fonts

Figure 10-10

2. In the Font dialog that appears (refer to **Figure 10-10**), tap the button with a small *A* on the left to use smaller text, or tap the button with the large *A* on the right to use larger text.

3. Tap Fonts. The list of fonts shown in **Figure 10-11** appears.

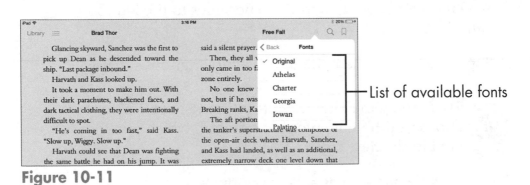

List of available fonts

Figure 10-11

4. Tap a font name to select it. The font changes on the book page.

5. If you want to add a sepia tint to the pages or to reverse black and white, which can be easier on the eyes, tap the Themes button and then tap White, Sepia, or Night to choose the theme you want to display.

6. Tap outside the Font dialog to return to your book.

 Some fonts appear a bit larger on your screen than others because of their design. If you want the largest font, use Iowan.

 If you're reading a PDF file, you're reading a picture of a document rather than an electronic book, so be aware that modifying the page's appearance might work a bit differently.

Search in Your Book

1. You may want to find a certain sentence or reference in your book. To do so, with the book displayed, tap the Search button, shown in **Figure 10-12**. The onscreen keyboard appears.

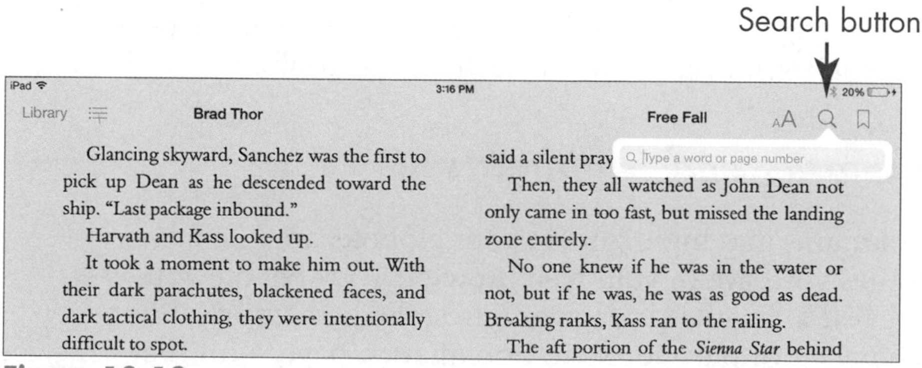

Search button

iPad 📶   3:16 PM   20% 🔋

Library ⋮≡   **Brad Thor**   **Free Fall**   ᴀA 🔍 🔖

Glancing skyward, Sanchez was the first to pick up Dean as he descended toward the ship. "Last package inbound."

Harvath and Kass looked up.

It took a moment to make him out. With their dark parachutes, blackened faces, and dark tactical clothing, they were intentionally difficult to spot.

said a silent pray   🔍 Type a word or page number

Then, they all watched as John Dean not only came in too fast, but missed the landing zone entirely.

No one knew if he was in the water or not, but if he was, he was as good as dead. Breaking ranks, Kass ran to the railing.

The aft portion of the *Sienna Star* behind

Figure 10-12

2. Type a search term (or tap the Dictation key on the onscreen keyboard and speak the term) and then tap the Search key on the keyboard. iBooks searches for any matching entries.

3. Use your finger to scroll down the entries (see **Figure 10-13**) and tap one to go to that spot in the book.

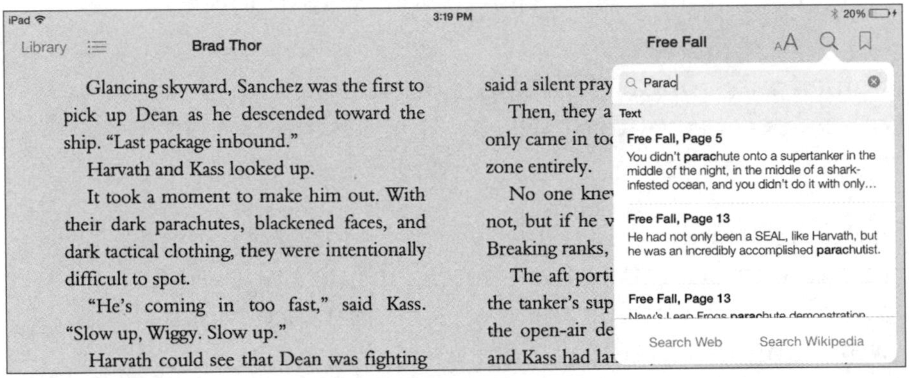

Figure 10-13

4. You can tap either the Search Web or Search Wikipedia button at the bottom of the Search dialog if you want to search for information about the search term online.

> You can also search for other instances of a particular word by pressing your finger on the word and tapping Search on·the toolbar that appears. If what you're looking for is a definition of the word, consider tapping Define rather than Search on this toolbar.

Use Bookmarks and Highlights

1. Bookmarks and highlights in your e-books are like favorite sites you save in your web browser: They enable you to revisit a favorite passage or refresh your memory about a character or plot point. To bookmark a page, with that page displayed, just tap the Bookmark button in the top-right corner (see **Figure 10-14**). A red ribbon appears in the top-right corner of the page.

Bookmark button

Figure 10-14

2. To highlight a word or phrase, press a word until the toolbar shown in **Figure 10-15** appears.

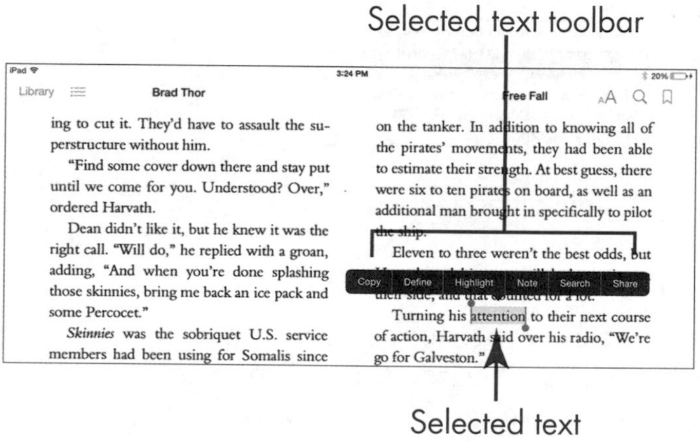

Selected text toolbar

Selected text

Figure 10-15

3. Tap the Highlight button. A colored highlight is placed on the word.

4. To change the color of the highlight or remove it, tap the highlighted word, and then tap the Highlight button.

5. Tap one of these options:

- *The Colors button:* Tap the Color button. The toolbar shown in **Figure 10-16** appears. Tap any colored circle to change the highlight color.

- *The Remove Highlight button:* Tapping the little trash can removes the highlight (or underline).

- *The Note button:* Tap the Note button to add a note to the item.

- *The Share button:* Tap this button to share the high-lighted text via Mail, Twitter, or Facebook.

Highlighted text toolbar

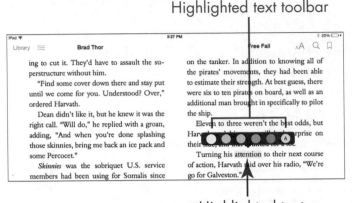

Highlighted text

Figure 10-16

6. You can also tap the button at the right end of the tool-bar to access Copy, Define, and Search tools. Tap outside the highlighted text to close the toolbar. Tap outside the highlighted text to close the toolbar.

7. To go to a list of bookmarks and highlights, tap the Table of Contents button on a book page.

8. In the table of contents, tap the Bookmarks or Notes tab. As shown in **Figure 10-17,** all bookmarks or notes (which include highlights) are displayed on their respec-tive tabs.

9. Tap a bookmark or highlight in one of these lists to go to that location in the book.

The iPad automatically bookmarks the place where you left off reading in a book so you don't have to do it man-ually. Because that information is stored in the iTunes Store, you can even pick up where you left off on your iPhone, Mac, iPod touch, or another iPad.

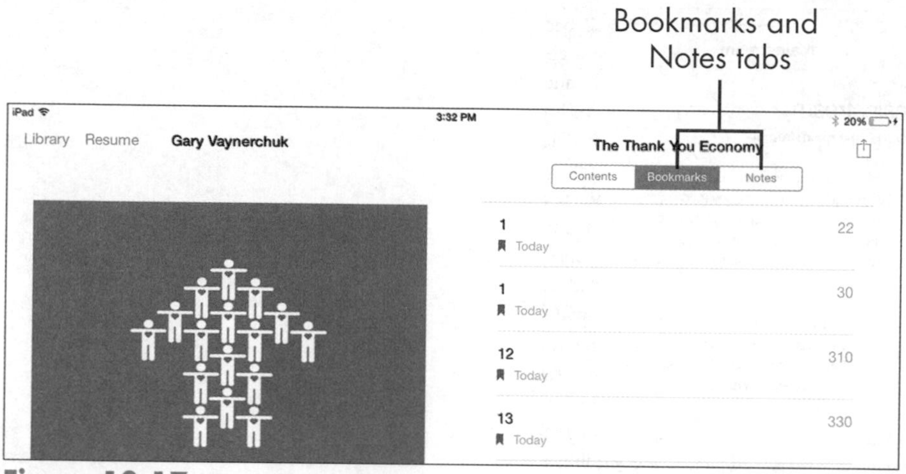

Bookmarks and
Notes tabs

Figure 10-17

Check Words in the Dictionary

1. As you read a book, you may come across unfamiliar words. Don't skip them; take the opportunity to learn new words! With a book open, press a word and hold it until the toolbar shown in **Figure 10-18** appears.

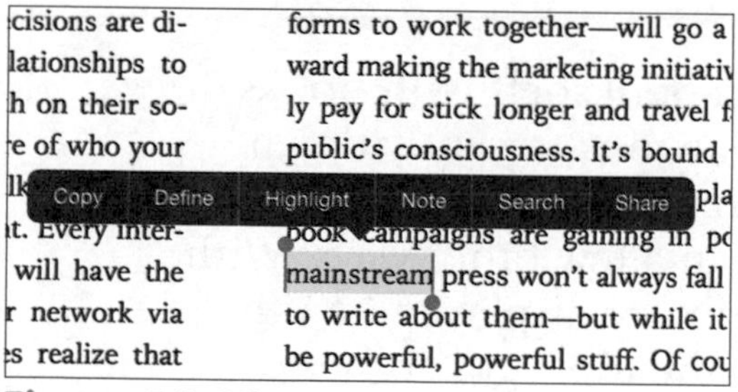

Figure 10-18

2. Tap the Define button. A definition dialog appears, as shown in **Figure 10-19**.

3. Tap the definition, and scroll down to view more.

4. When you finish reviewing the definition, tap anywhere on the page, and the definition disappears.

Figure 10-19

 You can also tap the Search Web button to look for information about a word from web sources or tap the Manage button to choose which dictionary your definitions come from.

Organize Your Library

1. Your iPad's library looks like a bookshelf with books stored on it by default, with the most recently downloaded title in the top-left corner. However, if you prefer, you can view your library in a few other ways. With the bookshelf version of the library displayed, tap the List View button, shown near the top-right corner of **Figure 10-20**.

Figure 10-20

2. Your books appear in a list, as shown in **Figure 10-21**. To organize the list alphabetically by title or author, tap the appropriate button at the bottom of the screen.

iPad	3:37 PM		⚡ 21% ⊡+
Store Collections	**Books**		⊞ Edit

FREE 25 Language Phrasebook
MobileReference
Reference

Free Fall
Brad Thor
Fiction & Literature

Gluten Free Cookbook
Kate Shean
Cookbooks, Food & Wine

How to Be Free
Joe Blow
Psychology

Stardrop Graphic Novel Free
Mark Oakley
Graphic Novels

The Thank You Economy
Gary Vaynerchuk
Business & Personal Finance

Winnie the Pooh
A. A. Milne
Children's Fiction

Figure 10-21

3. To organize by category, tap the Categories button at the bottom of the page. Your titles are divided into categories such as Fiction, Mysteries & Thrillers, and Literary.

4. To return to Bookshelf view at any time, tap the Bookshelf View button at the upper right of the screen.

 Tap the Bookshelf tab at the bottom to remove categories and list the most recently downloaded book first.

 Tap the Edit button in List view to display small circles to the left of all books in the list. Tap any of the circles and then tap the Delete button at the top of the page to delete books. Tap the Done button to exit the Edit function.

Organize Books in Collections

iBooks lets you create collections of books to help you organize them by your own logic, such as Tear Jerkers, Work-Related, and Recipes Dave Likes. You can place a book in only one collection, however. After you create several collections, you can drag left and right in iBooks to move among them.

1. To create a collection from the Library bookshelf, tap Edit.

2. In the dialog that appears, tap a book and then tap Move.

3. In the Collections screen, shown in **Figure 10-22**, tap New Collection.

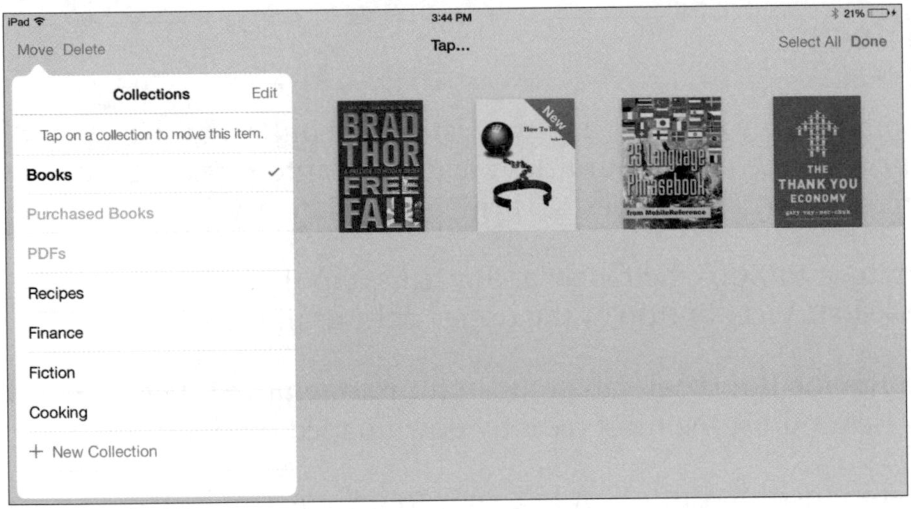

Figure 10-22

4. On the blank line that appears, type a name (see **Figure 10-23**) and then tap Done.

5. Tap outside the dialog to close the dialog and return to the library.

6. To add a book to your new collection from the library, tap Edit, tap the title, and then tap the Move button that appears in the top-left corner of the screen. In the dialog that appears (see **Figure 10-24**), tap the collection where you want to move the book.

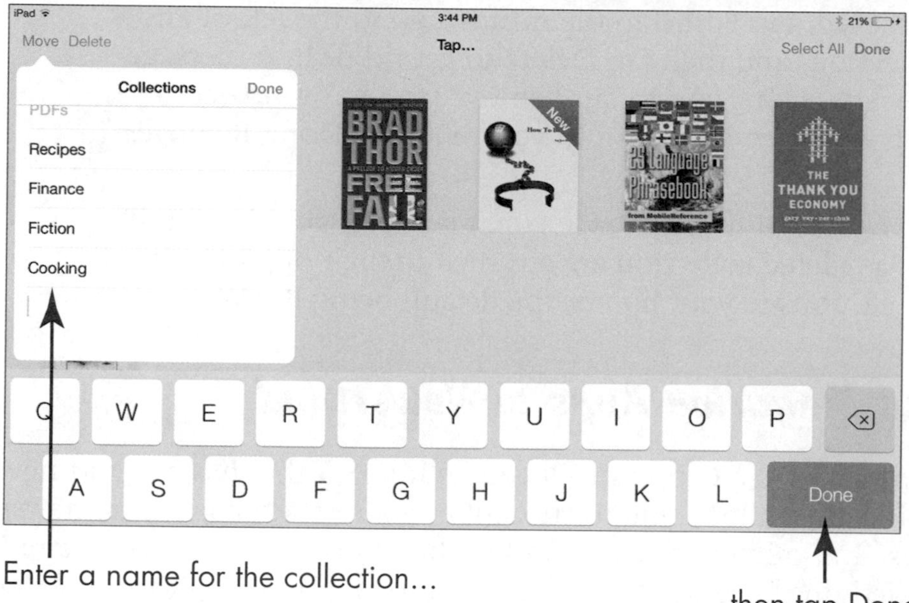

Enter a name for the collection...

then tap Done

Figure 10-23

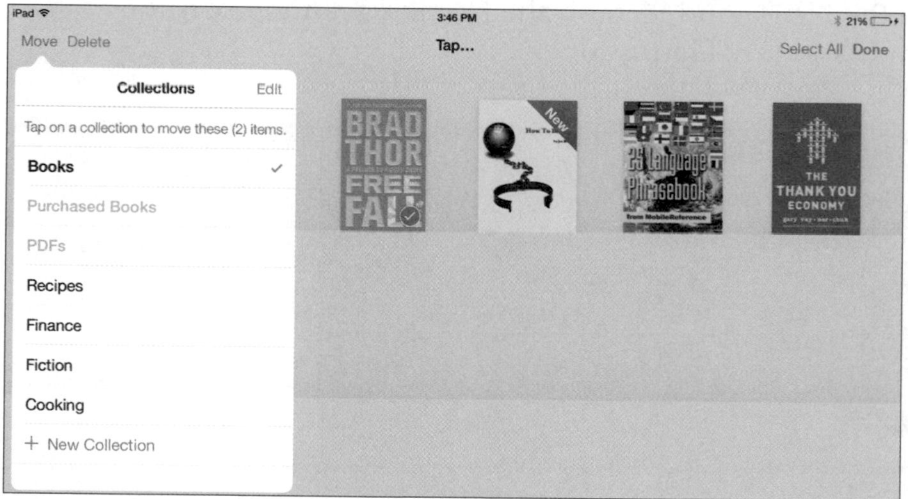

Figure 10-24

7. To delete a book, tap Edit, tap the book, and then tap
Delete.

displayed, tap Edit. Tap the minus sign to the left of any collection, and then tap Delete to get rid of it. A message appears, asking you to tap Remove (to remove the contents of the collection from your iPad) or Don't Remove.

 Note that if you choose Don't Remove, all titles within a deleted collection are returned to their original collections in your library, the default being Books.

Download Magazine Apps to Newsstand

Newsstand is an app introduced with iOS 5 that has a brand-new look in iOS 7. It allows you to subscribe to and read magazines, newspapers, and other periodicals rather than books. The app comes preinstalled on the iPad. When you download a free publication, you're actually downloading an app to Newsstand. You can then tap that app to buy individual issues, as covered in the next task.

1. Tap the Newsstand icon on the Home screen to open Newsstand (see **Figure 10-25**).

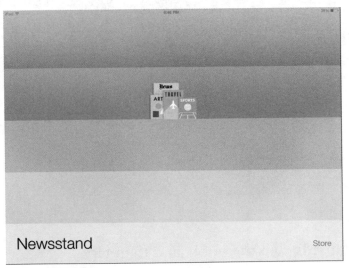

Figure 10-25

2. Tap the Store button. The store opens, offering buttons labeled Featured, Top Charts, and Near Me (which shows periodicals popular in your geographic region) at the bottom of the screen. Along the top of the screen are categories for your shopping pleasure (see **Figure 10-26**).

3. Tap any of the items displayed, tap the arrow buttons to move to other choices, or tap the Search field at the top and enter a search term to locate a publication you're interested in.

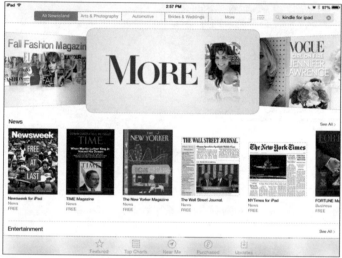

Figure 10-26

 If you tap other icons at the bottom of the screen, such as Top Charts or Purchased, you're taken to types of content other than periodicals. Also, if you tap Featured again after tapping one of these icons, you're taken to apps other than periodicals. Your best bet: Stay on the screen that appears when you tap the Store button in Newsstand.

4. When you find an item, tap it to view a detailed description (see **Figure 10-27**).

5. Tap the Free button and then tap Install. The app downloads to Newsstand.

Free button

Figure 10-27

Buy Issues

1. Tap a periodical app that you've added in Newsstand.

2. You can tap the publication's latest issue, or tap similar buttons for recent or special issues (see **Figure 10-28**).

3. Tap the Price button, and in the confirming dialog, tap Buy.

4. You may be asked to enter your ID again, tap OK, and tap Yes in one more confirming dialog. After you do, the issue is charged to your iTunes account and downloaded to your iPad.

Figure 10-28

Read Periodicals

1. If you buy a periodical or download a free preview, you can tap the publication app in Newsstand and then tap the edition you want to view **(see Figure 10-29)**.

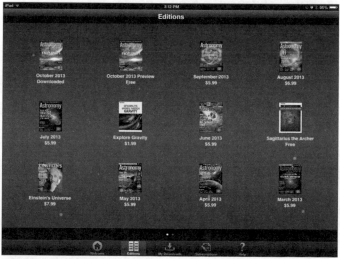

Figure 10-29

2. In the publication that appears, use your finger to swipe left, right, or up and down to view more of the pages, or tap a link, such as those in the publication contents page (see **Figure 10-30**).

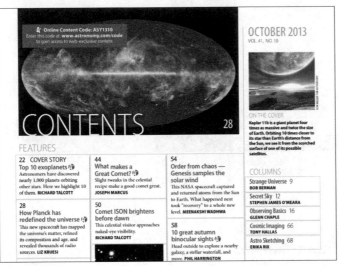

Figure 10-30

 Note that different publications offer different options for subscribing, buying issues, navigating, and organizing issues. Think of Newsstand as a central collection point for apps that allows you to preview and buy content in each publication's store.

Playing Music on the iPad

Chapter 11

*i*Pad includes an iTunes-like app called Music that allows you to take advantage of the iPad's amazing little sound system to play your favorite music, podcasts, and audiobooks.

In this chapter, you get acquainted with the Music app and its features that allow you to sort and find music and control playback. You also get an overview of AirPlay, which you can use to access and play your music over a home network. Finally, I introduce you to iTunes Radio, coming to the iPad with iOS 7.

View the Library Contents

1. Tap the Music app icon, located on the Dock on the Home screen. The Music library appears. **Figure 11-1** shows the library in Albums view.

2. Tap the Playlists, Songs, Artists, Genre, Composer, Compilations (like the Best of British Rock), and Albums buttons at the bottom of the library to view your music according to these criteria (refer to **Figure 11-1**).

Get ready to...

iPad 🤝	10:48 AM		97%

0:00 | -5:05
◀◀ ▶ ▶▶   Bebe Neuwirth & Rob Fisher **All That Jaz**   Repeat   Shuffle

Store	Albums		Now Playing ❯
Abbey Road	The Beatles	1 song, 3 min	
Chicagô - The Músical	Various Artists	1 song, 5 min	
Greatest Hits, Vols. 1 & 2	Billy Joel	25 songs, 113 min	
In the Mood	Glenn Miller and His Orchestra	1 song, 3 min	

Radio   Playlists   Artists   Songs   Albums   Genres   Compilations   Composers

Figure 11-1

You can tap the Store button to go to the iTunes Store to buy additional music.

3. Tap the Radio button (see **Figure 11-2**) to view this new feature of iOS 7, discussed in more detail later in this chapter.

iTunes has several free items you can download and use to play around with the features in Music. You can also sync content stored on your computer or other Apple devices to your iPad and play that content using the Music app. (See Chapter 3 for more about syncing and Chapter 8 for more about getting content from iTunes.)

Apple offers a service called iTunes Match (www.apple.com/itunes/itunes-match). You pay $24.99 per year for the capability to match the music you've bought from other providers or recorded yourself (and stored on your computer)

with what's in the iTunes catalog. If iTunes Match finds a match (and it usually does), that content is added to your iTunes library (up to 25,000 tracks). Then, using iCloud, you can sync the content among all your Apple devices.

Figure 11-2

Create Playlists

1. You can create your own playlists to put tracks from various sources in collections of your choosing. In the Music app, tap the Playlists button at the bottom of the screen.

2. Tap New Playlist.

3. In the dialog that appears, enter a name for the playlist, and tap Save.

4. In the list of selections that appears (see **Figure 11-3**), tap the plus sign next to each item you want to include.

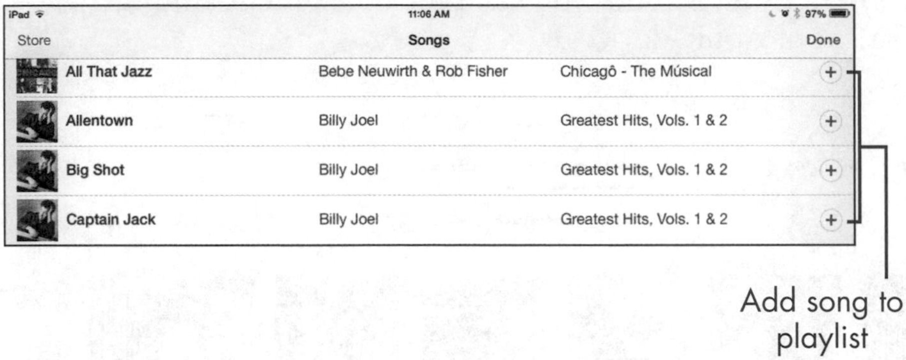

iPad 🖙	11:06 AM		⚡ ❤ ⚓ 97% ▪▪▪
Store	**Songs**		Done
All That Jazz	Bebe Neuwirth & Rob Fisher	Chicagô - The Músical	⊕
Allentown	Billy Joel	Greatest Hits, Vols. 1 & 2	⊕
Big Shot	Billy Joel	Greatest Hits, Vols. 1 & 2	⊕
Captain Jack	Billy Joel	Greatest Hits, Vols. 1 & 2	⊕

Add song to playlist

Figure 11-3

5. Tap the Done button.

6. Tap the Playlists button at the bottom of the screen. Your playlist appears in the list, and you can play it by tapping first the list's name and then the Play button.

 To delete a song from the playlist, swipe left to right across the name of the song you want to delete and then tap the Delete button.

Search for Audio

1. You can search for an item in your Music library by using the Search feature. With Music open, tap the Search field (see **Figure 11-4**) to open the onscreen keyboard.

2. Enter a search term in the Search field, or tap the Dictation key on the onscreen keyboard (see **Figure 11-5**) and speak the search term. Then tap the Search button on the onscreen keyboard. Results display, narrowing as you type.

3. Tap an item to play it.

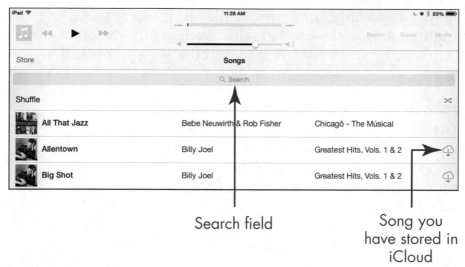

Search field   Song you
                                have stored in
                                iCloud

Figure 11-4

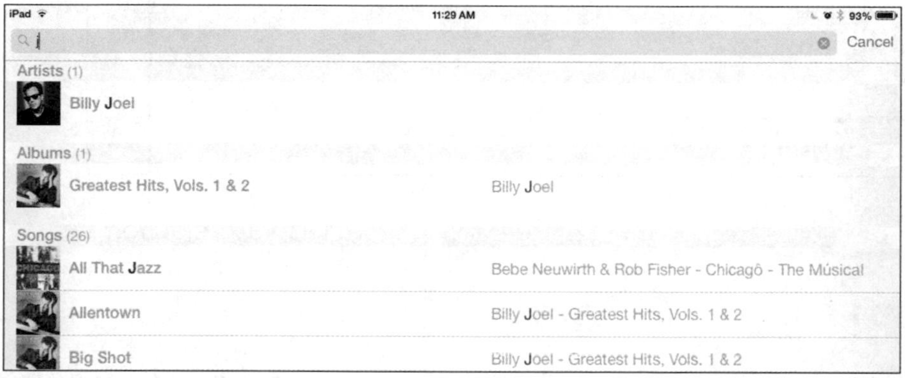

Figure 11-5

 You can enter (or speak) an artist's name, an author's
or a composer's name, or a word from the item's title
in the Search field to find what you're looking for.

Play Music and Other Audio

1. Locate the song or audiobook you want to play, using the
methods described in previous tasks in this chapter.

2. Tap the item you want to play. *Note:* If you're displaying
the Songs tab, you don't have to tap an album to open a

song; you need only tap a song to play it. If you're using any other tab, you have to tap items such as albums or multiple songs from one artist to find the song you want to hear.

3. Tap the item you want to play in the list that appears (see **Figure 11-6**). If the item is stored on iCloud, you may have to tap the iCloud symbol next to it to download it (refer to **Figure 11-4**). The item begins to play. Tap Now Playing to display the album cover full-screen (see **Figure 11-7**).

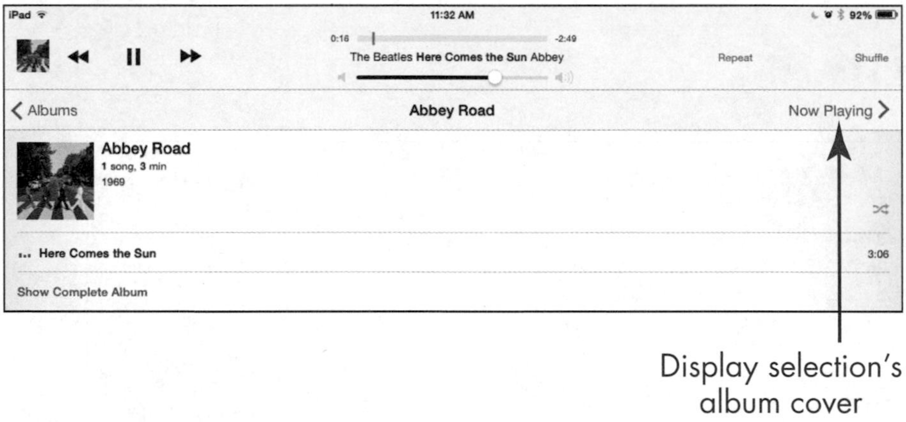

Display selection's
album cover

Figure 11-6

4. Use the Previous and Next buttons to navigate the audio file that's playing. The Previous button takes you back to the beginning of the item that's playing or the previous track if you're at the beginning; the Next button takes you to the next item.

5. Tap the Pause button to pause playback.

6. Tap and drag the line that indicates the current playback location on the Progress bar to the left or right to "scrub" to another location in the song.

7. If you don't like what's playing, here's how to make another selection: Tap the Back to Library arrow in the top-left

corner to return to Library view, or tap the Album List button in the upper-right corner to show other albums.

Back to Library

Album List button

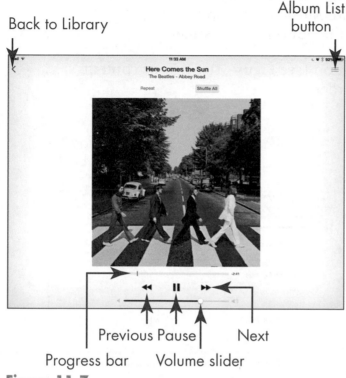

Previous Pause Next

Progress bar Volume slider

Figure 11-7

 You can tell Siri to play music. Just press and hold the Home button, and when Siri appears, say something like "Play Take the A Train" or "Play the White Album."

 The Home Sharing feature of iTunes allows you to share music among devices that have Home Sharing turned on. To use the feature, each device has to have the same Apple ID on your network. After you set up the feature via iTunes, you can retrieve music and videos from your iTunes shared library to any of the devices. For more about Home Sharing, visit www. apple.com/support/homesharing.

Shuffle Music

1. If you want to play a random selection of the music you've purchased or synced to your iPad, you can use the Shuffle feature. With Music open, tap the Songs or Albums button at the bottom of the screen.

2. Tap the Shuffle button (see **Figure 11-8**). Your content plays in random order.

Randomize
playback

Figure 11-8

Adjust the Volume

1. Music offers its own volume control that you can adjust during playback. This volume is set relative to the system volume you control using iPad's Settings. If you set it to

50%, it plays at 50 percent of the system's volume setting. With Music open, tap a piece of music to play it.

2. In the controls that appear onscreen (see **Figure 11-9**), press and drag the button on the Volume slider to the right for more volume or to the left for less volume.

Use the Volume slider to
adjust the volume

Figure 11-9

 If the volume is set high, but you're still having trouble hearing, consider getting a headset. It cuts out extraneous noises and may improve the sound quality of what you're listening to. I recommend that you use a 3.5mm stereo headphone; insert it into the headphone jack at the top of your iPad.

Use AirPlay

The AirPlay streaming technology is built into the iPhone, iPod touch, and iPad. *Streaming* technology allows you to send media files from one device to play on another. You can send, say, a movie you've purchased on your iPad or a slideshow of your photos to your TV — and control the TV playback from your iPad. You can also send music to play over speakers.

You can take advantage of AirPlay in a few ways: Purchase Apple TV and stream video, photos, and music to the TV, or purchase AirPort Express and attach your speakers to it to play music. Finally, if you buy AirPort-enabled wireless speakers, you can stream audio directly to them. Because this combination of equipment varies, my advice — if you're interested in using AirPlay — is to visit your nearest Apple Store or certified Apple Reseller and find out which hardware combination will work best for you.

 If you get a bit antsy watching a long movie, one of the beauties of AirPlay is that you can still use your iPad to check e-mail, browse photos or the Internet, or check your calendar while the media file is playing.

Play Music with iTunes Radio

1. You can access iTunes Radio with any Apple device that has iOS 7 or a computer running iTunes 11 or later. Begin by tapping the Music icon on the Home screen.

2. Tap the Radio button at the bottom of the screen that appears.

3. Tap a Featured Station (see **Figure 11-10**). A featured song begins to play.

Figure 11-10

4. Use the tools at the bottom of the screen, shown in **Figure 11-11**, to control playback.

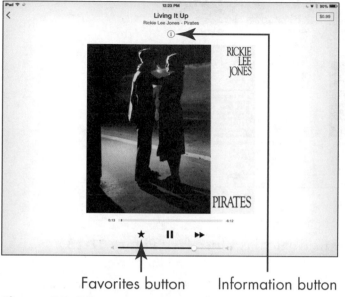

Favorites button   Information button

Figure 11-11

5. Tap the Information button at the top center of the screen to display options. You can choose New Station from Artist, New Station from Song, or Share Station via AirDrop, Mail, Twitter, or Facebook.

 The more you use iTunes Radio, the better it gets at building stations that fit your taste.

Create Stations

1. You can create a station of your own. To do so, first tap the Music icon on the Dock.

2. Tap Radio.

3. On the iTunes Radio home page, tap the New Station button, which has a bright red cross on it (see **Figure 11-12**).

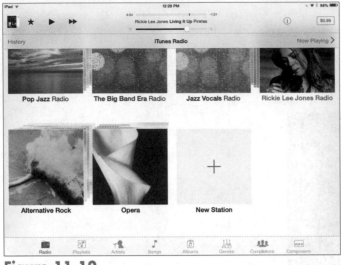

Figure 11-12

4. Tap a category of music, such as Blues (see **Figure 11-13**).

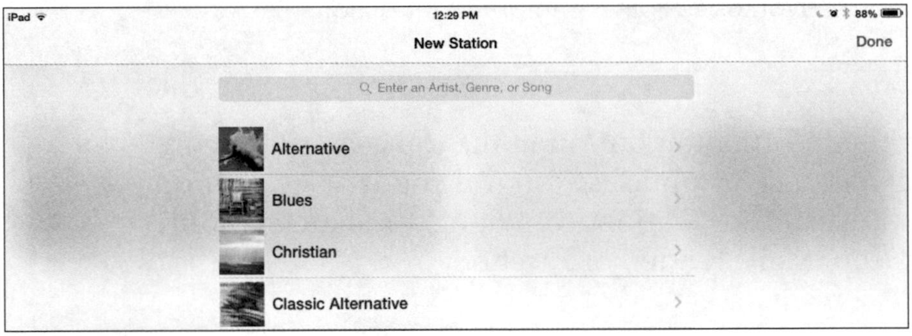

Figure 11-13

5. If subcategories are offered, tap the one you prefer and then tap the Add New button that appears to the right of the category. The category is added to your station.

View Your iTunes Radio History

1. iTunes Radio offers a great way to see where you've been and where you're going, musically speaking, with its

History and Wish List features. To use it, tap the Music icon on the Dock.

2. In the screen that appears (see **Figure 11-14**), tap History in the top-left corner.

Figure 11-14

3. Tap the Wish List tab (see **Figure 11-15**) to see items you've added to your Wish List.

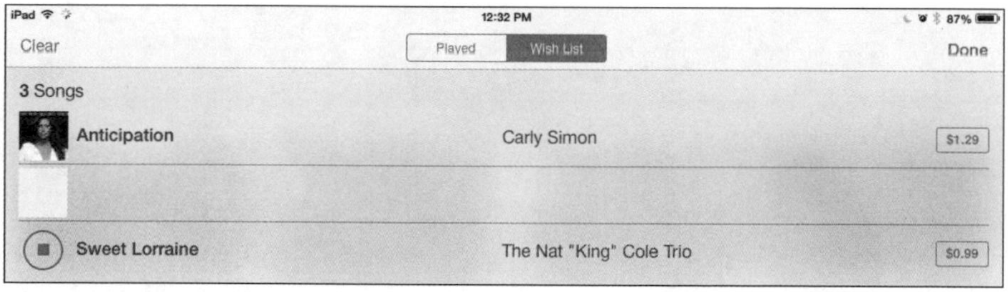

Figure 11-15

4. Tap the Played tab to see the music you've listened to.

 Wish List is a feature you can use to add songs to a list to buy at a later time. To add a radio station to your Wish List tap on it in the iTunes Radio home screen, and then tap the Favorites button (shaped like a star; refer to **Figure 11-11**). Tap Add to iTunes Wish List in the menu that appears.

Playing with Photos

With its gorgeous screen, the iPad is a natural for taking and viewing photos. It supports most common photo formats, such as JPEG, TIFF, and PNG. You can shoot your photos by using the iPad's built-in cameras with built-in square or panorama modes, and you can edit your images using filters that are new with the Photos and Camera apps that come with iOS 7. You can also sync photos from your computer, iPhone, or digital camera. You can save images you find online or receive by e-mail to your iPad.

If you have the third- or fourth-generation iPad or iPad mini, its rear-facing camera is a built-in iSight camera. This improvement on previous iPad cameras is a 5-megapixel beauty with an illumination sensor that adjusts for whatever lighting is available. Face detection balances focus across as many as ten faces in your pictures. The video camera option offers 1080p high-definition (HD) video with video stabilization that makes up for some shaking as you hold the device to take videos.

When you have photos to play with, the Photos app lets you organize photos from Camera Roll and view photos in albums, individually, or in a slideshow. A new feature lets you view photos by the years they were taken,

Get ready to . . .

with images divided into collections based on where or when you took them. You can also AirDrop, e-mail, message, or post photos to Facebook; tweet photos to friends; print photos; or use your expensive gadget as an electronic picture frame. The Photo Stream feature lets you share groups of photos with people using iCloud on an iOS 6 or later device or on a Mac computer with the Mountain Lion or Mavericks OS installed. And if you like to play around with photo effects, you'll enjoy the photo-editing features, as well as the preinstalled Photo Booth app. You can read about all these features in this chapter.

Take Pictures with the iPad Cameras

1. The cameras in the iPad (except the original iPad) are just begging to be used, so let's get started! Tap the Camera app icon on the Home screen to open the app.

2. If the orange highlighted word below the Capture button (see **Figure 12-1**) is *Video*, tap the row of words and slide up to set Photo (the still camera) as the active setting.

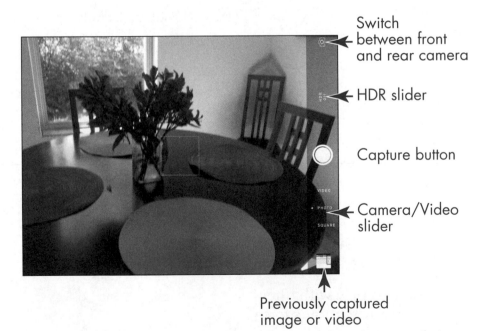

Switch between front and rear camera

HDR slider

Capture button

Camera/Video slider

Previously captured image or video

Figure 12-1

3. You can set the Square option by tapping the row of words below the Capture button and sliding up again. This setting lets you create square images like those you see on the popular Instagram site.

4. Move the camera around until you find a pleasing image.

5. You can do a couple of things at this point to help you take your photo:

- Tap the area of the grid where you want the camera to autofocus.

- Pinch the screen to display a zoom control; then drag the circle in the zoom bar to the right or left to zoom in or out on the image.

6. Press the Capture button on the right-center side of the screen and release it when you have the image in view. You've just taken a picture (see **Figure 12-1**), and that picture has been stored in the Photos app's gallery automatically.

 You can also use the up switch on the volume rocker on the right side of your iPad to capture a picture or start or stop video camera recording.

7. Tap the icon in the top-right corner to switch between the front camera and rear camera. Now you can take pictures of yourself, so go ahead and tap the Capture button to take another picture.

8. To view the last photo taken, swipe from left to right, or tap the thumbnail of the latest image in the bottom-right corner of the screen. The Photos app opens and displays the photo (see **Figure 12-2**).

Images slider   Delete

Figure 12-2

9. Tap the Done button to return to the Camera app.

10. Press the Home button to close the Camera app and return to the Home screen.

Import Photos from an iPhone, iPod, or Digital Camera

1. You can find information in Chapter 3 about syncing your computer with your iPad through either iTunes or iCloud to import photos. However, your computer isn't the only photo source available to you. You can also import photos from a digital camera or an iPhone if you buy the iPad Camera Connection Kit from Apple. The kit contains two adapters (see **Figure 12-3**): a USB Camera Connector to import photos from a digital camera or an iPhone/iPod touch, and an SD Card Reader to import image files from an SD card. Start the import process by putting your iPad to sleep.

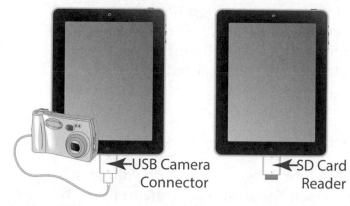

Figure 12-3

2. Insert the USB Camera Connector into the Lightning Connector slot of your iPad.

3. Connect the USB end of the cord that came with your digital camera or iPad into the USB Camera Connector.

4. Connect the other end of the cord that came with your camera or iPad into that device.

5. Wake your iPad. The Photos app opens and displays the photos on the digital camera or iPad.

6. Tap Import All on your iPad, or — if you want to import only selected photos — tap those photos and then tap Import. The photos are saved to the Last Import album.

7. Disconnect the cord and the adapter. You're done!

You can also import photos stored on a *secure digital (SD)* memory card, often used by digital cameras as a storage medium. Simply put the iPad to sleep, insert the SD Card Reader into the iPad, insert the SD card containing the photos, and then follow Steps 5 through 7 in the preceding list.

Remember that with AirDrop on an iPad mini or fourth-generation iPad and later, you can quickly send photos directly from your iPhone to your iPad as long as the devices are within about 12 feet of each other.

Save Photos from the Web

1. The web offers a wealth of images you can download to your Photo Library. Open Safari, and navigate to the web page containing the image you want.

2. Press and hold the image. A menu appears, as shown in **Figure 12-4.**

Figure 12-4

3. Tap Save Image. The image is saved to your Camera Roll album in the Photos app.

 For more about how to use Safari to navigate to or search for web content, see Chapter 5.

Many sites protect their photos from being copied by applying an invisible overlay. This blank overlay image ensures that you don't actually get the image you think you're tapping. Even if a site doesn't take these precautions, be sure that you don't save images from the web and use them in ways that violate the rights of the person or entity that owns them.

View an Album

1. The Photos app organizes your pictures into albums, using such criteria as the folder on your computer from which you synced the photos or photos captured with the iPad's camera (which go to Camera Roll). You may also have albums for images you synced from devices such as your iPhone or digital camera. To view your albums, start by tapping the Photos app icon on the Home screen.

2. If Photos is selected when the Photos app opens, as shown in **Figure 12-5**, tap the Albums button to display your albums.

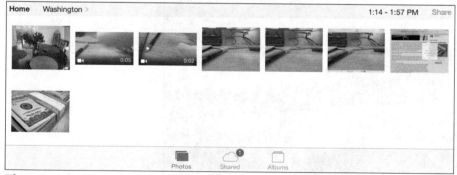

Figure 12-5

3. Tap an album. The photos in it are displayed.

View Individual Photos

1. Tap the Photos app icon on the Home screen. The Photos app opens.

2. Tap the Albums button at the bottom of the screen. Your photos are displayed in collections, such as Camera Roll (see **Figure 12-6**).

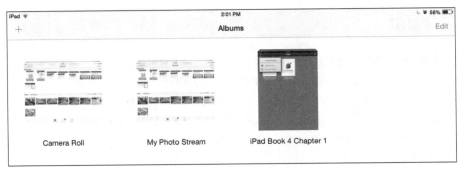

Figure 12-6

3. To view a photo, tap to expand a collection and then tap the photo to view it (see **Figure 12-7**). Place your fingers on the photo and then spread your fingers apart. The picture expands.

Figure 12-7

4. Flick your finger to the left or right to scroll through the album and look at the individual photos in it.

5. To reduce the individual photo and return to the multi-picture view, place two fingers on the photo and then pinch them together. You can also tap the arrow button in the top-left corner (which may display different words depending on where you are in a collection of photos) to view the next-highest level of your photo collection.

 You can place a photo from the Photos app on a person's information page in the Contacts app. For more about how to do it, see Chapter 18.

Edit Photos

1. The Photos app also lets you edit photos. Tap the Photos app on the Home screen to open it.

2. Using methods previously described in this chapter, locate a photo you want to edit.

3. Tap the Edit button. The Edit Photo screen, shown in **Figure 12-8**, appears.

Photo-editing options

Figure 12-8

4. At this point, you can take five possible actions:

- *Rotate:* Tap the Rotate button to rotate the image 90 degrees at a time. Continue to tap the button to move another 90 degrees.

- *Enhance:* Tap Enhance to turn Auto-Enhance on or off. This feature optimizes the crispness of the image.

- *Filters:* Apply any of nine filters (such as Fade, Mono, and Noir) to change the feel of your image. These effects adjust the brightness of your image or apply a black-and-white tone to your color photos. Tap the Filters button in the middle of the tools at the bottom of the screen, and scroll to view available filters. Tap one and then tap Apply to apply the effect to your image. Filters work on all but first generation iPads with the iOS 7 Camera app installed.

- *Red-Eye:* Tap Red-Eye if a person in a photo has that dreaded red-eye effect. When you activate this feature, simply tap each eye that needs clearing up.

- *Crop:* To crop the photo to a portion of its original area, tap the Crop button. Then tap any corner of the image and drag inward or outward to remove areas of the photo. Tap Crop and then tap Save to apply your changes.

 Each of the five editing features has a Cancel, an Undo, and a Revert to Original button. If you don't like the changes you made, tap these buttons to stop making changes or undo the changes you've already made.

Organize Photos in Camera Roll

1. If you want to create your own album, display the Camera Roll album.

2. Tap the Select button in the top-right corner and then tap individual photos to select them. Small check marks appear on the selected photos (see **Figure 12-9**).

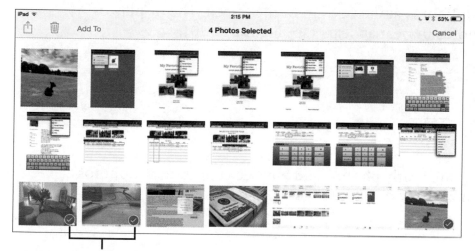

Check marks indicate selected photos

Figure 12-9

3. Tap the Add To button; then tap Add to Album (which appears only if you've previously created albums) or New Album.

4. Tap an existing album or enter a name for a new album (depending on your previous selection), and tap Save. If you created a new album, it appears in the Photos main screen with the other albums that are displayed.

 You can also tap the Share or Delete button after you select photos in Step 2 of this task. Doing this allows you to share or delete multiple photos at the same time.

View Photos by Year and Location

1. New with Photos and iOS 7 is the capability to view your photos in logical categories such as Years and Moments. These so-called *smart groupings* let you, for example, view all photos taken this year or all the photos from your summer vacation. Tap Photos on the Home screen to open the Photos app.

2. Tap Photos at the bottom of the screen. The display of photos by year appears (see **Figure 12-10**).

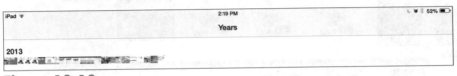

iPad 📶 2:19 PM 52% 🔋

Years

2013

Figure 12-10

3. Tap the yearly photos, and you see collections of photos arranged by date (see **Figure 12-11**).

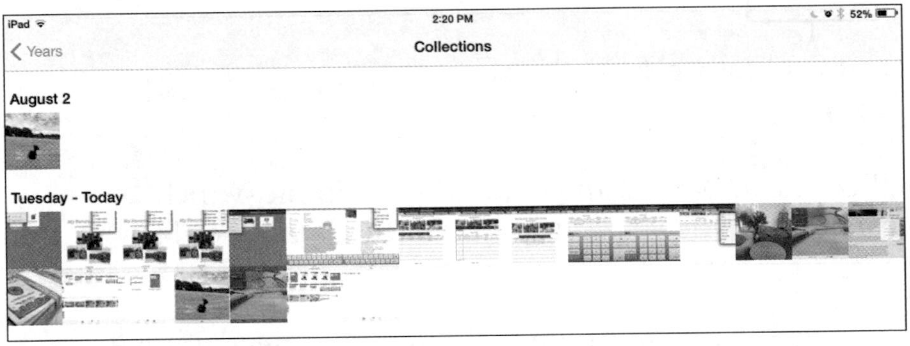

iPad 📶 2:20 PM 52% 🔋

< Years **Collections**

August 2

Tuesday - Today

Figure 12-11

4. Tap a collection to view the individual "moments" in that collection broken down day by day.

To go back to larger groupings, such as from a moment in a collection to the larger collection to the entire past year, just keep tapping the back button in the top-left corner of the screen (which will be named after the next collection up in the hierarchy, such as Collections or Years).

Share Photos with Mail, Twitter, and Facebook

1. You can easily share photos stored on your iPad by sending them as e-mail attachments, posting them to Facebook, or tweeting them via Twitter. You have to go to Facebook or Twitter in a web browser and set up an account before you can use this feature. First, tap the Photos app icon on the Home screen.

2. Tap the Photos or Albums button, and locate the photo you want to share.

3. Tap the photo to select it and then tap the Share icon. (It looks like a box with an arrow jumping out of it.) The menu shown in **Figure 12-12** appears.

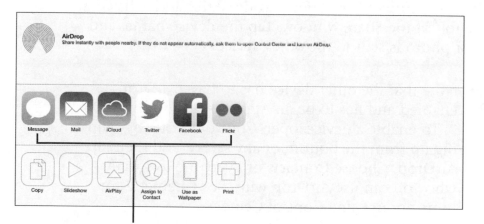

Social sharing options

Figure 12-12

4. Tap Mail, Twitter, or Facebook.

5. In the message form that appears, make any modifications you want in the To, Cc/Bcc, or Subject field; then type a message for e-mail or enter your Facebook post or tweet text.

6. Tap the Send button. The message and photo go on their way.

 You can also copy and paste a photo into documents such as those created in the available Pages word processor application. To do this, press and hold a photo in Photos until the Copy command appears. Tap Copy; then, in the destination application, press and hold the screen, and tap Paste.

Share Photos with AirDrop

 1. AirDrop provides a way to share content such as photos with others who are nearby and have AirDrop-enabled devices. Follow the steps in the previous task to locate a photo you want to share, and tap the Share icon.

2. If an AirDrop-enabled device is in your immediate vicinity (say, within 12 or so feet), you see the device listed at the top of the Share window. Tap the device name, and your photo is sent to the other device.

Note that the other device has to have AirDrop enabled and has to be an Apple device running iOS 7. To enable a device, open Control Center by swiping up from the bottom of any screen and then tap AirDrop. Choose Contacts or Everyone to specify who you can use AirDrop with. See Chapter 2 for more about using Control Center.

Share Photos with Photo Stream

1. Photo Stream allows you to automatically send copies of any new photos to any iCloud devices and to share photo streams with others. You can also subscribe to another person's photo stream if he or she shares it with you. To set up Photo Stream, tap Settings⇨Photos & Camera; then tap the On/Off button for My Photo Stream to share among your devices, and tap Photo Sharing to share with others.

2. To share a photo stream with somebody else, return to the Home screen, and tap Photos. Locate a photo you want to share, tap the Share icon, and then tap iCloud.

3. In the form that appears (see **Figure 12-13**) enter a photo-stream name and then tap Next.

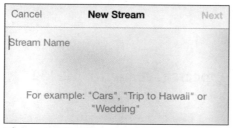

Figure 12-13

4. Enter a recipient's email address and then tap Create.

5. If you want to, enter a comment in the following dialog and then tap Post. The photo is posted. Your contact receives an e-mail message with a link that allows him or her to join your photo stream.

Print Photos

1. If you have a wireless printer that's compatible with Apple AirPrint technology or you use an app such as Printopia or HandyPrint with a shared printer connection, you can print photos from your iPad. With Photos open, locate the photo you want to print, and tap it to maximize it.

2. Tap the Share icon and then tap Print (see **Figure 12-14**).

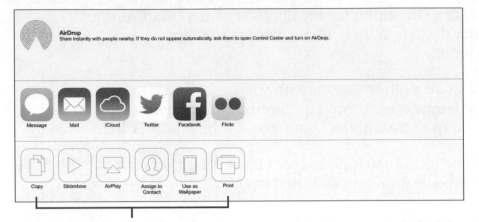

Image and device utilities options

Figure 12-14

3. In the Printer Options dialog that appears (see **Figure 12-15**), tap Select Printer. The iPad searches for any compatible wireless printers on your local network.

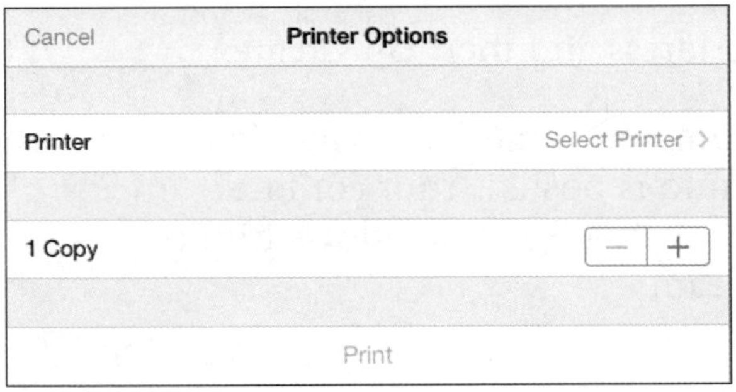

Cancel	Printer Options	
Printer		Select Printer >
1 Copy		− +
	Print	

Figure 12-15

4. Tap the plus or minus symbol in the Copy field to set the number of copies to print.

5. Tap the Print button. Your photo goes on its way to the printer.

Run a Slideshow

1. You can run a slideshow of your images in Photos and even play music and choose transition effects for the show. Tap the Photos app on the Home screen.

2. Tap the Photos button (refer to **Figure 12-5**) and then tap a slide in a collection.

3. Tap the Share icon and then tap Slideshow to see the Slideshow Options dialog, shown in **Figure 12-16**.

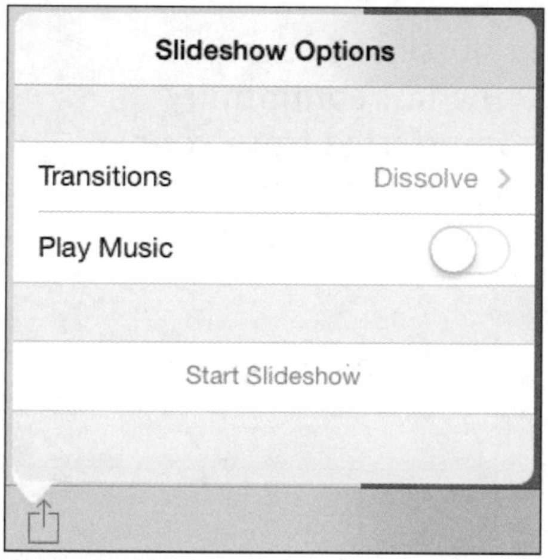

Slideshow Options

Transitions   Dissolve >

Play Music

Start Slideshow

Figure 12-16

4. If you want to play music along with the slideshow, tap the Play Music field's On/Off button.

5. To choose music to play along with the slideshow, tap Music, and in the list that appears, tap any selection in your Music library.

6. In the Slideshow Options dialog, tap Transitions and then tap the transition effect you want to use for your slideshow.

7. Tap the Start Slideshow button. The slideshow begins.

8. To stop the show tap anywhere on the screen.

 To run a slideshow that includes only the photos contained in a particular album, tap the Albums button instead of the Photos button in Step 2, tap an album to open it, and then tap the Slideshow button to choose settings and run a slideshow.

Delete Photos

1. You may find that it's time to get rid of some of those old photos of the family reunion or the last community-center project. If the photos weren't transferred from your computer but were downloaded or captured as screen shots on the iPad, you can delete them. Tap the Photos app's icon on the Home screen.

2. Tap the Albums or Photos button; then, if you've opened Albums, tap an album to open it.

3. Tap the Trash icon.

4. Tap Delete Photo (see **Figure 12-17**).

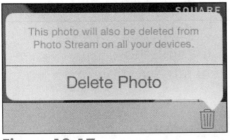

This photo will also be deleted from Photo Stream on all your devices.

Delete Photo

Figure 12-17

5. Tap the Delete Photo/Selected Photos button that appears to finish the deletion.

 To delete more than one photo, with a collection or album displayed, tap Select; then tap all the photos you want to delete before tapping the Trash icon.

Play around with Photo Booth

1. Photo Booth is a photo-manipulation app that's provided with every iPad from the iPad 2 on and works with the iPad cameras. You can use this app to capture photos using various fun effects. To open Photo Booth, tap its icon on the Home screen. The various effects that you can use in the current view of the camera appear (see **Figure 12-18**).

Figure 12-18

2. Tap an effect and then tap the Capture button (see **Figure 12-19**) to capture an image with that effect applied. The image appears within a filmstrip of the other images you've taken in Photo Booth.

3. If you want to delete a photo, tap it, tap the Trash icon, and then tap Delete Photo.

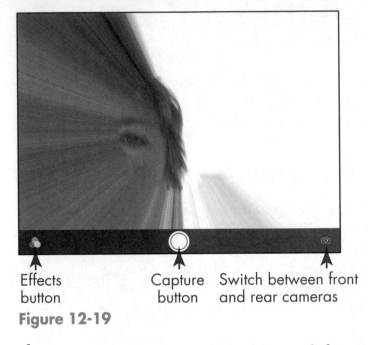

Effects   Capture   Switch between front
button   button   and rear cameras

Figure 12-19

4. Tap the Effects button in the bottom-left corner of the
screen to return to the various effects, or press the Home
button to return to the Home screen. Your photos are
available in the Camera Roll album of the Photos app.

Getting the Most Out of Video Features

*U*sing the Videos app, you can watch downloaded movies or TV shows, as well as media you've synced from iCloud or your Mac or PC.

In addition, all iPads (except the original iPad) sport two video cameras you can use to capture your own videos. If you own a third- or fourth-generation iPad, an iPad Air, or an iPad mini with Retina Display, you can take advantage of the rear-facing iSight camera, which can record video in 1080p high definition (HD), with video stabilization to prevent those wobbly video moments. You can also benefit from the Retina display on fourth-generation and later iPads to watch videos with super-high resolution, which simply means that those videos will look very, very good.

By purchasing the iMovie app (a more limited version of the longtime mainstay on Mac computers), you add the capability to edit those videos.

In this chapter, I explain all about shooting and watching video content from a variety of sources. For practice, you may want to refer to Chapter 8 first to purchase or download one of many available free TV shows or movies, and see Chapter 9 for help with downloading the iMovie app.

Capture Your Own Videos with the Built-in Cameras

1. To capture a video, tap the Camera app on the Home screen. The Camera app opens.

 On all iPads except the original iPad, two video cameras can capture video from either the front or back of the device and make it possible for you to edit the videos with third-party video apps or share them with others. (See more about this topic in the next task.)

2. Tap the row of words below the Capture button and slide up to switch from the still camera to the video camera (see **Figure 13-1**).

Switch between front and rear cameras

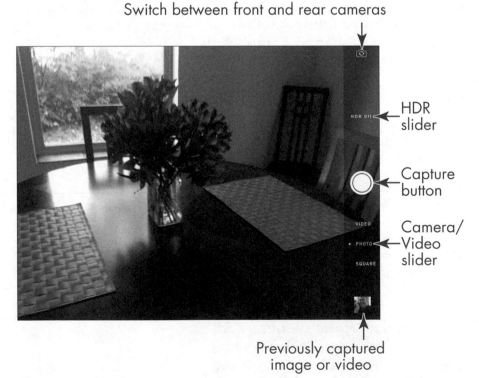

HDR slider

Capture button

Camera/ Video slider

Previously captured image or video

Figure 13-1

3. If you want to switch between the front and back cameras, tap the icon near the top-right corner of the screen (refer to **Figure 13-1**).

4. Tap the red Record button shown in **Figure 13-2** to begin recording the video. (This button turns into a red square when the camera is recording.)

Record button

Figure 13-2

5. When you're finished, tap the Record button again. Your new video is listed in the bottom-left corner of the screen.

6. Tap the video to play it, share it, or delete it. In the future you can find and play the video in your Camera Roll when you open the Photos app.

 Before you start recording, remember that when you're holding the iPad in portrait orientation, the camera lens is in the top-right corner of the back. You could easily put your fingers directly over the lens!

Play Movies, Podcasts, or TV Shows with Videos

1. When you first open the Videos app by tapping its button
on the Dock of any Home screen, you may see a relatively blank screen with a note that reads you don't have
any videos on your iPad and a link to the iTunes Store.
After you've purchased TV shows and movies or rented
movies from the iTunes Store (see Chapter 8 to find out
how) or other sources, you'll see tabs listing the different
kinds of content you own. Tap the Videos app icon on
the Home screen to open the application.

2. On a screen like the one shown in **Figure 13-3**, tap the
appropriate category at the top of the screen (TV, Podcasts,
or Movies, depending on the content you've downloaded).

Figure 13-3

3. Tap an item to open it. A description appears, as shown
in **Figure 13-4**. TV Shows include Episodes, Details, and
Related tabs; Movies contain Details, Chapters, and
Related tabs.

Play button

iCloud
button

Figure 13-4

4. For a TV show, tap the Episodes tab to display episodes, each of which has a Play button; for a movie, the Play button appears no matter which tab is selected. When you tap the Play button for the content you want to watch, the movie, TV show, or podcast begins playing. (If you see a small cloud-shaped icon instead of a Play button, tap it to download the content from iCloud.) The progress of the playback is displayed on the Progress bar (see **Figure 13-5**), showing how many minutes you've viewed and how many remain. If you don't see the bar, tap the screen once to display it briefly, along with a set of playback tools at the bottom of the screen.

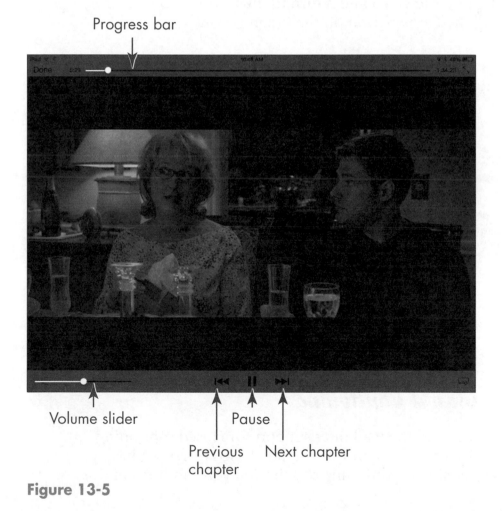

Progress bar

Volume slider

Pause

Previous chapter

Next chapter

Figure 13-5

5. With the playback tools displayed, take any of these actions:

- Tap the Pause button to pause playback.

- Tap either Go to Previous Chapter or Go to Next Chapter to move to a different location in the video playback.

- Tap the circular button on the Volume slider and drag the button left or right to decrease or increase the volume, respectively.

6. To stop the video and return to the information screen, tap the Done button on the Progress bar.

 If you've watched a video and stopped it partway, it opens by default to the last spot you viewed. To start a video from the beginning, tap and drag the circular button on the Progress bar all the way to the left.

 If your controls disappear during playback, just tap the screen to make them reappear.

 If you like to view things on a bigger screen, you can use the iPad's AirPlay feature to send your iPad movies and photos to your TV via the Apple Digital AV Connector (a $39.95 accessory) or Apple TV (a device that costs $99). Depending on your TV model, you may need the Composite connector (for virtually any analog set rather than the Digital AV Connector, which is used only for HD TV).

Turn on Closed Captioning

1. iTunes and the iPad offer support for closed captioning and subtitles. If a movie you purchased or rented has either closed captioning or subtitles, you can turn on this feature in iPad. Look for the "CC" logo on media you download to use this feature; be aware that video you record won't have this capability. Begin by tapping the Settings icon on the Home screen.

2. Tap General⇨Accessibility. On the screen that appears, tap Subtitles & Captioning (see **Figure 13-6**).

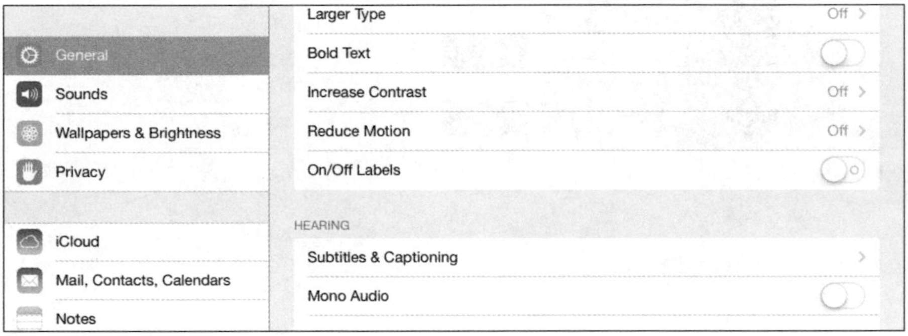

	Larger Type	Off >
⚙ General	Bold Text	⬭
🔊 Sounds	Increase Contrast	Off >
❄ Wallpapers & Brightness	Reduce Motion	Off >
✋ Privacy	On/Off Labels	⬭
	HEARING	
☁ iCloud	Subtitles & Captioning	>
✉ Mail, Contacts, Calendars	Mono Audio	⬭
📓 Notes		

Figure 13-6

3. On the menu that appears on the right side of the screen, tap the Closed Captions + SDH On/Off button to turn on the feature. Now when you play a movie with closed captioning, you can tap the Audio and Subtitles button to the left of the playback controls to manage this feature.

Go to a Movie Chapter

1. Tap the Videos app icon on the Home screen.

2. Tap the Movies tab, if it isn't already displayed.

3. Tap the title of the movie you want to watch. Information about the movie is displayed (refer to **Figure 13-4**).

4. Tap the Chapters tab. A list of chapters is displayed, as shown in **Figure 13-7**.

Figure 13-7

5. Tap a chapter to play it.

 You can also use the playback tools to go back one chapter or forward one chapter. See the "Play Movies, Podcasts, or TV Shows with Videos" task earlier in this chapter for more information.

 If you buy a video using iTunes, sync to download it to your iPad and then delete it from your iPad, it's still saved in your iTunes library. You can sync your computer and iPad again to download the video once more at no additional charge. Remember, however, that rented movies are gone with the wind when you delete them.

 The iPad has much smaller storage capacity than your typical computer, so downloading lots of TV shows or movies can fill its storage area quickly. If you don't want to view an item again, delete it to free space.

Share Your Favorite Videos

1. You can share your opinion about a video by using Mail, Twitter, or Facebook. Tap the Videos app to open it and then tap the Store button.

2. Find and tap a video that you want to share.

3. In the information screen shown in **Figure 13-8**, tap the Share icon (a box with an arrow at the top of it at the top of the screen).

Share

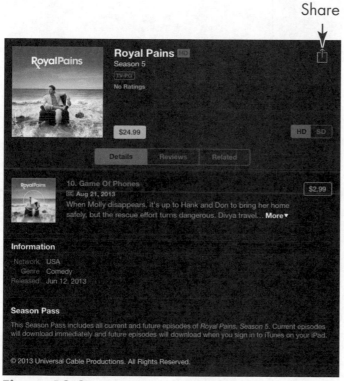

Figure 13-8

4. In the resulting menu, tap Mail, Twitter, or Facebook to use one of these methods of sharing your enthusiasm for the item (see **Figure 13-9**).

Figure 13-9

5. In the form that appears, enter a recipient in the To: field and add to the message, if you like. If you chose to post to your Facebook page, enter your message in the Facebook form.

6. Tap the appropriate Send button to send your recommendation by your preferred method.

 When you're viewing information about a video in the iTunes Store, you can tap the Related tab to find information about other movies or TV shows watched by those who watched this one.

Playing Games

*T*he iPad is super for playing games, with its bright screen (especially bright if you're using the Retina display on a third-generation or later iPad) and great sound system, as well as its capability to rotate the screen as you play and track your motions. You can download game apps from the App Store and play them on your device. You can also use the preinstalled Game Center app to find and buy games, add friends to play against, and track and share scores.

In this chapter, you get an overview of game playing on your iPad, including opening a Game Center account, adding a friend, purchasing and downloading games, and playing basic games solo or against friends.

 You can also download games from the App Store and play them on your iPad without having to use Game Center. What Game Center provides is a place where you can create a gaming profile, add a list of gaming friends, keep track of and share your scores and perks, and shop for games (and only games) in the App Store, along with listings of top-rated games and game categories to choose among.

Chapter 14

Get ready to . . .

Open an Account in Game Center

1. On the Home screen, tap the Game Center icon. If you've never used Game Center, you're asked whether to allow *push* notifications. If you want to receive these notices alerting you that your friends want to play a game with you, tap OK. You should be aware, however, that push notifications can drain your iPad's battery more quickly.

2. Sign in on the Game Center opening screen (see **Figure 14-1**). If you want to use Game Center with another Apple ID, tap Create New Apple ID and follow the onscreen instructions, which ask you to enter your birthdate, agree to terms, choose a security question, and so on. Otherwise, tap in the ID and Password fields and enter your current account information using the onscreen keyboard that appears, and then tap the Go key on the keyboard. The screen that appears shows games you've downloaded, requests from other players, friends, and so on.

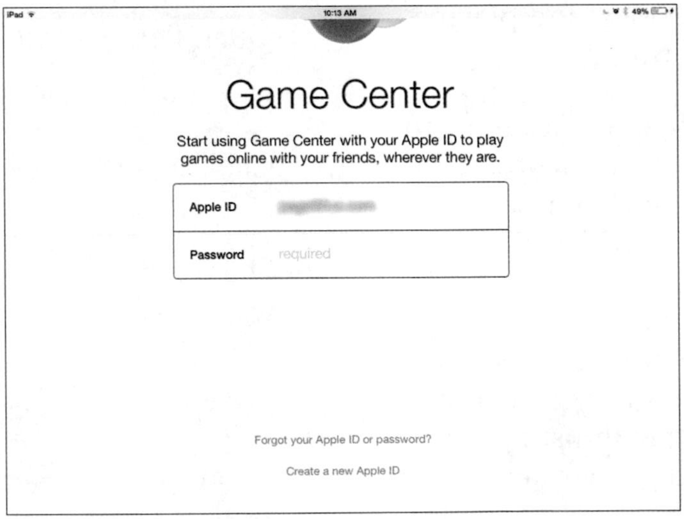

Figure 14-1

3. Tap any of the floating balloons to get to any of the displayed categories, or tap a button along the bottom of the screen (see **Figure 14-2**).

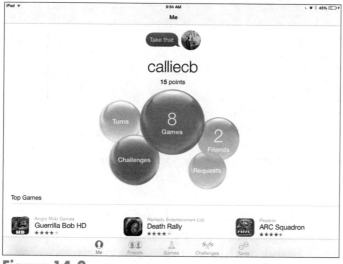

Figure 14-2

 When you first register for Game Center, if you use an e-mail address other than the one associated with your Apple ID, you may have to create a new Apple ID and verify it by responding to an e-mail message that's sent to your e-mail address. See Chapter 3 for more about creating an Apple ID when opening an iTunes account.

Create a Profile

1. When you have an account with which you can sign in to Game Center, you're ready to specify some account settings. On the Home screen, tap Settings.

2. Tap Game Center.

3. In the dialog that appears (see **Figure 14-3**), specify whether you want other players to be able to invite you to play games when Game Center is open. Tap the Allow Invites Off/On button to turn off this feature.

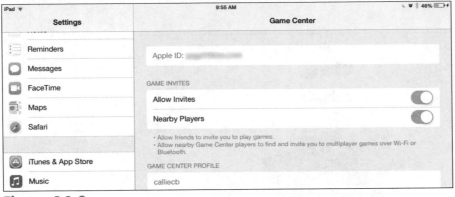

Figure 14-3

4. If you want your friends to be able to send you requests for playing games via e-mail, check to see whether the primary e-mail address listed in this dialog is the one you want them to use. If not, tap the current Apple ID, and in the dialog that appears, tap Sign Out. On the screen that appears, tap the Apple ID field and enter another account, or tap Create a New Apple ID.

5. Tap the Nearby Players On/Off button (refer to **Figure 14-3**) if you want others to be able to find you and invite you to games.

6. If you want others to see your profile, including your real name, scroll down to tap the current profile; then tap the Public Profile On/Off button to turn on your public profile.

7. Press the Home button when you finish choosing the settings. You return to the Home screen.

8. Tap Game Center. You return to Game Center, already signed in to your account, with information displayed about your friends, games, and gaming achievements (all set to zero initially).

After you create an account and a profile, whenever you go to Game Center, you log in by entering your e-mail address and password and then tapping Sign In.

Add Friends

1. If you want to play Game Center games with others who have an Apple ID and an iPhone, iPod touch, or iPad, add them as friends so that you can invite them to play. (Game Center is also available on Macs with the Mountain Lion OS and later, but few cross-platform games are available for it at this time.) On the Game Center home screen, tap the Friends button at the bottom of the screen.

2. On the Friends page, tap the Add Friends button in the top-left corner (shaped like a plus sign).

3. Enter an e-mail address in the To: field and then enter an invitation, if you like (see **Figure 14-4**).

Figure 14-4

4. Tap the Send button. After your friend accepts your invitation, his or her name is listed on the Friends screen.

 With iOS 5, Game Center gained a Friend Recommendations feature. Tap the Friends tab and then tap the A-Z button in the top-left corner. A Recommendations section appears above the list of your current friends. These people play the same games as you, or similar ones, so if you like, try adding one or two as friends. You can tap the Points tab to view the points these folks have accumulated so you can stay in your league.

 You'll probably receive requests from friends who know that you're on Game Center. When you get such an e-mail invitation, be sure that you know the person sending it before you accept it — especially if you've allowed e-mail access in your account settings. If you don't double-check, you could be allowing a stranger into your gaming world.

Purchase and Download Games

1. Time to get some games to play! Remember that you can buy any game app from the App Store or other sources and simply play it by tapping to open it on your iPad. But if you want to use Game Center to buy games, here are the steps involved. Open Game Center, and sign in to your account.

2. Tap the Games button at the bottom of the screen, and in the Recommended category, tap Show More.

3. Scroll through the list of featured games that appears, and tap one that appeals to you. Tap the price/free button (see **Figure 14-5**) to display details about it.

![Screenshot of Game Center showing Bag It! FREE by Hidden Variable Studios, with a Free App button, 49 ratings, and tabs for Leaderboards, Achievements, and Players.]

Figure 14-5

4. To buy a game, tap the button labeled with either the text *Free App* or the price (such as $1.99).

5. In the detailed app page that appears, tap the button again and then tap the Buy or Install button. A dialog may appear, asking for your Apple ID password. Enter it and then tap OK.

6. Follow the instructions on the next couple of screens to enter your password and verify your payment information if this is the first time you've signed in to your account from this device.

7. When the verification dialog appears, tap Buy. The game downloads.

 If you've added friends to your account, you can go to the Friends page and view games that your friends have downloaded. To purchase one of these games, just tap it in your friend's list.

Master iPad Game-Playing Basics

It's almost time to start playing games, but first, let me give you an idea of the iPad's gaming strengths. For many reasons, such as the following, the iPad may be the ultimate gaming device:

➡ **Fantastic-looking screen:** The high-resolution, 9.7-inch iPad screen (7.9 inch for iPad mini) has a backlit LED display that Apple describes as "remarkably crisp and vivid." The The third- and fourth-generation iPad and the iPad Air with Retina display takes this crisp screen to the max. In-plane switching (IPS) technology lets you hold your iPad at almost any angle (it has a 178-degree viewing angle) and still see good color and contrast.

➡ **Faster processor:** The dual-core A6X chip in the fourth-generation iPad and the A7 chip in the iPad Air are super-fast processors that make the iPad ideal for gaming.

➡ **Game play in full-screen mode:** Rather than play on a small iPhone screen, you can play most games designed for the iPad in full-screen mode. Seeing the full screen brings the gaming experience to you in an even more engaging way than a small screen ever could.

➡ **Ability to drag elements onscreen:** Though the iPad's Multi-Touch screen is based on the same technology that's in the iPhone, it has been redone from the ground up for the iPad. The newer screen is responsive — and when you're about to be zapped by virtual aliens in a fight to the death, responsiveness counts.

➡ **Ten-hour battery life:** A device's long battery life means that you can tap energy from it for many hours of gaming fun. Even with the extra power required for the Retina display of third-generation and later iPads, Apple managed to maintain this excellent battery life.

➡ **Specialized game-playing features:** Some newer games have features that take full advantage of the iPad's capabilities. One example is N.O.V.A. (from Gameloft), which features Multiple Target Acquisition, letting you target multiple bad guys in a single move to blow them out of the water with one shot. In Real Racing 3 (Firemint), you can look in your rearview mirror as you're racing to see what's coming up behind you — a feature made possible by the iPad's larger screen.

➡ **Stellar sound:** The built-in iPad speakers are powerful, but if you want an experience that's even more up-close and personal, you can plug a headphone, some speaker systems, or a microphone into the built-in jack.

 The iPad has a built-in motion sensor — the *three-axis accelerometer* — as well as a gyroscope. These features provide lots of fun for people who develop apps for the iPad because they use the automatically rotating screen to become part of the gaming experience. A built-in compass device, for example, reorients itself automatically as you switch your iPad from land-scape to portrait orientation. In some racing games, you can grab the iPad as though it were a steering wheel and rotate the device to simulate the driving experience.

Play against Yourself

Many games allow you to play a game all on your own. Each game has different rules and goals, so study a game's instructions to learn how to play it. Here's some general information about games:

⟹ Often, a game can be played in two modes: with oth-ers or in a solitaire version, in which you play against yourself or the computer.

⟹ Many games that you may be familiar with in the offline world, such as Carcassonne and Scrabble, have online versions. You already know the rules of play, so you simply need to figure out the exe-cution. In the online Carcassonne solitaire game, for example, you tap to place a tile on the board, tap the placed tile to rotate it, and then tap the check mark to complete your turn and reveal another tile.

⟹ Game Center records the scores of all the games you play on your own, so you can track your progress.

Challenge Friends in Game Center

1. After you've added a friend and both of you have down-loaded the same games, you can challenge your friend to beat your scores. Tap the Game Center app icon on the Home screen and sign in, if necessary.

2. Tap Me and then tap the Games bubble.

3. In the My iOS Games section, tap a game.

4. In the resulting screen, tap the Achievements tab and then tap an achievement (see **Figure 14-6**).

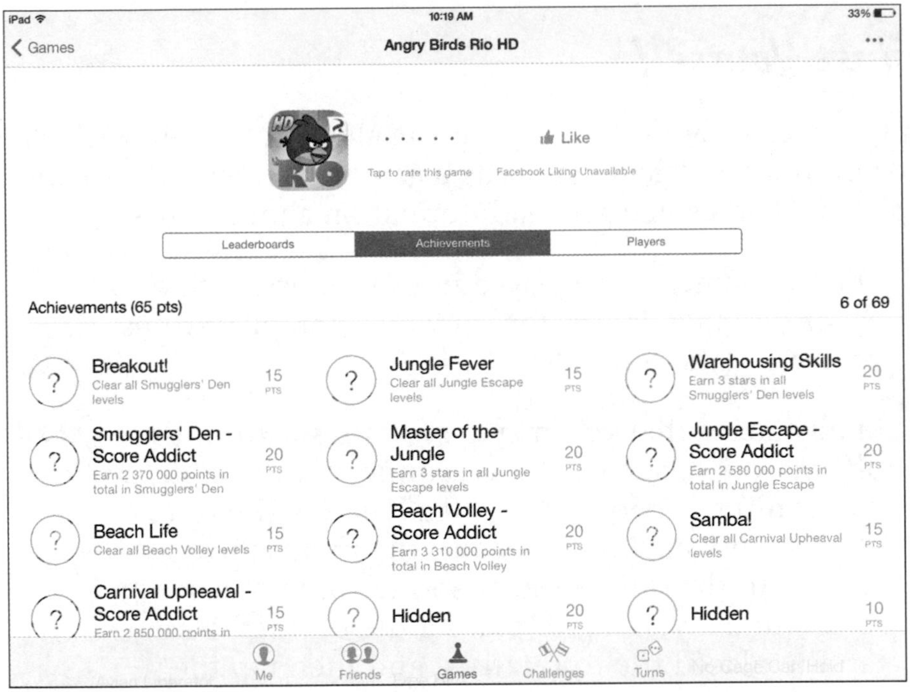

iPad 🔋   10:19 AM   33% 🔋

< Games   Angry Birds Rio HD   •••

👍 Like

Tap to rate this game   Facebook Liking Unavailable

| Leaderboards | Achievements | Players |

Achievements (65 pts)   6 of 69

?	**Breakout!** Clear all Smugglers' Den levels	15 PTS	?	**Jungle Fever** Clear all Jungle Escape levels	15 PTS	?	**Warehousing Skills** Earn 3 stars in all Smugglers' Den levels	20 PTS
?	**Smugglers' Den - Score Addict** Earn 2 370 000 points in total in Smugglers' Den	20 PTS	?	**Master of the Jungle** Earn 3 stars in all Jungle Escape levels	20 PTS	?	**Jungle Escape - Score Addict** Earn 2 580 000 points in total in Jungle Escape	20 PTS
?	**Beach Life** Clear all Beach Volley levels	15 PTS	?	**Beach Volley - Score Addict** Earn 3 310 000 points in total in Beach Volley	20 PTS	?	**Samba!** Clear all Carnival Upheaval levels	15 PTS
?	**Carnival Upheaval - Score Addict** Earn 2 850 000 points in	15 PTS	?	**Hidden**	20 PTS	?	**Hidden**	10 PTS

Me   Friends   Games   Challenges   Turns

Figure 14-6

5. At this point, some games offer you an option to challenge your friend. To do so, tap the Challenge Friends bubble.

6. On the screen that appears, tap a friend and then tap Next.

7. In the form that appears enter a message, if you like, and then tap Send (see **Figure 14-7**).

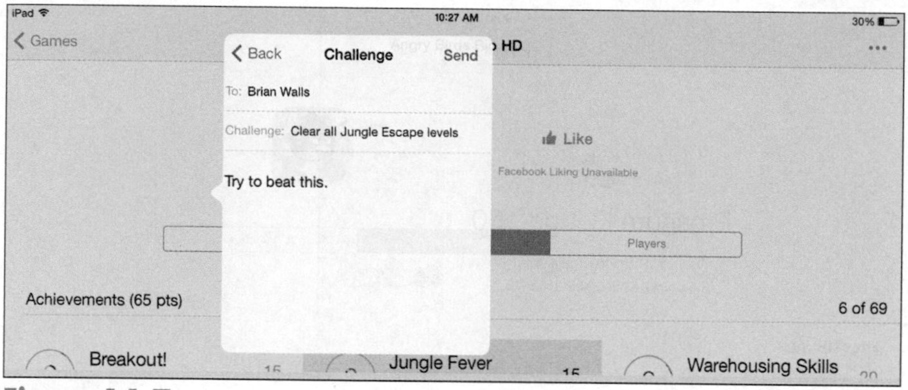

Figure 14-7

If your friends aren't available, you can play a game by tapping its icon on the Home screen. You can then return to Game Center and compare your scores with others around the world who have also played the game.

Share High Scores with Friends

1. It's fun to share your best scores with friends. Tap Game Center on the Home screen; then tap Me and tap the Games bubble.

2. In the My iOS Games section, tap a game.

3. Tap the Achievements tab, tap an achievement in the list, and then tap the Share bubble.

4. In the dialog that appears (see **Figure 14-8**), tap AirDrop (iPad fourth-gen and later), Message, Mail, Twitter, or Facebook.

5. Depending on what method you chose for sharing, enter an e-mail address and edit the message (see **Figure 14-9**), or enter account information and then follow directions to forward your score.

iPad
10:37 AM
Games
Ticket to Ride
Info
Like
Facebook Liking Una
Pressure Gauge 160
You Scored 160+
9 points earned May 15, 2013
Achievements (104 pts)
Conductor Lev
You played 20 games
evel 2
6
PTS
Message
Mail
Twitter
Conductor Lev
Play 5,000 games
evel 5
72
PTS
Cancel
Pressure Gauge 120
You Scored 120+
3
PTS
Pressure Gauge 160
You Scored 160+
9
PTS

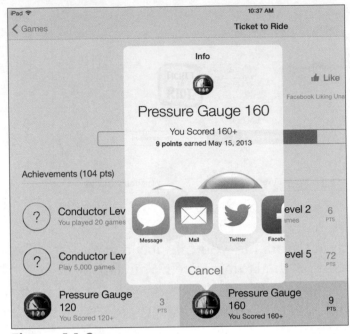

Figure 14-8

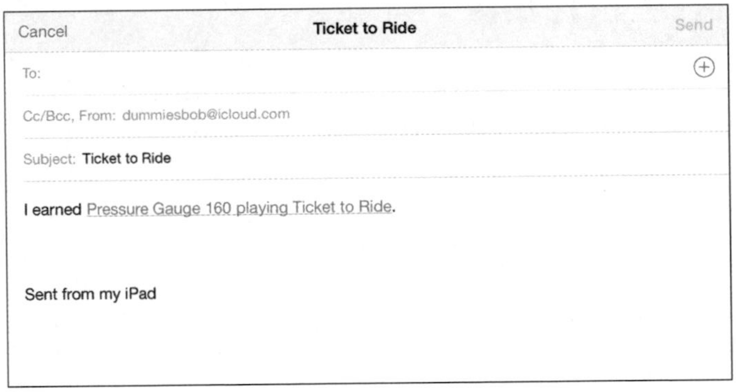

Cancel
Ticket to Ride
Send
To:
Cc/Bcc, From: dummiesbob@icloud.com
Subject: Ticket to Ride
I earned Pressure Gauge 160 playing Ticket to Ride.
Sent from my iPad

Figure 14-9

Finding Your Way with Maps

*Y*ou may have used a maps app on a smartphone before. The big difference with the iPad is its large screen, on which you can view all the beautiful map visuals, traffic flow, and maps in standard views and even 3-D as long as you have an Internet connection. You can also display the map and written directions simultaneously or have Maps speak your directions, guiding you as you drive.

If you're new to the Maps app, you'll find that it has lots of useful functions. You can find directions with suggested alternative routes from one place to another. You can bookmark locations to return to them again. Also, the Maps app makes it possible to get information about locations, such as the phone numbers and web links to businesses. You can even add a location to your Contacts list or share a location with a buddy by using Mail, Messages, Twitter, or Facebook.

Be prepared: This application is seriously cool, and you're about to have lots of fun exploring it in this chapter.

Go to Your Current Location

1. The iPad can figure out where you are at any time and display your current location as long as you have an Internet connection and have turned Location Services on in Privacy Settings. On the Home screen, tap the Maps icon.

2. Tap the Current Location icon (the small arrow in the bottom-left corner; see **Figure 15-1**). Your current location is displayed with a pin in it and a blue circle around it. The circle indicates how accurate the location is; it can be anywhere within the area of the circle.

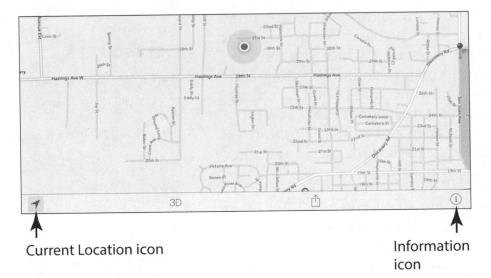

Current Location icon   Information
                                         icon

Figure 15-1

3. Double-tap the screen to zoom in on your location. (Additional methods of zooming in and out are covered in the "Zoom In and Out" task later in this chapter.)

 If you don't have a 3G or 4G iPad, your current location is a rough estimate based on a triangulation method. Only 3G- and 4G-enabled iPads with the Global Positioning System (GPS) can pinpoint where you are. Still, if you type a starting location and an ending location to get directions, you can get pretty accurate results even with a Wi-Fi–only iPad.

Change Views

1. The Maps app offers three views: Standard, Satellite, and Hybrid. iPad displays Standard view (the top-left image in **Figure 15-2**) by default the first time you open Maps. To change views, with Maps open, tap the Information icon in the bottom-right corner of the screen. The Maps menu appears, as shown in the bottom image in **Figure 15-2**.

Standard view   Satellite view

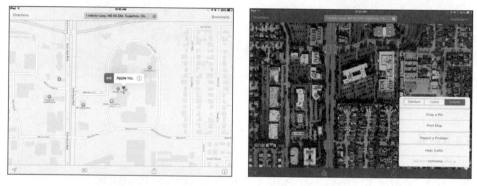

Hybrid view

Figure 15-2

2. Tap the Satellite option. Satellite view (refer to the top-right image in **Figure 15-2**) appears.

3. Tap the Information icon again and then tap Hybrid. Satellite view is displayed with street names superimposed (refer to the bottom-left image in **Figure 15-2**).

4. Finally, you can display a 3D effect (see **Figure** 15-3) on any view by tapping the 3D icon at the bottom of the screen.

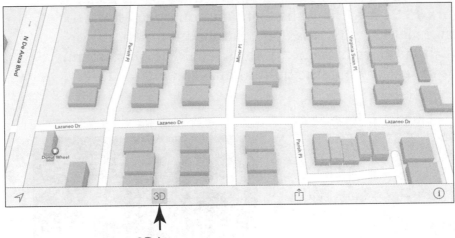

3D icon

Figure 15-3

 The Maps menu also has a traffic-overlay feature. If you live in a larger metropolitan area (this feature doesn't really work in small towns or rural settings), turn on this feature by tapping the Show Traffic button. The traffic overlay shows red dashes on roads indicating accidents or road closures to help you navigate your rush-hour commute or trip to the mall.

 You can drop a pin to mark a location on a map that you can return to. See the task "Drop a Pin," later in this chapter, for more about this topic.

 To print any displayed map to an AirPrint-compatible printer, just tap the Print button on the Maps menu.

Zoom In and Out

1. You'll appreciate the Zoom feature because it gives you the capability to zoom in and out to see more or less detailed maps and move around a displayed map. With a map displayed, double-tap with a single finger to zoom in.

2. Double-tap with two fingers to zoom out, revealing less detail.

3. Place two fingers together on the screen and move them apart to zoom in.

4. Place two fingers apart on the screen and then pinch them together to zoom out.

5. Press your finger to the screen and drag the map in any direction to move to an adjacent area.

 It can take a few moments for the map to redraw itself when you enlarge, reduce, or move around it, so have a little patience. Areas that are being redrawn look like blank grids that fill in eventually. Also, if you're in Satellite or Hybrid view, zooming in may take some time; wait, because the blurred image resolves itself.

Go to Another Location

1. With Maps open, tap the Search field. The keyboard opens. If you've displayed directions for a route you won't see the Search field; tap the Clear button on a directions screen to get back to the Search field.

2. Type a location, using a street address with city and state, a stored contact name, or a destination such as *Empire State Building* or *Detroit airport*. Maps may make suggestions (see **Figure 15-4**) as you type if it finds any logical matches. Tap the Search key on the keyboard, and the location appears, with a pin inserted into it and a label with the location and an Information icon.

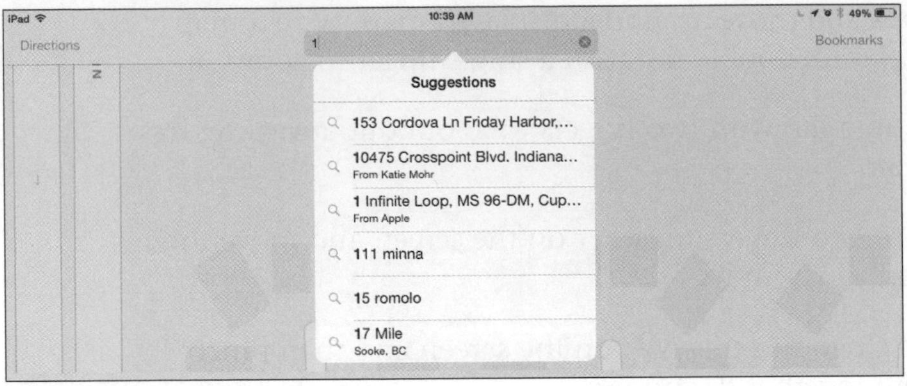

Figure 15-4

3. Tap the Information icon to see more about the destination
(see **Figure 15-5**). Note that if several locations match your
search term, several pins may display in a suggestions list.

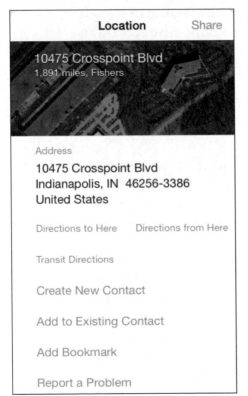

Figure 15-5

On iPad 3 and later you can tap the Dictation key on the onscreen keyboard and speak a location to the iPad if you prefer. Tap the Search field, tap the Dictation key, speak the location, and then tap the Dictation key or the Search field again. What you've spoken appears there. Next, tap the Search button on the keyboard to display the location.

Try double-pressing the Home button and asking Siri for a type of business or location by zip code. If you crave something with pepperoni, for example, say "Find pizza in 99208 zip code." The results typically display a small map you can tap to open the Maps app to find your way there. See Chapter 19 for more about using Siri.

4. Tap the screen and drag in any direction to move to a nearby location.

5. Tap Bookmarks in the top-right corner (refer to **Figure 15-4**) and at the bottom of the Bookmarks dialog that appears tap Recents to reveal recently visited sites. Tap a bookmark to go there.

If you enter a destination such as *Bronx Zoo*, you may want to enter its city and state as well. Entering just *Bronx Zoo* landed me in Woodland Park Zoo in Tacoma, Washington, because Maps looks for the closest match to your geographical location in a given category.

Drop a Pin

1. *Pins* are markers. A green pin marks a start location, a red pin marks a search result, and a blue pin (referred to as the *blue marker*) marks your iPad's current location. If you drop a pin yourself, it appears in a lovely purple. Display a map that contains a spot where you want to drop a pin to help you find directions to or from that site. If you need to, you can zoom in to a more detailed map to see a better view of the location you want to pin.

2. Press and hold your finger on the screen at the location where you want to place the pin. The pin appears.

3. Tap the Information icon to display details about the pin's location (see **Figure 15-6**).

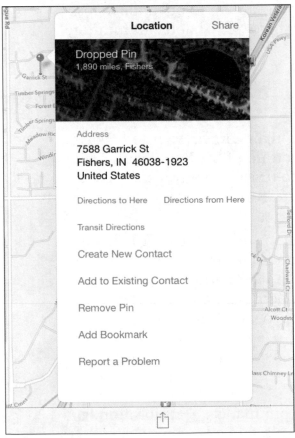

Figure 15-6

If a site has associated reviews on the restaurant review site Yelp (www.yelp.com), you can tap the More Info on Yelp button in its Information dialog to install the Yelp app and read those reviews.

Add and View a Bookmark

1. A *bookmark* provides a way to save a destination so that you can display a map or directions to it quickly. To add a bookmark to a location, first place a pin on it, as described in the preceding task.

2. Tap the Information icon to display the Information dialog.

3. Tap Add Bookmark (refer to **Figure 15-6**). The Add Bookmark dialog shown in **Figure 15-7** and the keyboard appear.

Figure 15-7

4. If you like, modify the name of the bookmark.

5. Tap Save.

6. To view your bookmarks, tap Bookmarks in the top-right corner of the Maps screen (refer to **Figure 15-4**). Select the Bookmarks tab at the bottom of the dialog that appears.

7. Tap a bookmark to go to that location in Maps.

You can also view recently viewed locations, even if you haven't bookmarked them. Tap Bookmarks and then, at the bottom of the Bookmarks dialog that appears, tap Recents. Locations that you've visited recently are listed. Tap a location to return to it in Maps.

Delete a Bookmark

1. Tap Bookmarks in the upper-right corner and then tap the Bookmarks tab at the bottom of the dialog that appears, to be sure you're viewing bookmarks.

2. Tap the Edit button. A red minus icon appears to the left of each bookmark, as shown in **Figure 15-8**.

Done	**Bookmarks**	
Current Location		
⊖ 7588 Garrick St	>	≡

Figure 15-8

3. Tap a red minus icon.

4. Tap Delete. The bookmark is removed.

 You can also use a touchscreen shortcut after you've displayed the bookmarks in Step 1. Simply swipe across a bookmark and then tap the Delete button that appears.

 You can also clear all recent locations stored by Maps to give yourself a clean slate. Tap Bookmarks and then tap the Recents tab. Tap Clear and then confirm by tapping Clear All Recents.

Find Directions

1. You can get directions in a couple of ways. With at least one pin on your map in addition to your current location, tap the Directions button and then tap Route. A line appears, showing the route between your current location and the closest pin for the selected transportation method: by car, on foot, or via public transit (see **Figure 15-9**).

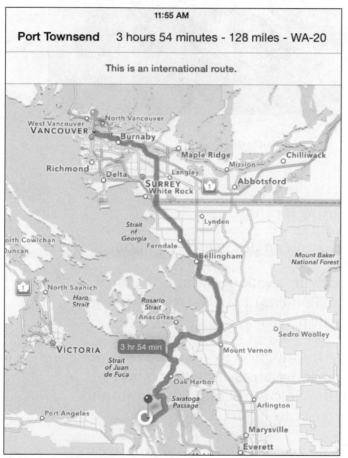

Figure 15-9

2. To show directions from your current location to another pin, tap Clear; then tap the starting point and tap Directions. In the dialog that appears, tap the location of the other pin. The route is redrawn.

3. You can also enter two locations to get directions from one to the other. Tap the Directions button in Maps and then tap the Start field (see **Figure 15-10**). The keyboard appears.

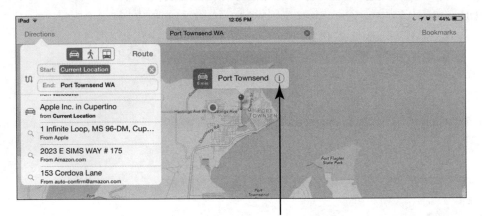

Information icon

Figure 15-10

4. Enter a different starting location.

5. Tap the End field and enter a destination location.

6. If you like, tap the driving, walking, or public transit button and then tap the Route button. The route between the two locations is displayed.

7. You can also tap the Information icon on the information bar that appears above any selected pin and use the Directions To Here or Directions From Here button to generate directions (refer to **Figure 15-6**).

8. When a route is displayed, an information bar appears along the top of the Maps screen, telling you the distance and the time it takes to travel between the two locations.

If alternative routes are available, Maps notes the time it takes to travel any alternative routes. Tap a route's timing to make that route the active route.

View Information about a Location

1. In earlier tasks in this chapter, you display the Information dialog for locations to add a bookmark or get directions. In this task, you focus on the useful information displayed there. Go to a location, and tap the pin.

2. On the information bar that appears above the pinned location, tap the Information icon (refer to **Figure 15-10**).

3. In the Information dialog (see **Figure 15-11**), tap the web address listed in the Home Page field to be taken to the location's web page, if it has one associated with it.

4. You can also press and hold either the Phone (refer to **Figure 15-11**) or Address field and use the Copy button to copy the phone number, for example, so that you can place it in a Notes document for future reference.

5. Tap outside the Information dialog to close it.

 Rather than copy and paste information, you can easily save all information about a location in your Contacts address book. See the next task, "Add a Location to a Contact," to find out how.

Add a Location to a Contact

1. Tap a pin to display the information bar.

2. Tap the Information icon.

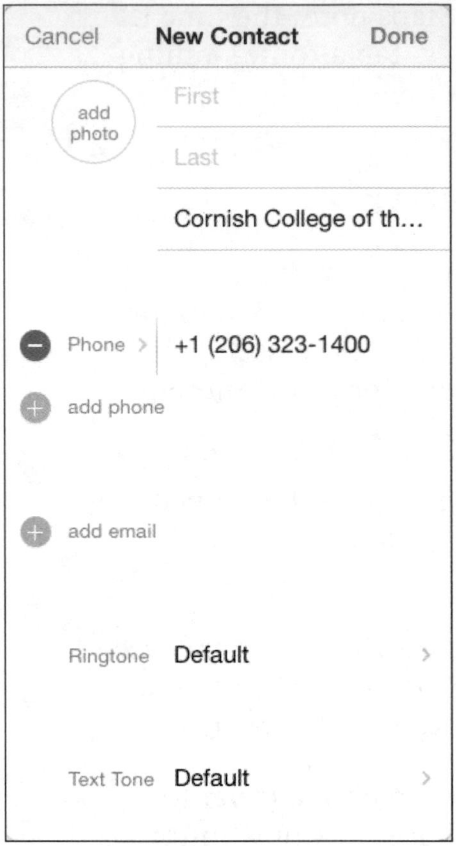

Figure 15-11

3. In the Information dialog that appears, tap Create New Contact.

4. In the resulting dialog, whatever information was available about the location has already been entered. Enter any additional information you need, such as name, phone, or e-mail address (refer to **Figure 15-11**).

5. Tap Done. The information is stored in your Contacts address book.

If you tap Add to Existing Contact instead in Step 3, you can choose a contact from your Contacts list to add the location information to.

 You can choose a distinct ringtone or text tone for a new contact. Just tap the Ringtone or Text Tone field in the New Contact form to see a list of options. When that person calls via FaceTime or texts you via iMessage, you'll recognize him or her from the tone that plays.

Share Location Information

1. Tap a pin to display the information bar.

2. Tap the Information icon.

3. In the Information dialog that appears, tap the Share icon at the bottom of the Maps screen and then tap Selected Location.

4. In the resulting dialog (see **Figure 15-12**), you can choose to share via AirDrop, Mail, Twitter, or Facebook. Tap Mail to see how this option works.

5. On the form that appears, use the onscreen keyboard to enter the recipient's information. (If you chose Facebook or Twitter in Step 4, you'd enter recipient information as appropriate to the service you chose.) Then tap Send to share the map.

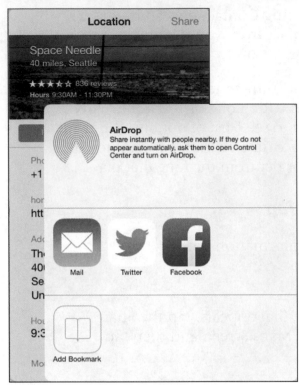

Figure 15-12

 You may have to install and set up the Twitter or Facebook app before sharing Maps content with those services. You also must have an account with these services to use them to share content.

Get Turn-by-Turn Navigation Help

1. When you've entered directions for a route and displayed that route, you can begin listening to turn-by-turn navigation instructions that can be helpful as you're driving. Tap the Start button in the top-right corner to start. The narration begins, and large text instructions are displayed, as shown in **Figure 15-13**.

2. Continue driving according to the route until the next instruction is spoken.

Figure 15-13

3. For an overview of your route at any time, tap the
Overview button in the top-right corner. Tap Resume to
go back to the step-by-step instructions.

 To adjust the volume of the spoken navigation aid,
tap Settings➪Maps and then adjust the Navigation
Voice Volume settings to No Voice, Low, Normal, or
Loud.

 To change route information from miles to kilometers, tap Settings➪Maps, and tap In Kilometers to
change the setting.

Part IV
Managing Your Life and Your iPad

Keeping On Schedule with Calendar and Clock

W hether you're retired or still working, you have a busy life full of activities (even busier if you're retired, for some unfathomable reason). You may need a way to keep on top of all those activities and appointments. The Calendar app on your iPad is a simple, elegant, electronic daybook that helps you do just that.

In addition to being able to enter events and view them by the day, week, month, or year, you can set up Calendar to send alerts to remind you of your obligations and search for events by keywords. You can even set up repeating events, such as weekly poker games, monthly get-togethers with the girls or guys, or weekly babysitting appointments with your grandchild. To help you coordinate calendars on multiple devices, you can also sync events with other calendar accounts or use iCloud to sync calendars between supported devices.

A preinstalled app that arrived on the iPad with iOS 6 is Clock. Though simple to use, Clock helps you view the time in multiple locations, set alarms, and use a timer.

In this chapter, you master the simple procedures for getting around your calendar, entering and editing events, setting up alerts, syncing, and searching. You also learn the simple ins and outs of using Clock.

View Your Calendar

1. Calendar offers several ways to view your schedule. Start by tapping the Calendar app icon on the Home screen to open it. Depending on what you last had open, you may see today's calendar, an open event, or the Search screen with all appointments displayed.

2. Tap the Today button at the bottom of the screen to display Today's view (if it's not already displayed) and then tap the Search button to see all appointments. This view, shown in **Figure 16-1,** displays your daily appointments with times listed on the left page and an hourly breakdown of the day on the right page. Tap an event on this list to view more details.

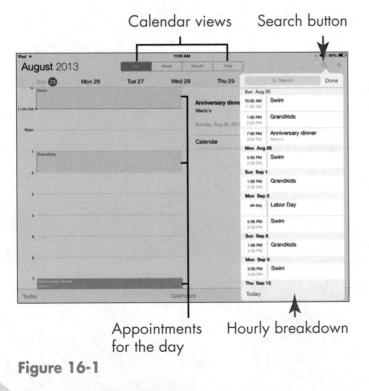

Calendar views   Search button

Appointments for the day   Hourly breakdown

Figure 16-1

3. Tap the Week button to view all events for the current week, as shown in **Figure 16-2**. In this view, appointments appear against the times listed along the left side of the screen.

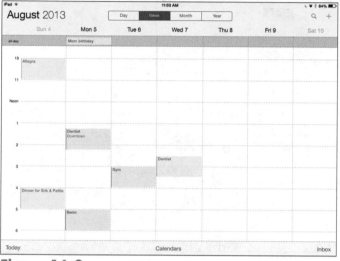

Figure 16-2

4. Tap the Month button to get an overview of your busy month (see **Figure 16-3**). In this view, you see the name and timing of each event.

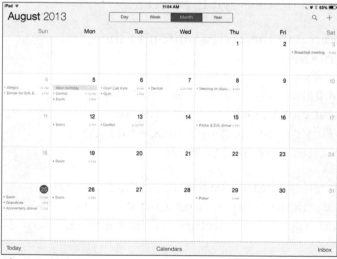

Figure 16-3

5. Tap the Year button to see all months in the year so you can quickly move to one, as shown in **Figure 16-4**.

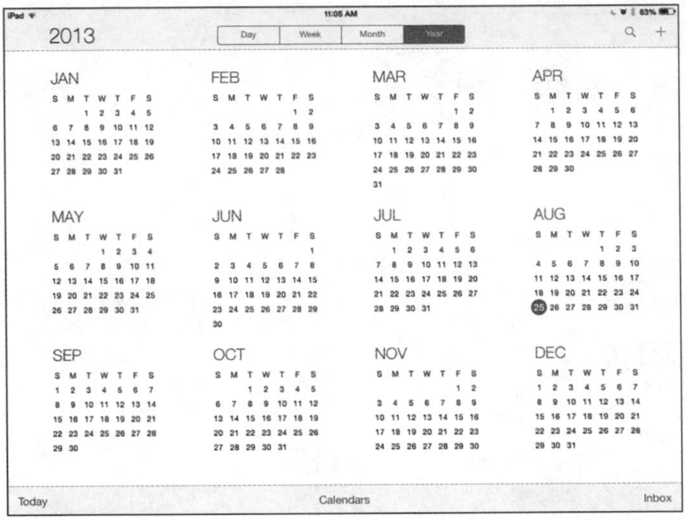

Figure 16-4

6. In any calendar view, tap the Search button to see List view, which lists all your commitments to the right, as shown in **Figure 16-5**.

7. To move from one day, week, month, or year to another, use your finger to scroll up or down the screen.

8. To jump back to today, tap the Today button in the bottom-left corner of Calendar.

For the feel of a paper calendar book, rotate your screen to landscape orientation when you use the Calendar app. This orientation provides a nice book-like experience, especially in Day view.

To view any invitation that you accepted, which placed an event on your calendar, tap Inbox; a list of invitations is displayed. Tap Done to return to the calendar.

Search button

Add button

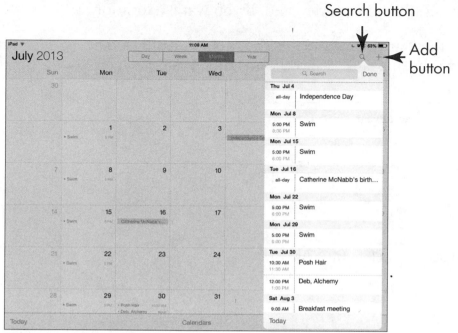

Figure 16-5

Add Calendar Events

1. With any view displayed, tap the Add button (refer to **Figure 16-5**) to add an event. The Add Event dialog, shown in **Figure 16-6**, appears.

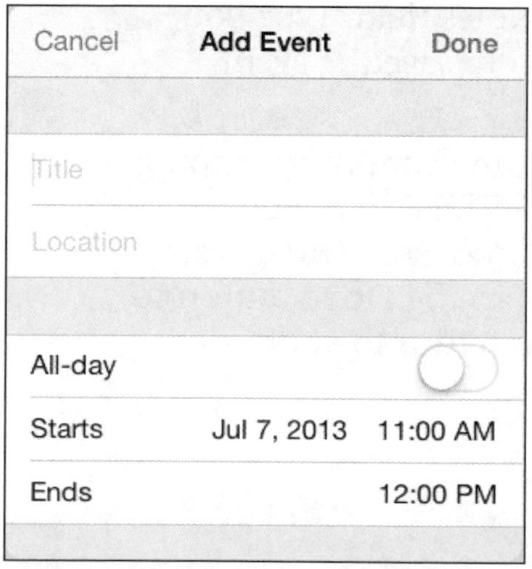

Cancel	**Add Event**	Done
Title		
Location		
All-day		
Starts	Jul 7, 2013	11:00 AM
Ends		12:00 PM

Figure 16-6

2. Enter a title for the event and, if you want, a location.

3. Tap the Starts or Ends field. The tool for setting a date and time appears, as shown in **Figure 16-7**.

Cancel	**Add Event**	Done

All-day

Starts	Jul 7, 2013	11:00 AM

Thu Jul 4	8	57	
Fri Jul 5	9	58	
Sat Jul 6	10	59	
Sun Jul 7	**11**	**00**	**AM**
Mon Jul 8	12	01	PM
Tue Jul 9	1	02	
Wed Jul 10	2	03	

Figure 16-7

4. Place your fingertip on the date, hour, minute, or AM/PM column, and move your finger to scroll up or down. (Note that if the event will last all day, you can simply tap the All-Day On/Off button and forget about setting start and end times.)

5. If you want to add notes, use your finger to scroll down in the Add Event dialog and tap the Notes field. Type your note and then tap the Done button to save the event.

You can edit any event at any time simply by tapping it in any view of your calendar. The Edit dialog appears, offering the same settings as the Add Event dialog (refer to **Figure 16-6**). Tap the Done button to save your changes or Cancel to return to your calendar without saving any changes.

Add Events Using Siri

1. Press and hold the Home button.

2. Say "Create Meeting October 3rd at 2:30 p.m."

3. When Siri asks you whether you're ready to schedule the event, say "Yes."

 You can schedule an event with Siri in several ways because the feature is pretty flexible. You can say "Create event," and Siri asks you first for a date and then for a time. Or you can say "I have a meeting with John on April 1st," and Siri may respond by saying "I don't find a meeting with John on April 1st; shall I create it?" You can say "Yes" to have Siri create it. Play around with this feature and Calendar; it's a lot of fun!

Create Repeating Events

1. If you want an event to repeat, such as a weekly or monthly appointment, you can set a repeating event. With any view displayed, tap the Add button to add an event. The Add Event dialog appears (refer to **Figure 16-6**).

2. Enter a title and location for the event, and set the start and end dates and times, as shown in the earlier task "Add Calendar Events."

3. Scroll down the page, if necessary, and tap the Repeat field. The Repeat dialog, shown in **Figure 16-8**, is displayed.

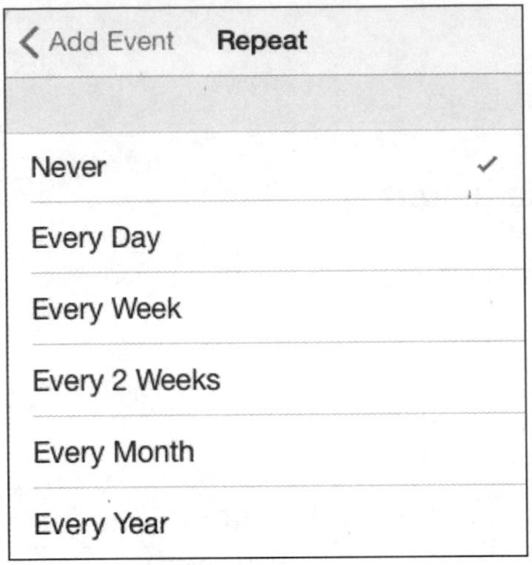

‹ Add Event	**Repeat**
Never	✓
Every Day	
Every Week	
Every 2 Weeks	
Every Month	
Every Year	

Figure 16-8

4. Tap a preset time interval: Every Day, Week, 2 Weeks, Month, or Year.

5. Tap Done. You return to the calendar.

 Other calendar programs may give you more control of repeating events. You may be able to make a setting to repeat an event every Tuesday or the 1st and 3rd Sunday of the month, for example. If you want a more robust calendar feature, consider setting up your appointments in iCal/Calendar or Outlook and then syncing them to iPad. But if you want to create a simple repeating event in the iPad's Calendar app, simply add the first event on a Tuesday and make it repeat every week. Easy, huh?

Add Alerts

1. If you want your iPad to alert you when an event is coming up, you can use the Alert feature. First, tap the Settings icon on the Home screen, and choose Sounds.

2. Scroll down to Calendar Alerts and then tap any Alert Tone, which causes the iPad to play the tone for you.

3. Press the Home button; tap Calendar; and create an event in your calendar or open an existing one for editing, as covered in earlier tasks in this chapter.

4. In the Add Event dialog (refer to **Figure 16-6**) or the Edit dialog, tap the Alert field. The Event Alert dialog appears, as shown in **Figure 16-9**. Note that if you want to set two alerts — say, one the day before the event and one an hour before it — you can repeat this procedure by using Second Alert instead.

5. Tap any preset interval, from 5 Minutes to 2 Days Before or at the time of the event. You return to the Edit dialog.

6. Tap Done to save the alert.

7. Tap the Day button to display Day view of the date of your event and then tap the event. The alert information is included in that view, as shown in **Figure 16-10**.

 If you work for an organization that uses a Microsoft Exchange server, you can set up your iPad to receive and respond to invitations from colleagues in your company. When somebody sends an invitation that you accept, it appears on your calendar. Check with your company network administrator (who will jump at the chance to get her hands on your iPad) or the *iPad User Guide* to set up this feature if it sounds useful to you. Or you can check into using iCloud, which does pretty much the same thing, minus the IT person.

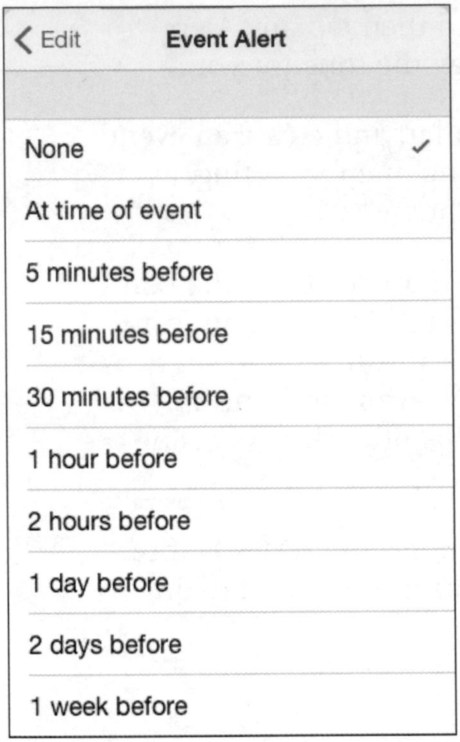

< Edit	**Event Alert**	
None		✓
At time of event		
5 minutes before		
15 minutes before		
30 minutes before		
1 hour before		
2 hours before		
1 day before		
2 days before		
1 week before		

Figure 16-9

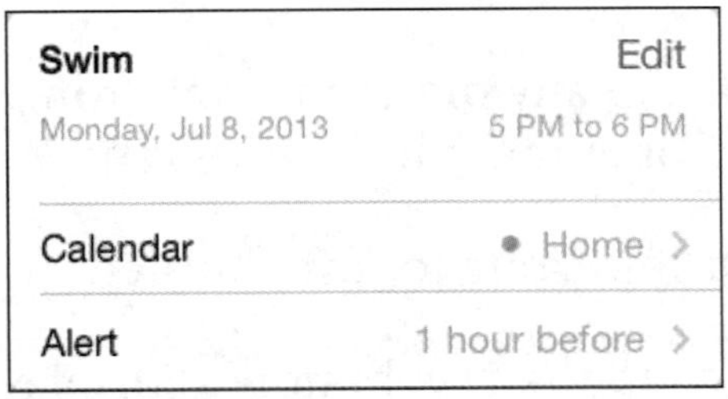

Swim	Edit
Monday, Jul 8, 2013	5 PM to 6 PM
Calendar	• Home >
Alert	1 hour before >

Figure 16-10

Search Calendars

1. With Calendar open in any view, tap the Search button in the top-right corner (refer to **Figure 16-5**).

2. Tap the Search field (the onscreen keyboard appears), type a word or words to search by, and then tap the Search key. While you type, the Results dialog appears, as shown in **Figure 16-11**.

3. Tap any result to display it in the view you were in when you started the search. The Edit dialog appears.

4. Use the Edit dialog to edit the event, if you want.

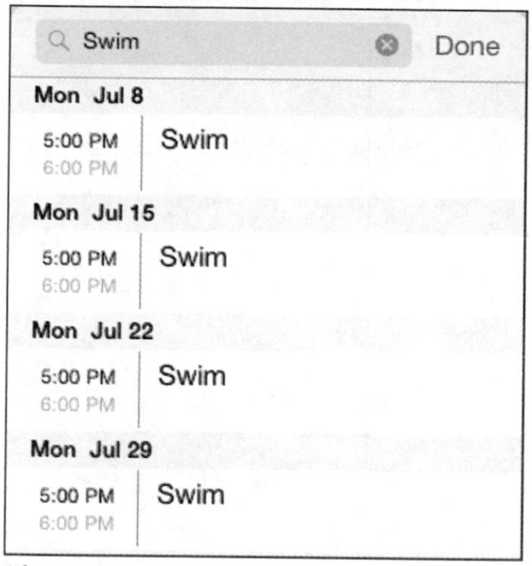

Q Swim	⊗	Done
Mon Jul 8		
5:00 PM 6:00 PM	Swim	
Mon Jul 15		
5:00 PM 6:00 PM	Swim	
Mon Jul 22		
5:00 PM 6:00 PM	Swim	
Mon Jul 29		
5:00 PM 6:00 PM	Swim	

Figure 16-11

Subscribe To and Share Calendars

1. If you use a calendar from an online service such as Yahoo! or Google, you can subscribe to that calendar to read events saved there on your iPad. Note that you can only read, not edit, these events. Tap the Settings icon on the Home screen to get started.

2. Tap the Mail, Contacts, Calendars option on the left.

3. Tap Add Account. The Add Account options, shown in **Figure 16-12,** appear.

4. Tap an e-mail choice, such as Gmail or Yahoo!

5. In the dialog that appears (see **Figure 16-13**), enter your name, e-mail address, and e-mail account password.

6. Tap Next. The iPad verifies your address.

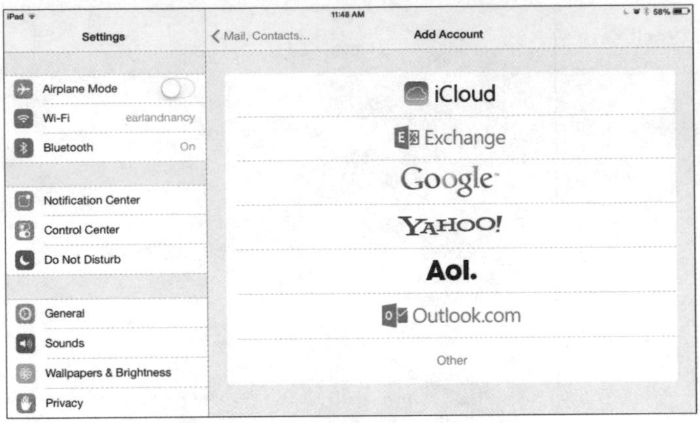

Figure 16-12

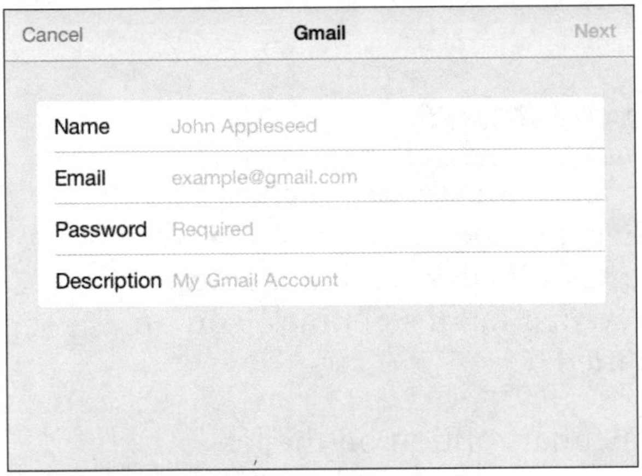

Figure 16-13

7. On the following screen, tap the On/Off button for the Calendars field. Your iPad retrieves data from your calendar at the interval you've set to fetch data. To review these settings, tap the Fetch New Data option in the Mail, Contacts, Calendars dialog.

8. In the Fetch New Data pane that appears (see **Figure 16-14**), be sure that the Push option's On/Off button is set to On and then choose the option you prefer for how frequently data is pushed to your iPad.

iPad 🛜		11:51 AM		🔋 58% 🔋
Settings	‹ Mail, Contacts...		**Fetch New Data**	

✈️ Airplane Mode ⚪	**Push** 🔵
📶 Wi-Fi earlandnancy	New data will be pushed to your iPad from the server when possible.
🔵 Bluetooth On	**iCloud** Push › Mail, Contacts, Calendars, Safari, Reminders, Notes, Photos, Find My iPad and 2 more...
📵 Notification Center	**Outlook** Push › Mail, Contacts, Calendars, Reminders

Figure 16-14

 If you use Microsoft Outlook's calendar or iCal/ Calendar on your main computer, you can sync it to your iPad calendar to avoid having to re-enter event information. To do this, use iCloud settings to sync automatically (see Chapter 3), sync wirelessly from the iPad, or connect your iPad to your computer with the Lightning to USB Cable (or Dock Connector to USB Cable) and use the settings in your iTunes account to sync with calendars. Click the Sync button, and your calendar settings are shared between your computer and iPad (in both directions). Read more in Chapter 3 about working with iTunes to manage your iPad content.

 If you store your contacts' birthdays in the Contacts app, the Calendar app displays each one when the day comes around so that you won't forget to pass on your congratulations . . . or condolences.

You can also have calendar events sent if you sub- scribe to a push service. This service can sync calen- dars from multiple e-mail accounts with your iPad calendar. Be aware that if you choose to have data pushed to your iPad, your battery may drain faster.

Delete an Event

1. When an upcoming luncheon or meeting is canceled, you may want to delete the appointment. With Calendar open, tap an event and then tap the Edit button on the information bar that appears. The Edit dialog opens.

2. In the Edit dialog, tap the Delete Event button (see **Figure 16-15**). Confirming options appear, including a Delete Event button.

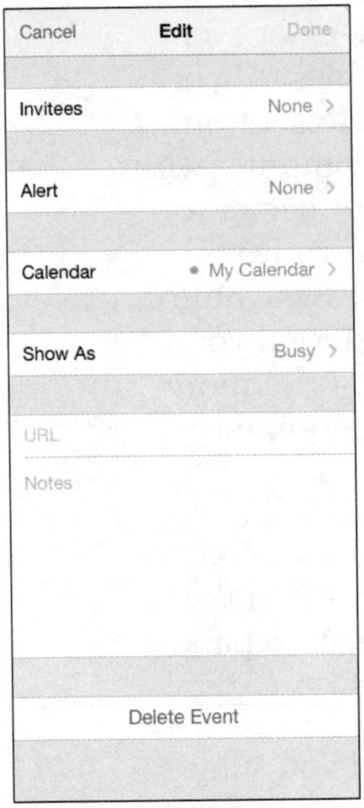

Cancel	**Edit**	Done
Invitees		None >
Alert		None >
Calendar	• My Calendar	>
Show As		Busy >
URL		
Notes		
	Delete Event	

Figure 16-15

3. If this event is a repeating event, you see two buttons that offer the option to delete this instance of the event or this instance and all future instances of the event (see **Figure 16-16**). Tap the button for the option you prefer. The event is deleted, and you return to Calendar view.

 If an event is moved but not canceled, you don't have to delete the old one and create a new one: Simply edit the existing event to change the day and time in the Edit dialog.

This is a repeating event.

Delete This Event Only

Delete All Future Events

Cancel

Figure 16-16

Display Clock

1. Clock is a preinstalled app that comes with iOS 7. You can access it from the Home screen that contains all the other preinstalled apps, such as Notes and Camera. Tap the Clock app to open it. In World Clock view, preset location clocks are displayed along the top of the screen, and the locations of these clocks are displayed on a world map below them.

2. Tap a clock at the top of the screen to display it full
screen (see **Figure 16-17**).

Figure 16-17

3. Tap the World Clock button to return to the World Clock
screen. (If the World Clock button isn't visible, tap the
screen to make it appear.)

 Clocks for cities that are currently in nighttime are
displayed in black. Clocks for cities that are currently
in daytime are displayed in white.

Add or Delete a Clock

1. You can add a clock for many (but not all) locations
around the world. With Clock open, tap Add on the
clock on the far-right side.

2. Tap a city in the resulting list, or tap a letter on the right
side of the screen to display locations that begin with
that letter. The clock appears in the last spot on the right
side of the screen, and the location is displayed on the
world map.

3. To remove a location's clock, tap the Edit button in the top-left corner of the World Clock screen. Then tap the minus symbol next to a location and tap the Delete button (see **Figure 16-18**).

Figure 16-18

Set an Alarm

1. With the Clock app open, tap the Alarm tab at the bottom of the screen.

2. Tap the Add button (a button with a plus symbol on it in the top-right corner).

3. In the Add Alarm dialog, shown in **Figure 16-19**, take any of the following actions, tapping the Back button after you make each setting to return to the Add Alarm dialog:

- Tap Repeat if you want the alarm to repeat at a regular interval, such as every Monday or every Sunday.

- Tap Label if you want the alarm to have a name such as "Take Pill" or "Call Mom."

- Tap Sound to choose the tone the alarm will play.

- Tap the On/Off button for Snooze if you want to use the Snooze feature.

4. Place your finger on the three wheels at the bottom of the dialog, scroll to set the time when you want the alarm to occur, and tap Save. The alarm appears on the calendar's Alarm tab.

 To delete an alarm, tap the Alarm tab and then tap Edit. All alarms appear. Tap the red circle with a minus in it next to the alarm and then tap the Delete button.

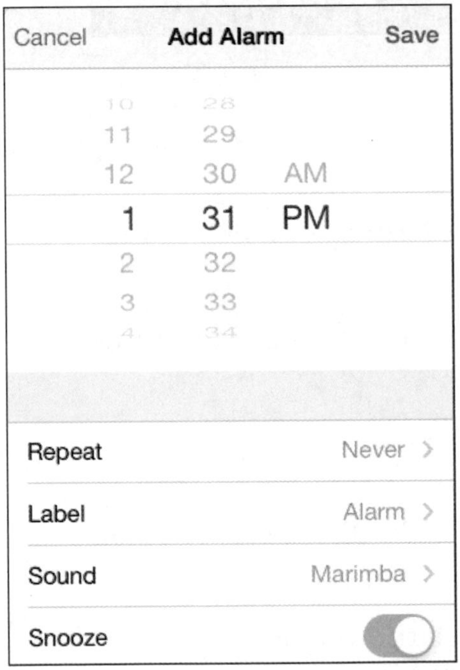

Cancel	**Add Alarm**	Save
	10 28	
	11 29	
	12 30 AM	
	1 31 PM	
	2 32	
	3 33	
	4 34	
Repeat		Never >
Label		Alarm >
Sound		Marimba >
Snooze		⬤

Figure 16-19

Use Stopwatch and Timer

Sometimes, life seems like a countdown or a ticking clock counting the minutes you've spent on a certain activity. You can use the Stopwatch and Timer tabs of the Clock app to count down to a specific time, such as the moment when your chocolate chip cookies are done, or to time a walk.

These two apps work similarly. Tap the Stopwatch or Timer tab and tap the Start button. When you set the Timer app, the iPad uses a sound to notify you when time's up. When you start the Stopwatch app, you have to tap the Stop button when the activity is done (see **Figure 16-20**).

Figure 16-20

 If you want to time incremental events, such as a series of laps you swim in a pool, with the Stopwatch running, tap the Lap button at the end of each segment and each segment is displayed in a list beneath the main timing field.

Working with Reminders and Notifications

With the arrival of iOS 5, the Reminders app and the Notification Center feature appeared, warming the hearts of those of us who occasionally have a "senior" moment.

Reminders is a kind of to-do list that lets you create tasks and set reminders so you don't forget important commitments.

Notifications allows you to review all the things you should be aware of in one place, such as new mail messages, text messages, calendar appointments, reminders, and alerts. You can also display weather and stock reports in Notification Center.

If you occasionally need to escape all your obligations, try the Do Not Disturb feature, new as of iOS 6. Turn this feature on, and you won't be bothered with alerts until you turn it off again.

In this chapter, you discover how to set up and view tasks in Reminders, and you see how Notification Center can centralize all your alerts, including the new Today, All, and Missed tabs that help you view all your notifications in an organized way, in one easy-to-find place.

Get ready to . . .

Create a Task in Reminders

1. Creating a task in Reminders is pretty darn simple. Tap Reminders on the Home screen.

2. On the screen that appears, tap Scheduled, or tap a category of reminders you've created (such as Exercise or Club), and then tap a blank slot in the displayed list to add a task (see **Figure 17-1**). The onscreen keyboard appears.

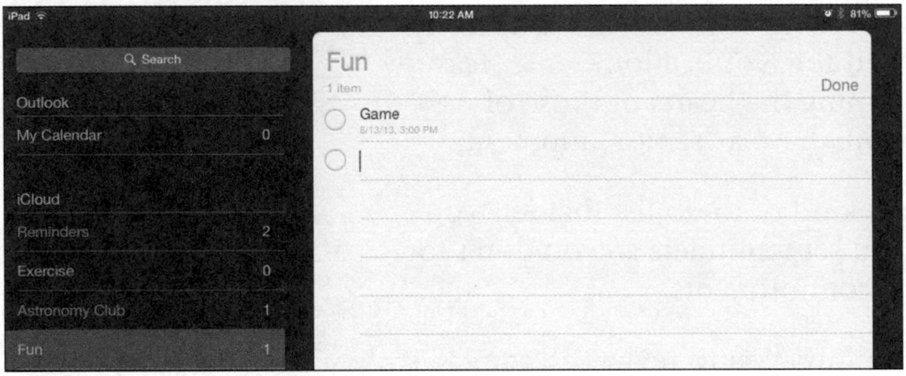

Figure 17-1

3. Enter a task name or description, and tap the Return button. The new task is added to the Reminders list.

 See the next task to discover how to add more specifics about an event for which you've created a reminder.

 Note that when you first use Reminders, you have only the Reminders list to add tasks to. However, you can create your own list categories. See the task "Create a List" later in this chapter to find out how to do this.

Edit Task Details

1. Tap a task and then tap the Information icon that appears to the right of it to open the Details dialog, shown in **Figure 17-2**. (I explain reminder settings in the task that follows.)

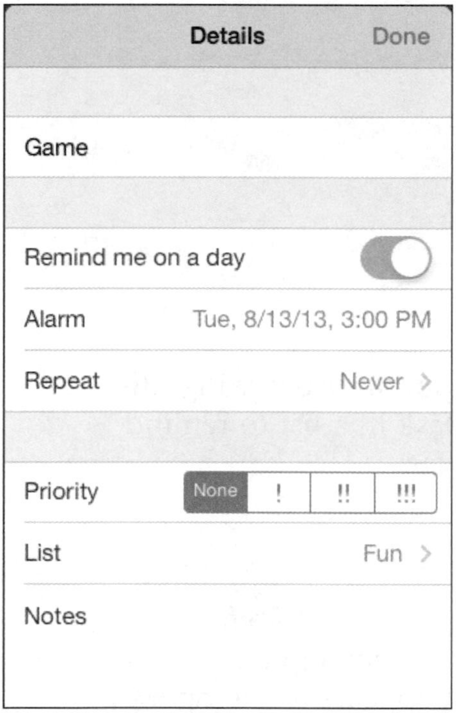

Details	Done
Game	
Remind me on a day	⬤
Alarm	Tue, 8/13/13, 3:00 PM
Repeat	Never >
Priority	None ! !! !!!
List	Fun >
Notes	

Figure 17-2

2. Tap a Priority (None, Low, Medium, or High).

3. Tap List, and then choose any list name to access the tasks from that list.

4. Tap Notes and then, using the onscreen keyboard, enter a note about the task (see **Figure 17-3**).

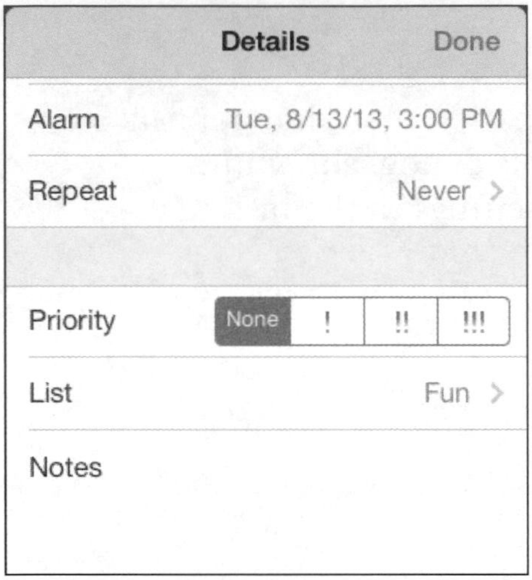

Details	**Done**
Alarm	Tue, 8/13/13, 3:00 PM
Repeat	Never >
Priority	None ! !! !!!
List	Fun >
Notes	

Figure 17-3

5. Tap Done to save the task details.

 In the current version of the app, priority settings display exclamation points on a task in a list to remind you of the importance of that task.

Schedule a Reminder

1. One of the major purposes of Reminders is to remind you of upcoming tasks. To set a reminder, tap a task and then tap the Information icon that appears to the right of the task.

2. In the Details dialog that appears, tap Remind Me On a Day to turn the feature on.

3. Tap the Alarm field that appears below this setting. The settings shown in **Figure 17-4** appear.

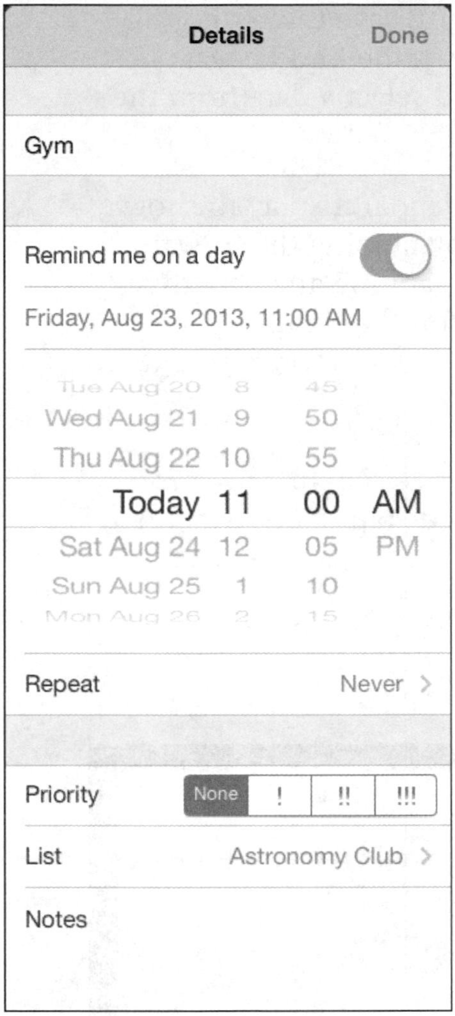

Details	Done

Gym

Remind me on a day ⬤

Friday, Aug 23, 2013, 11:00 AM

Tue Aug 20	8	45	
Wed Aug 21	9	50	
Thu Aug 22	10	55	
Today	**11**	**00**	**AM**
Sat Aug 24	12	05	PM
Sun Aug 25	1	10	
Mon Aug 26	2	15	

Repeat   Never >

Priority   None ! !! !!!

List   Astronomy Club >

Notes

Figure 17-4

4. Tap and flick the day, hour, and minutes fields to scroll to the date and time for the reminder.

5. Tap Done to save the settings for the reminder.

 If you want a task to repeat with associated reminders, tap the Repeat field in the Details dialog, and in the dialog that appears, tap Every Day, Week, 2 Weeks, Month, or Year (so you remember those annual meetings — or remember to buy your spouse an anniversary gift). Tap Done to save the setting. To stop the task from repeating, tap the End Repeat field, tap End Repeat Date, and select a date from the scrolling calendar.

 You can scroll the monthly calendar display to show months in the past or future by tapping the forward or backward arrows, and then tapping any date to show its tasks in the daily list on the right.

Create a List

1. You can create your own lists of tasks to help you keep different parts of your life organized. Tap Reminders on the Home screen to open it.

2. Tap Add List to display the New List form, shown in **Figure 17-5**.

Figure 17-5

3. Enter a name for the list, and tap a color. The list name appears in that color in List view.

4. Tap Done to save the list.

5. Tap a blank line to create a task.

Sync with Other Devices and Calendars

 To make all these settings work, you should set up your default Calendar and then set up your iCloud account by tapping Settings⇨Mail, Contacts, Calendars⇨Accounts⇨iCloud.

1. To determine which tasks are brought over from other devices or calendars such as Outlook or iCal/Calendar, tap the Settings icon on the Home screen.

2. Tap iCloud, and make sure that in the list that appears in the right pane, Reminders is set to On (see **Figure 17-6**).

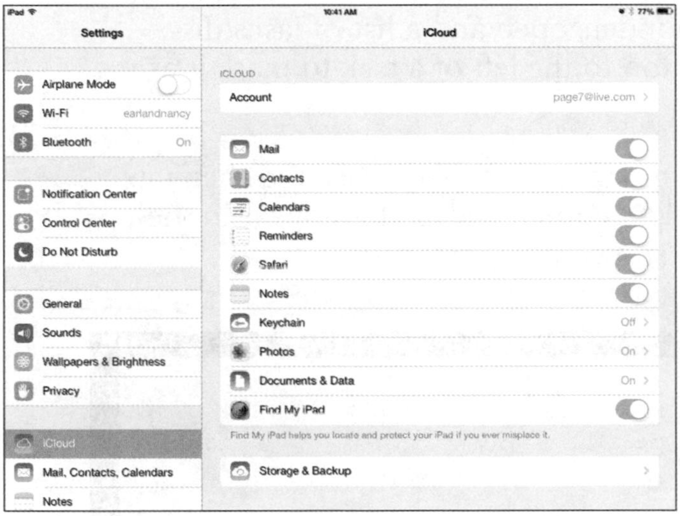

Figure 17-6

3. Also in the right pane, make sure that Calendars is set to On.

4. Tap Mail, Contacts, Calendars, and scroll down to the Calendars settings.

5. Tap the Sync field and then choose how far back to sync Reminders (see **Figure 17-7**).

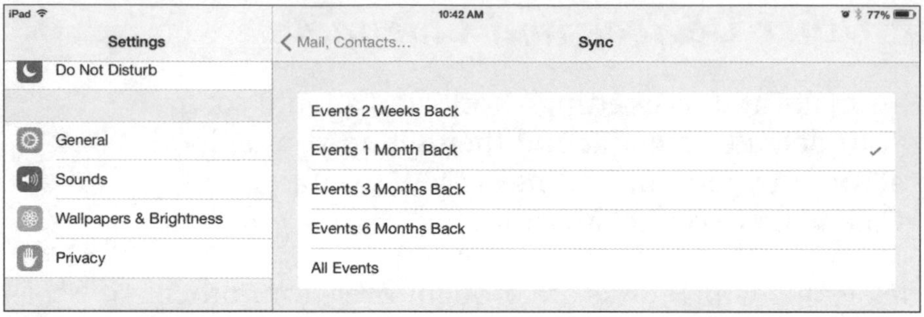

Figure 17-7

Mark As Complete or Delete a Reminder

1. You may want to mark a task as completed or just delete it entirely so you don't continue to get notifications about it. With Reminders open and a list of tasks displayed, tap the button to the left of a task to mark it as complete.

2. To delete more than one task, display a list and then tap Edit in the upper-right corner. Red circles appear to the left of the tasks, as shown in **Figure 17-8.**

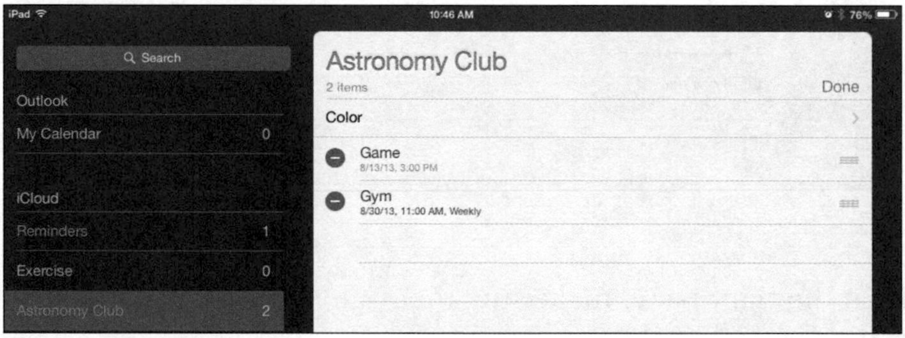

Figure 17-8

3. Tap the red circle to the left of the task and then tap the Delete button. The task is deleted.

4. Tap Done to return to the list.

Set Notification Types

1. Notification Center is a list of various alerts and appointments hat you can display by swiping down from the top of any iPad screen. Notification Center is on by default, but you can make settings to control what types of notifications are displayed. Tap Settings and then tap Notification Center.

2. In the settings that appear (see **Figure 17-9**), note the list of items you can set to be included in Notification Center — or not. Messages and Reminders may be included, for example, but alerts in game apps may not.

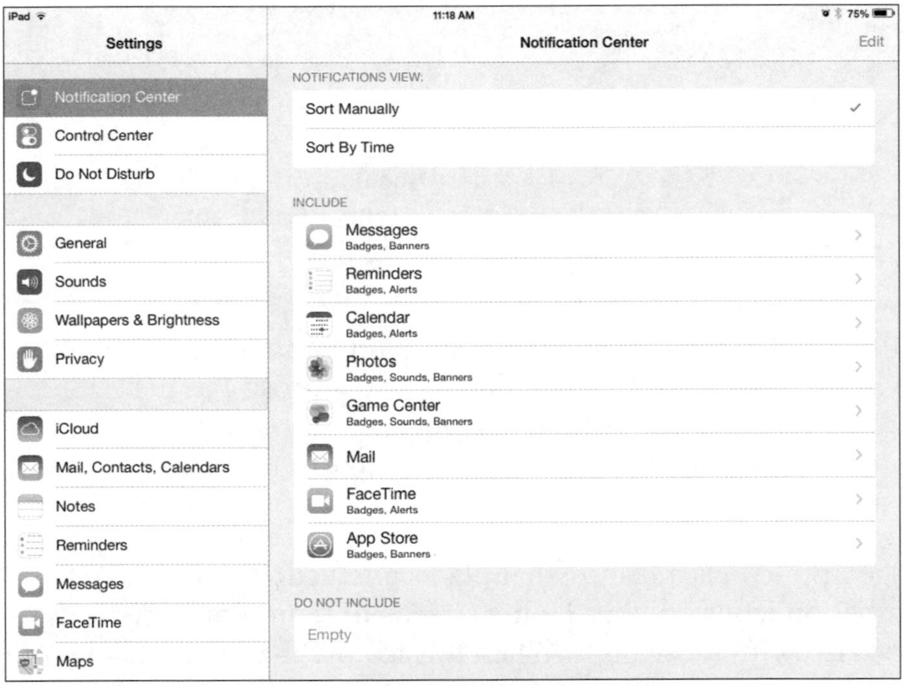

Figure 17-9

3. Tap any item, and in the settings that appear (see **Figure 17-10**), tap the Show in Notification Center On/ Off button to include that item in, or exclude it from, Notification Center.

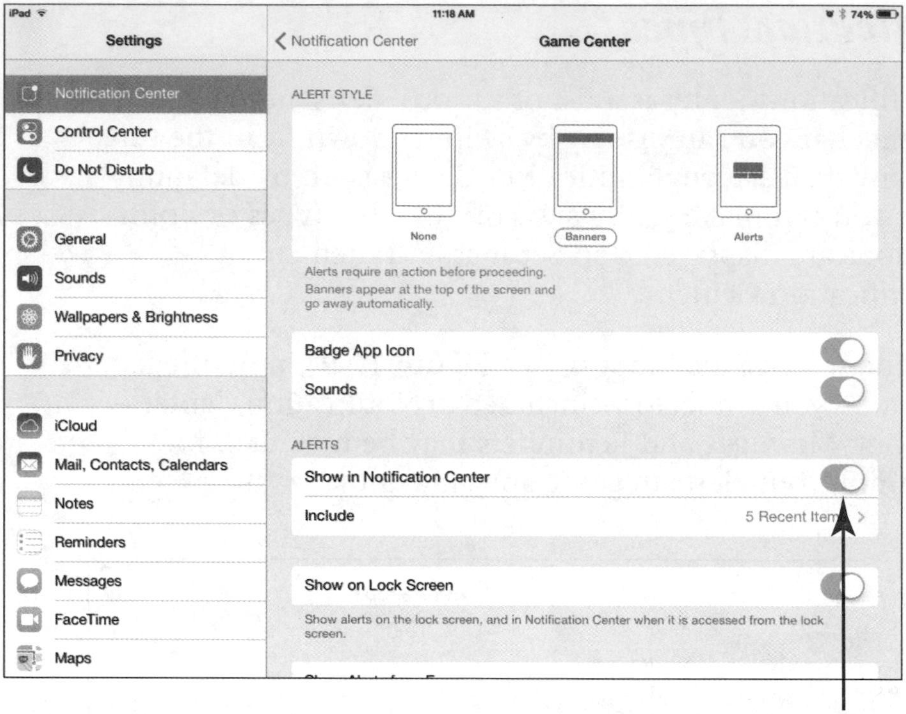

Include or exclude from
Notification Center

Figure 17-10

4. Tap an Alert Style to have no alert, a banner across the
top of the screen, or a boxed alert. If you choose Banner,
the banner appears and then disappears automatically. If
you choose Alerts, you have to take an action to dismiss
the alert when it appears.

5. Badge App Icon is a feature that places a red circle and
number on icons on your Home screens to represent alerts
associated with those apps. When this feature is turned on,
you might see an indication of how many new e-mails you
have waiting for you, for example. To turn this feature off,
tap the On/Off button for Badge App Icon.

6. If you want to be able to view alerts such as those about
new messages when the Lock screen is displayed, turn on
the Show on Lock Screen setting.

7. When you finish making settings for an individual app, tap the Notification Center button to go back to the Notification Center settings, or press the Home button to return to the Home screen.

View Notification Center

1. After you've made settings to specify what should appear in Notification Center, you'll want to take a look at those alerts and reminders regularly. On any screen, tap the black Status bar at the top and drag down to display Notification Center (see **Figure 17-11**). Note that items are divided into lists by type, such as Reminders, Mail, and Calendar.

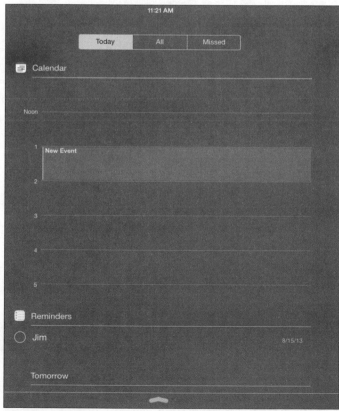

Figure 17-11

2. To close Notification Center, tap the bold arrow at the bottom center of the notification area and drag up toward the Status bar.

 To determine what's displayed in Notification Center, see the previous task.

 You can also view Notification Center from the Lock screen. Just swipe down from the top of the screen to reveal it, and swipe up to hide it again.

Check Out All and Missed Views

1. With the latest Notifications feature in iOS 7, you get three views to play with: Today, All, and Missed. Tap and swipe down from the top of the screen to display Notifications.

2. Tap the Today tab to show all Reminders and other items you've selected to display in Notification Center (see the previous task) that occur today.

3. Tap the All tab to see items for today plus missed and future items (see **Figure 17-12**).

Figure 17-12

4. Tap the Missed tab to see only those items that are in the past and that you never deleted or marked as complete in their originating apps.

Go to an App from Notification Center

1. You can easily jump from Notification Center to any app that caused an alert or reminder to appear. Tap the Status bar and drag down to display Notification Center.

2. Tap any item under a category, such as Reminders or Stocks; it opens in its originating app. If you've tapped a message such as an e-mail, you can then reply to the message by following the procedure described in Chapter 6.

Clear Notifications

1. To get rid of old notifications for an app, tap the Status bar and drag down to display Notification Center.

2. Tap the pale gray X to the right of a notification category such as Photos. The button changes to Clear (see **Figure 17-13**).

3. Tap the Clear button, and all items for that category are removed.

 If you change your mind about clearing all items in a group after you tap the Clear button, just close Notification Center.

Figure 17-13

Get Some Rest with Do Not Disturb

1. Do Not Disturb is a simple but useful setting you can use to stop any alerts and FaceTime calls from appearing or making a sound. You can make settings to allow calls from certain people through or to allow several repeat calls from the same person in a short period to come through. (Apple is assuming that such repeat calls may signal an emergency situation or an urgent need to get through to you.) Tap Settings and then tap Do Not Disturb.

2. Tap the Manual On/Off switch to turn the feature on.

3. In the other settings shown in **Figure 17-14,** do any of the following:

- Tap Scheduled to allow alerts during a specified time period to appear.

- Tap Allow Calls From, and in the next screen, select Everyone, No One, Favorites, or All Contacts.

- Tap Repeated Calls to allow a second call from the same person in a three-minute period to come through.

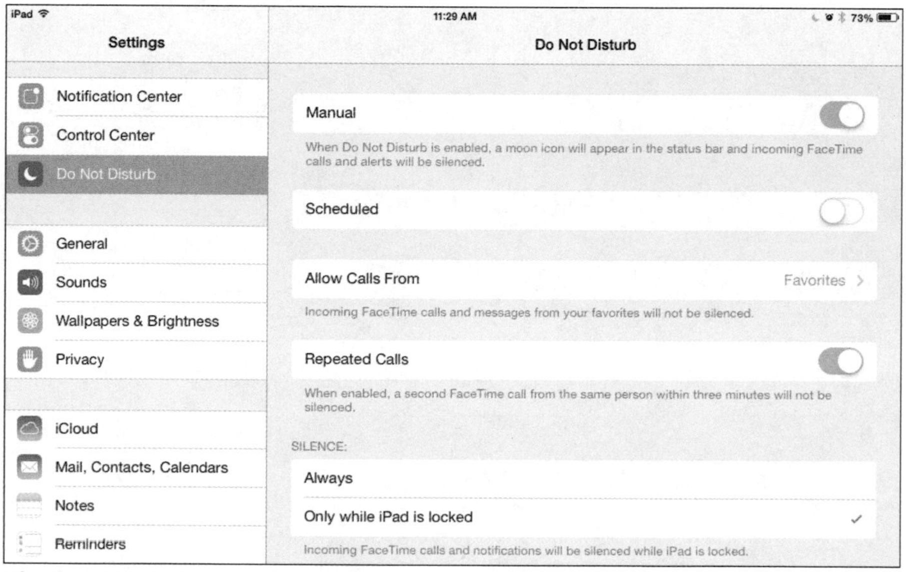

Figure 17-14

4. Press the Home button to return to the Home screen.

Managing Contacts

Chapter 18

*C*ontacts is the iPad equivalent of the dog-eared address book that sits by your phone. The Contacts app is simple to set up and use, and it has some powerful features beyond simply storing names, addresses, and phone numbers.

You can pinpoint a contact's address in the iPad's Maps application, for example. You can use your contacts to address e-mails, Facebook messages, and tweets quickly. If you store a contact record that includes a website, you can use a link in Contacts to view that website instantly. And, of course, you can easily search for a contact by a variety of criteria, including people related to you by family ties and mutual friends.

In this chapter, you discover the various features of Contacts, including how you can save yourself time by syncing many e-mail contacts lists to your iPad instantly.

Add a Contact

1. Tap the Contacts app icon on the Home screen to open the app. If you haven't entered any contacts yet, you see a blank address book (except for your own contact information, which may have been added when you set up your iPad), like the one shown in **Figure 18-1**.

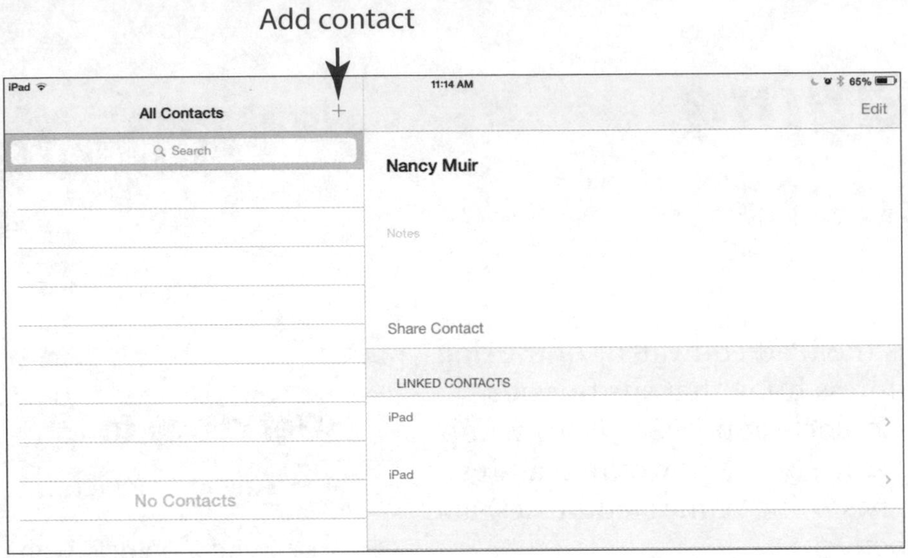

Add contact

Figure 18-1

2. Tap the Add button, which has a small plus sign (+) on
it. A blank Info page opens (see **Figure 18-2**), and the
onscreen keyboard displays.

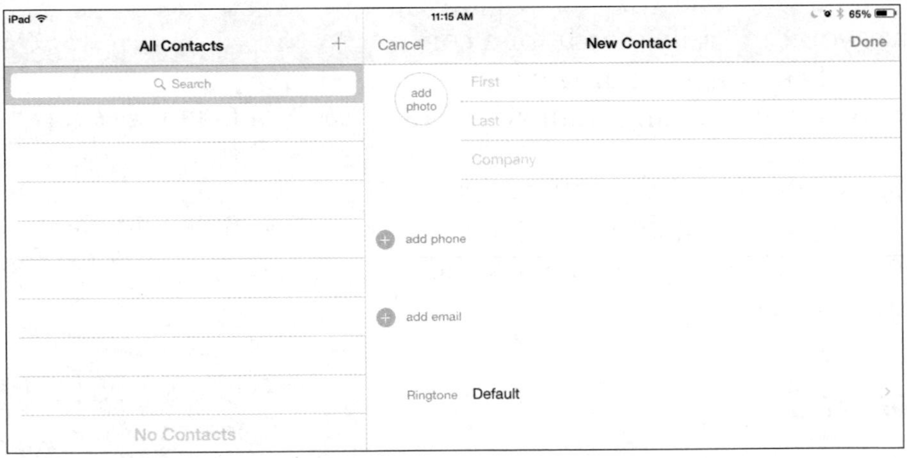

Figure 18-2

3. Enter any contact information you want. (You only have to enter first name, last name, or company to create a contact.)

4. To scroll down the contact page and see more fields, flick up on the page with your finger.

5. If you want to add information such as a mailing or street address, you can tap the related Add field, which opens additional entry fields.

6. To add another information field, such as Nickname or Job Title, tap Add Field toward the bottom of the screen. In the Add Field dialog that appears (see **Figure 18-3**), choose a field to add. (You may have to flick the page up with your finger to view all the fields.)

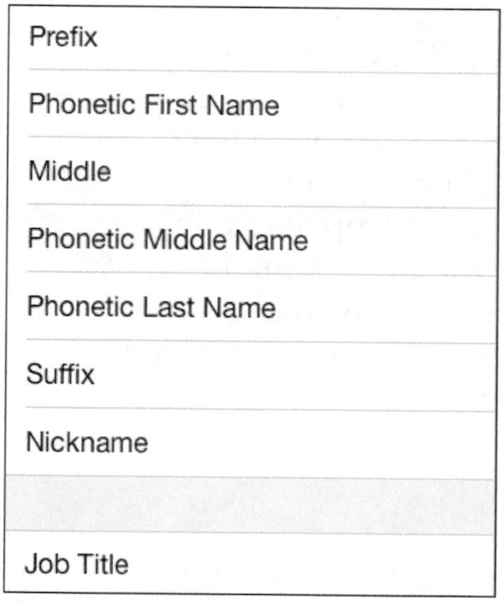

Prefix
Phonetic First Name
Middle
Phonetic Middle Name
Phonetic Last Name
Suffix
Nickname
Job Title

Figure 18-3

7. Tap the Done button when you finish making entries. The new contact appears in your address book.
Figure 18-4 shows an address book with entries added.

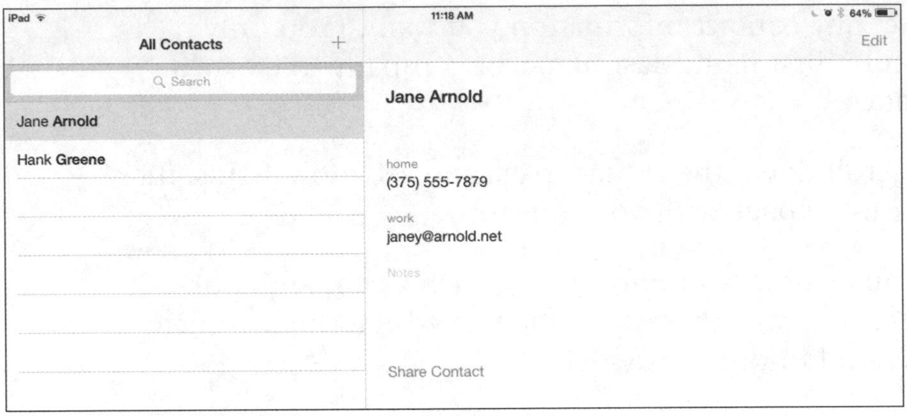

iPad 🕓	11:18 AM	⌕ ⦿ ✳ 64% ▬
All Contacts ＋		Edit

Q Search

Jane Arnold

Jane **Arnold**

Hank **Greene**

home
(375) 555-7879

work
janey@arnold.net

Notes

Share Contact

Figure 18-4

If your contact has a name that's difficult for you to pronounce, consider adding the Phonetic First Name or Phonetic Last Name field, or both, to that person's record (refer to Step 6).

If you want to add multiple e-mail addresses to a contact so that you can easily send e-mail to all of that contact's e-mail addresses, enter a work e-mail address in the preceding steps; another Add E-mail field, titled Other, opens. Tap the pop-up, enter an appropriate title, and then enter another e-mail address. Another Other field opens, and so on. Simply enter all e-mail addresses you want to include for that contact and then tap Done.

Sync Contacts with iCloud

1. You can use your iCloud account to sync contacts from your iPad to back them up. These contacts also become available to your iCloud e-mail account, if you set one up. Tap Settings on the Home screen and then tap iCloud.

2. In the iCloud settings shown in **Figure** 18-5, make sure the On/Off button for Contacts is set to On to sync contacts.

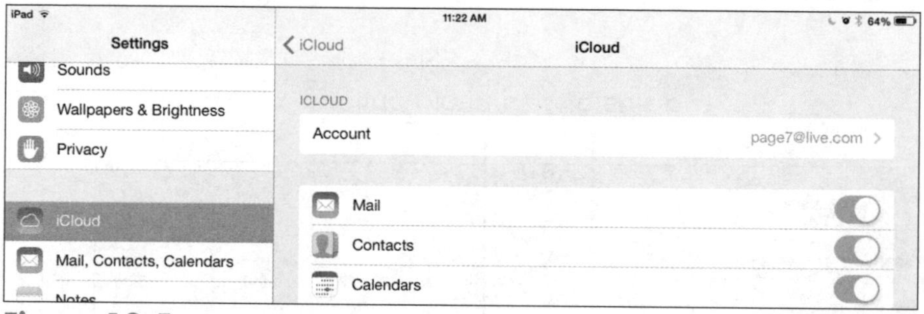

Figure 18-5

3. In the Merge with iCloud dialog that appears, tap Merge (see **Figure** 18-6) to merge your iPad Contacts with iCloud.

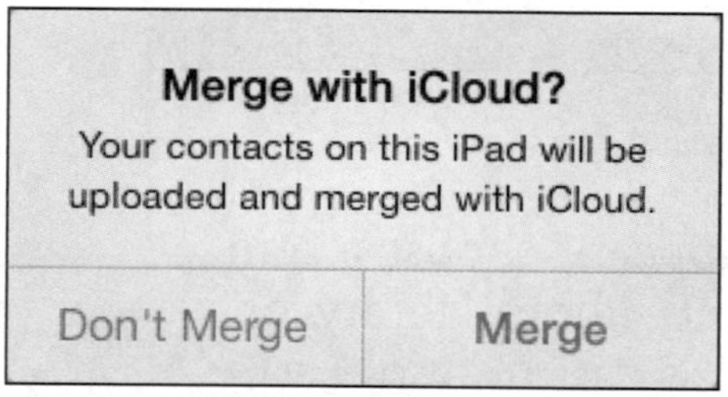

Merge with iCloud?
Your contacts on this iPad will be uploaded and merged with iCloud.

Don't Merge   Merge

Figure 18-6

 You can also use iTunes to sync contacts among all your Apple devices and even a Windows PC. See Chapter 3 for more about making iTunes settings.

Assign a Photo to a Contact

1. With Contacts open, tap a contact to whose record you want to add a photo.

2. Tap the Edit button.

3. On the Info page that appears, tap Add Photo.

4. In the dialog that appears (see **Figure 18-7**), tap Choose Photo to choose an existing photo from the Photos app's Camera Roll, an album, or Photo Stream. You can also choose Take Photo to take that contact's photo on the spot.

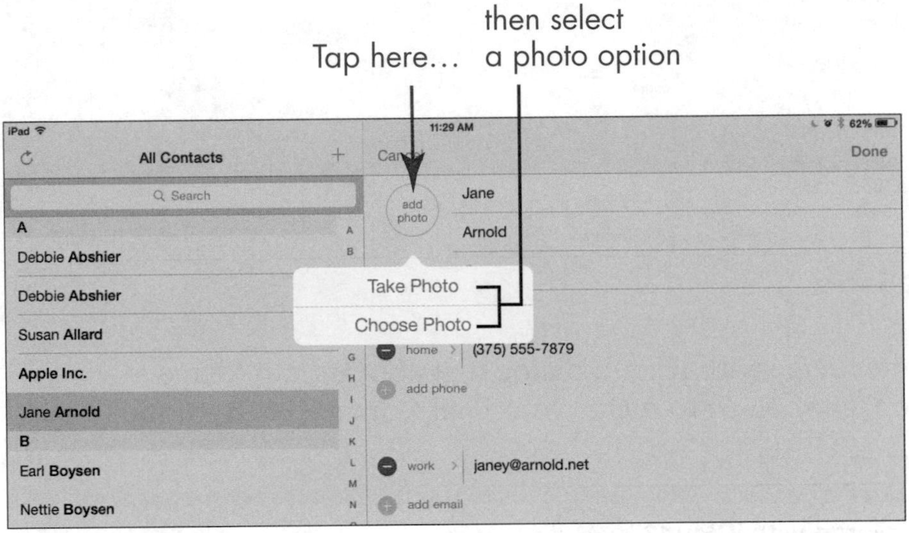

Tap here... then select
a photo option

Figure 18-7

5. In the Photo Albums dialog that appears, choose a source for your photo (such as Camera Roll, Photo Library, or Photo Stream) or a category (such as Last Import, Last 12 Months, or Flags).

6. In the photo album that appears, tap a photo to select it. The Choose Photo dialog, shown in **Figure 18-8,** appears.

7. Tap the Use button to use the photo for this contact. The photo appears on the contact's Info page (see **Figure 18-9**).

8. Tap Done to save changes to the contact.

Figure 18-8

Figure 18-9

 While you're in the Choose Photo dialog in Step 6, you can modify the photo before saving it to the contact information. You can unpinch your fingers on the screen to expand the photo. You can also move the photo around the selected area with your finger to focus on a particular section and then tap the Use button to use the modified version.

Add Twitter or Facebook Information

1. You can add Twitter information to a contact so that you can quickly tweet (send a short message to) contacts via Twitter or enter Facebook account information so that you can post a message to your contact's Facebook account. With Contacts open, tap a contact.

2. Tap the Edit button.

3. Scroll down and tap Add Social Profile.

4. In the list that appears (see **Figure 18-10**), enter a Twitter label.

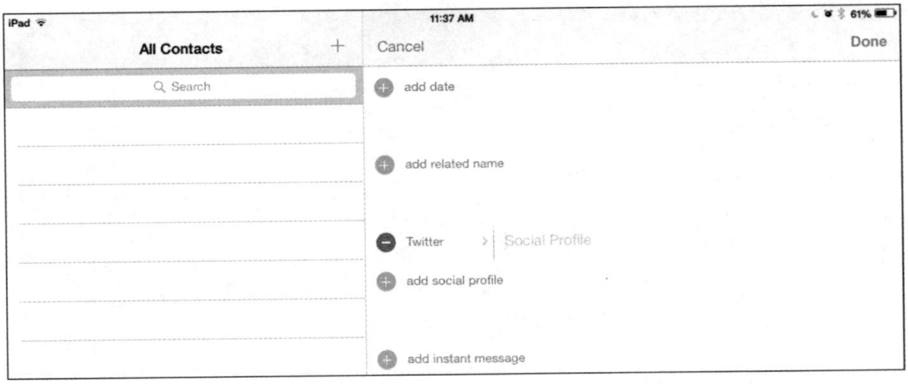

Figure 18-10

5. If you want to create a different social networking field, tap Add Social Profile. A Facebook field appears. You can tap again to get a Flickr account, a LinkedIn account, and so on.

6. Tap Done, and the information is saved. The account is now displayed when you select the contact, as shown in

Figure 18-11, and you can send a Twitter, Facebook, or other message simply by tapping the username for a service and choosing the appropriate command (such as Tweet).

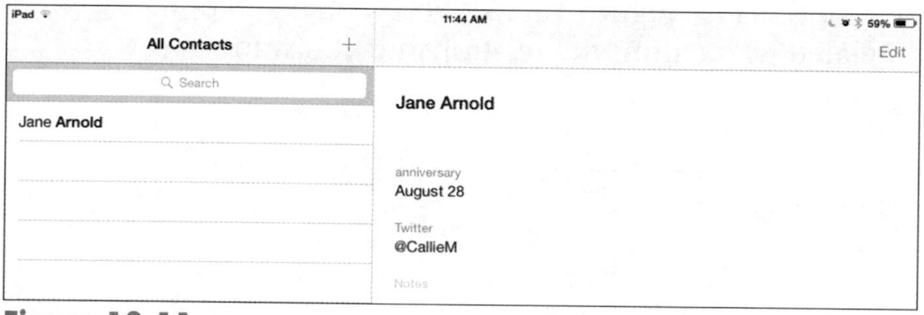

Figure 18-11

Designate Related People

1. You can quickly designate family relations in a contact record if those people are saved to Contacts. Tap a contact and then tap Edit.

2. Scroll down the record, and tap Add Related Name. A new field labeled Mother appears (see **Figure 18-12**).

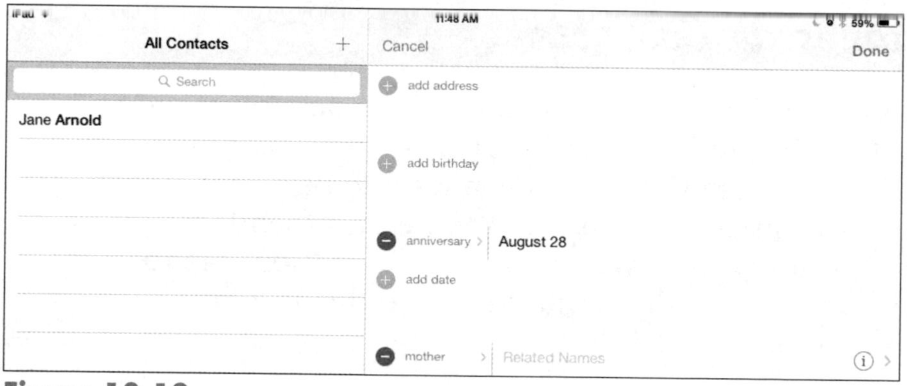

Figure 18-12

3. Enter the contact name for your mother, or tap the Information icon to the right of the field to see a list of your contacts from which you can choose your mother.

4. Tap Add Related Name again, and a new blank field titled Father appears (see **Figure 18-13**). You can keep tapping Add Related Name until the relationship you want appears.

iPad 🔋		11:50 AM		⏻ ❄ ⚫ 58% 🔋
All Contacts	+	Cancel		Done
🔍 Search				
Jane **Arnold**		⊖ anniversary ›	August 28	
		⊕ add date		
		⊖ mother ›	Jane Arnold	ⓘ ›
		⊖ father ›	Related Names	ⓘ ›
		⊕ add related name		

Figure 18-13

 After you add relations to a contact record, when you select the person in the Contacts main screen, all the related people for that contact are listed there.

Set Ringtones for Contacts

1. If you want to hear a unique tone when you receive a text or a FaceTime call from a particular contact, you can set up this feature in Contacts. If you want to be sure that you know instantly when your spouse, sick friend, or boss is calling, set a unique tone for that person. Tap to add a new contact or select a contact in the list of contacts and then tap Edit.

2. Tap the Ringtone field, and a list of tones appears (see **Figure 18-14**). You can also scroll to the top of the list and tap Buy More Tones to buy additional ringtones from Apple.

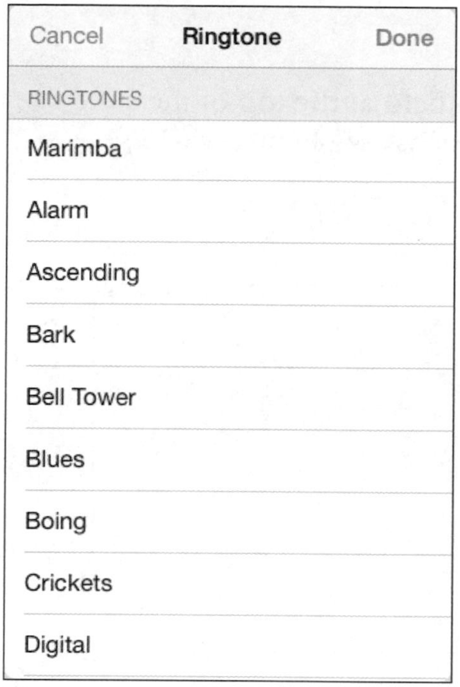

Cancel	**Ringtone**	Done
RINGTONES		
Marimba		
Alarm		
Ascending		
Bark		
Bell Tower		
Blues		
Boing		
Crickets		
Digital		

Figure 18-14

3. Tap a tone, and it previews.

4. When you hear a tone that you like, tap Done.

5. Tap Done again to close the contact form.

 You can set a custom tone for FaceTime calls and text messages by tapping Settings⇨Sounds.

 If your Apple devices are synced via iCloud, setting a unique ringtone for an iPad contact also sets it for your iPhone and iPod touch, as well as for FaceTime on a Mac. See Chapter 3 for more about iCloud.

Search for a Contact

1. With Contacts open, tap the Search field at the top of the left pane. The onscreen keyboard opens (see **Figure 18-15**).

Tap in the Search field

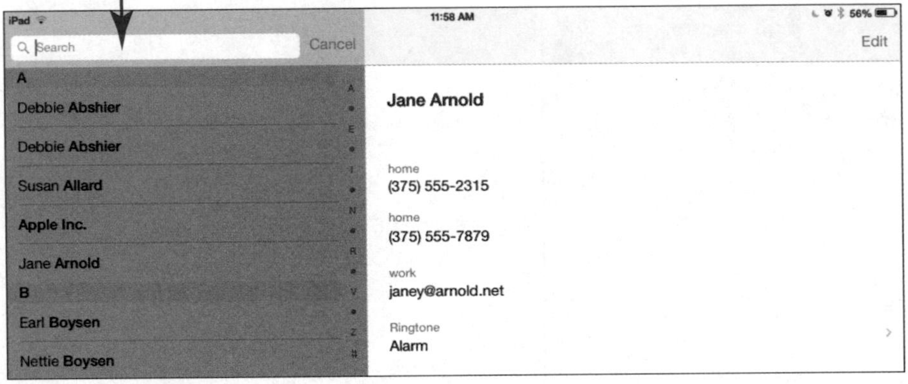

Figure 18-15

2. Type the first letter of the contact's first or last name or the contact's company. All matching results appear, as shown in **Figure 18-16**. In this example, pressing *J* displays *Jane Arnold* and *Ted and Joan Stier* in the results, all of which have *J* as the first letter of the first or last part of the name.

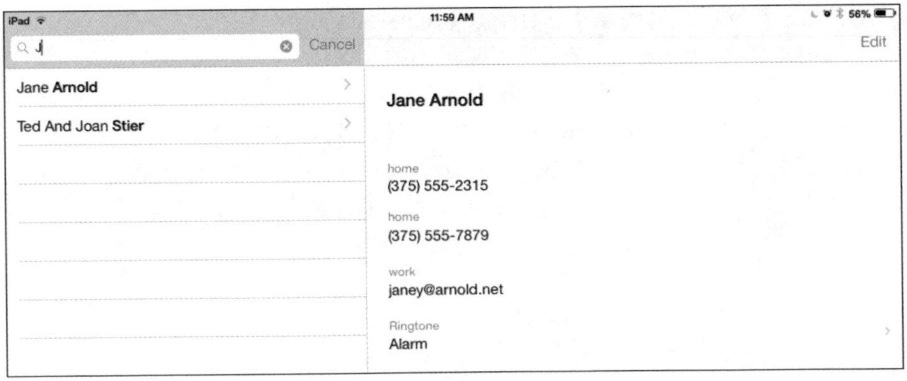

Figure 18-16

3. Tap a contact in the results to display that person's information in the pane on the right (refer to **Figure 18-16**).

 You can search by phone number, website, or address in Contacts as well as by name.

 You can also use the alphabetical listing to locate a contact. Tap and drag to scroll down the list of contacts on the All Contacts pane on the left. You can also tap on any tabbed letter along the left side of the page to scroll quickly to the entries starting with that letter.

Go to a Contact's Website

1. If you entered website information in the Home Page field of a contact record, it automatically becomes a link in the contact's record. Tap the Contacts app icon on the Home screen to open Contacts.

2. Tap a contact's name to display the person's contact information on the pane at the right and then tap the website link in the Home Page field (see **Figure 18-17**). The Safari browser opens, with the web page displayed (see **Figure 18-18**).

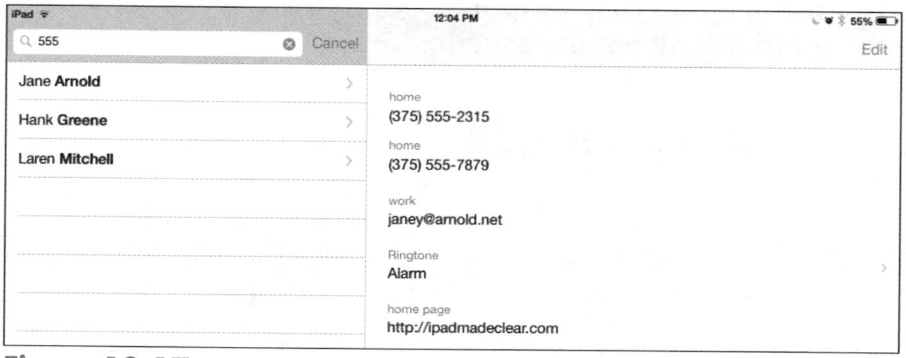

iPad 🤚	12:04 PM	📞 🤚 🔋 55% 🔋
🔍 555 ⊗ Cancel		Edit
Jane **Arnold** ＞		
Hank **Greene** ＞	home	
	(375) 555-2315	
Laren **Mitchell** ＞	home	
	(375) 555-7879	
	work	
	janey@arnold.net	
	Ringtone	
	Alarm	＞
	home page	
	http://ipadmadeclear.com	

Figure 18-17

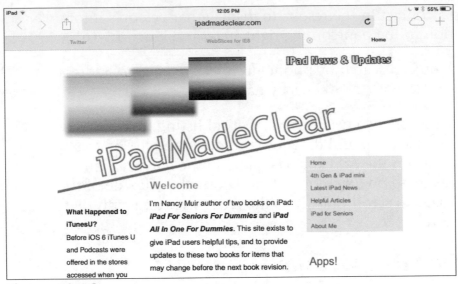

Figure 18-18

 You can't go directly back to Contacts after you follow a link to a website. You have to press the Home button and then tap the Contacts app icon again to re-enter the application, or use the multitasking feature by double-pressing the Home button and choosing Contacts from the icons that appear along the bottom of the screen. However, if you have gesture support turned on in General Settings, you can do the four-finger swipe to the left to return to the app you just left and keep swiping to go to the apps on the multitasking bar in sequence.

Address E-mail Using Contacts

1. If you entered an e-mail address for a contact, the address automatically becomes a link in the contact's record. Tap the Contacts app icon on the Home screen to open Contacts.

2. Tap a contact's name to display the person's contact information on the pane at the right and then tap the e-mail address link (labeled Work in the example shown in **Figure 18-19**). The New Message dialog appears, as shown in **Figure 18-20**. Initially, the title bar of this dialog reads New Message, but as you type a subject, New Message changes to the specific title.

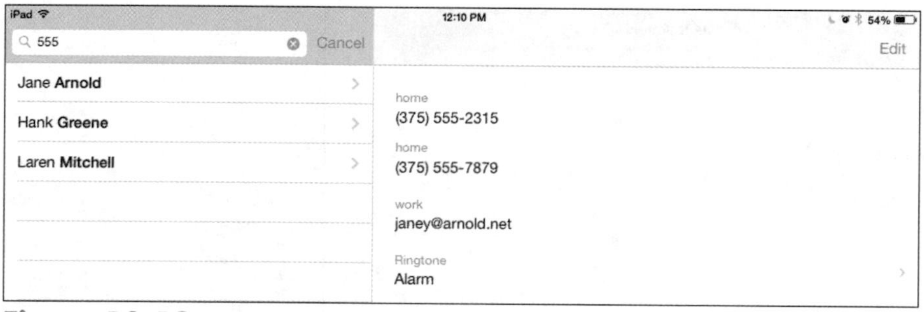

Figure 18-19

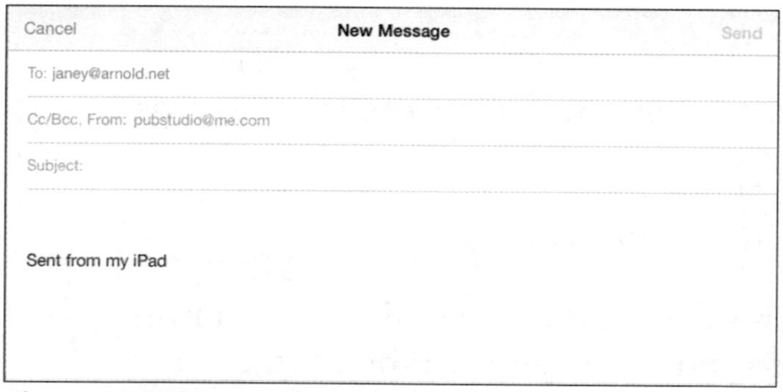

Figure 18-20

3. Use the onscreen keyboard to enter a subject and message.

4. Tap the Send button. The message goes on its way!

Share a Contact

1. After you've entered contact information, you can share it with others via an e-mail message. With Contacts open, tap a contact name to display its information.

2. On the Info page, tap the Share Contact button (refer to **Figure 18-4**).

3. In the dialog that appears, tap Mail. A New Message form appears, as shown in **Figure 18-21**).

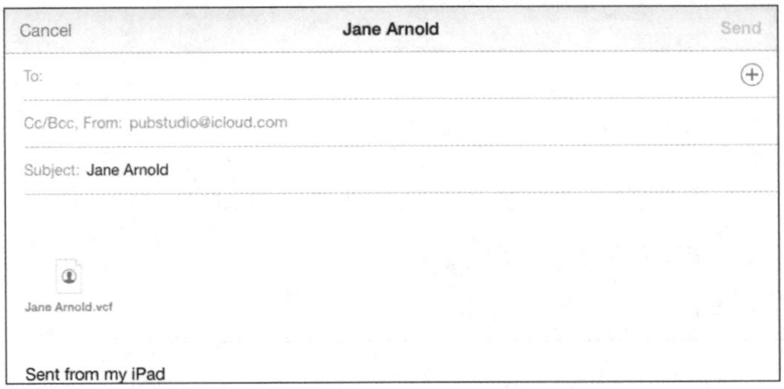

Cancel	**Jane Arnold**	Send
To:		⊕

Cc/Bcc, From: pubstudio@icloud.com

Subject: Jane Arnold

Jane Arnold.vcf

Sent from my iPad

Figure 18-21

4. Use the onscreen keyboard to enter the recipient's e-mail address. *Note:* If the person is saved in Contacts, just type his or her name here.

5. Enter information in the Subject field.

6. If you like, enter a message and then tap the Send button. The message goes to your recipient with the contact information attached as a .vcf file. (This *vCard* format is commonly used to transmit contact information.)

When somebody receives a vCard containing contact information, she needs only to click (or tap) the attached file to open it. At this point, depending on the recipient's e-mail or contact management program, she can perform various actions to save the content. Other Mac, iPhone, iPod touch, or iPad users can easily import .vcf records into their own Contacts apps. Even PC users can do this if their contact management programs support .vcf records.

In Step 2, with an iPad mini or fourth generation and later, you can select AirDrop and then tap the name of a device near to you to send the contact information to that device wirelessly.

View a Contact's Location in Maps

1. If you've entered a person's address in Contacts, you have a shortcut for viewing that person's location in the Maps application. Tap the Contacts app icon on the Home screen to open it.

2. Tap the contact you want to view to display his information.

3. Tap the address. Maps opens and displays a map to the address (see **Figure 18-22**).

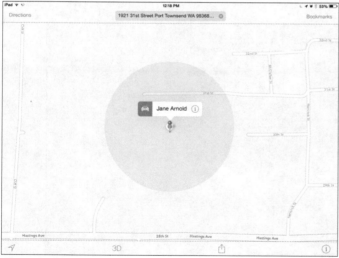

Figure 18-22

 This task works with more than just your friends' addresses. You can save information for your favorite restaurant, movie theater, or any other location and then use Contacts to jump to the associated website in the Safari browser or to the address in Maps. For more about using Safari, see Chapter 5. For more about the Maps application, see Chapter 15.

Delete a Contact

1. When you want to remove a name or two from your Contacts list, it's easy to do. With Contacts open, tap the contact you want to delete.

2. Tap the Edit button in the top-right corner of the screen (refer to **Figure 18-4**).

3. On the Info page that appears, drag your finger upward to scroll down and then tap the Delete Contact button at the bottom (see **Figure 18-23**). The confirming dialog shown in **Figure 18-24** appears.

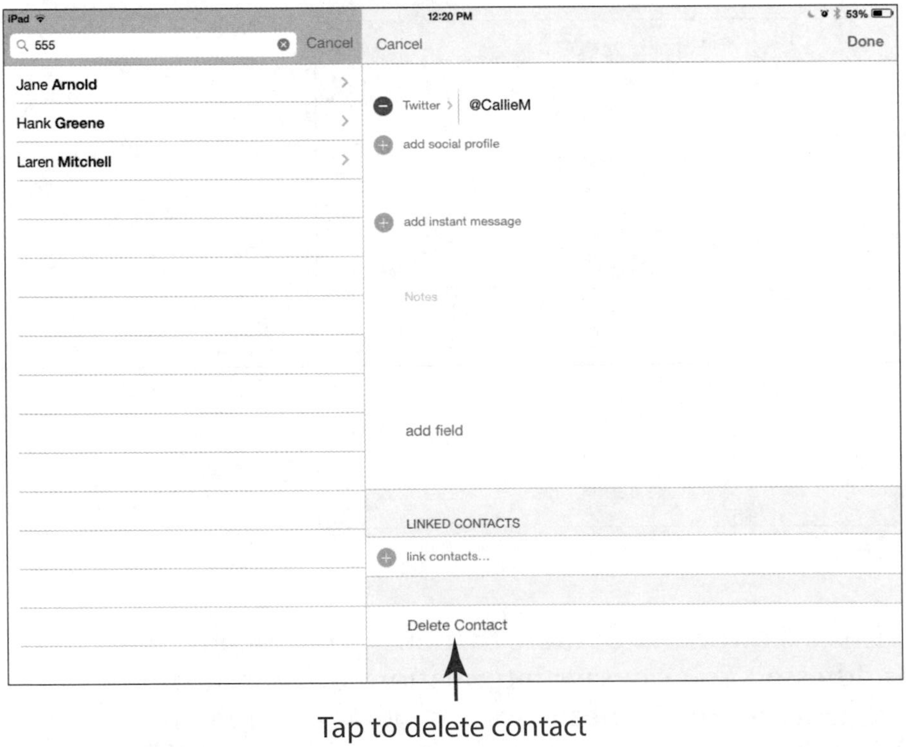

Tap to delete contact

Figure 18-23

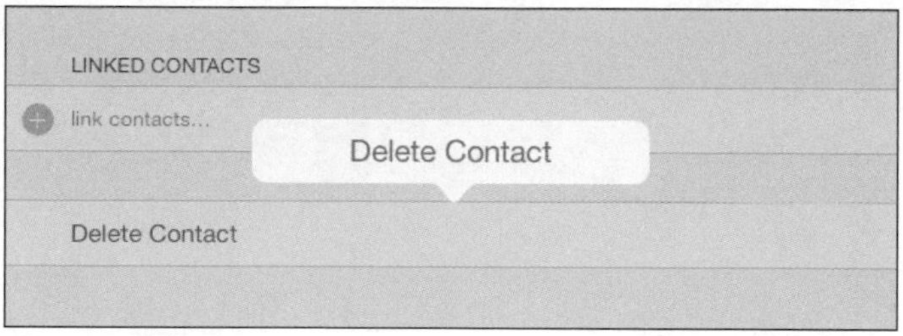

LINKED CONTACTS

link contacts...

Delete Contact

Delete Contact

Figure 18-24

4. Tap the Delete Contact button to confirm the deletion.

 During this process, if you change your mind before you tap Delete Contact, tap the Cancel button in Step 4. But be careful: After you tap Delete, there's no going back!

Talking to Your iPad with Siri

O ne of the biggest changes in iOS 6 for iPad was the addition of Siri, a personal-assistant feature of a third- and fourth-generation iPad, an iPad Air, or an iPad mini with Retina Display that responds to spoken commands. With Siri on your iPad, you can ask for nearby restaurants, and a list appears. You can dictate your e-mail messages rather than type them. FaceTiming your mother is as simple as saying "Call Mom." Want to know the capital of Rhode Island? Just ask. Siri checks several online sources to answer questions ranging from the result of a mathematical calculation to the size of Jupiter. You can also have Siri perform tasks such as returning calls and controlling iTunes Radio.

Activate Siri

Siri is a very useful feature for interacting with your iPad and getting information. You can use Siri to ask for a map to a nearby restaurant, send an e-mail, or tell you how far the Earth is from Pluto, for example. Siri will respond with an answer, display a map, or access web resources for you; see **Figure 19-1**.

Chapter 9

Get ready to . . .

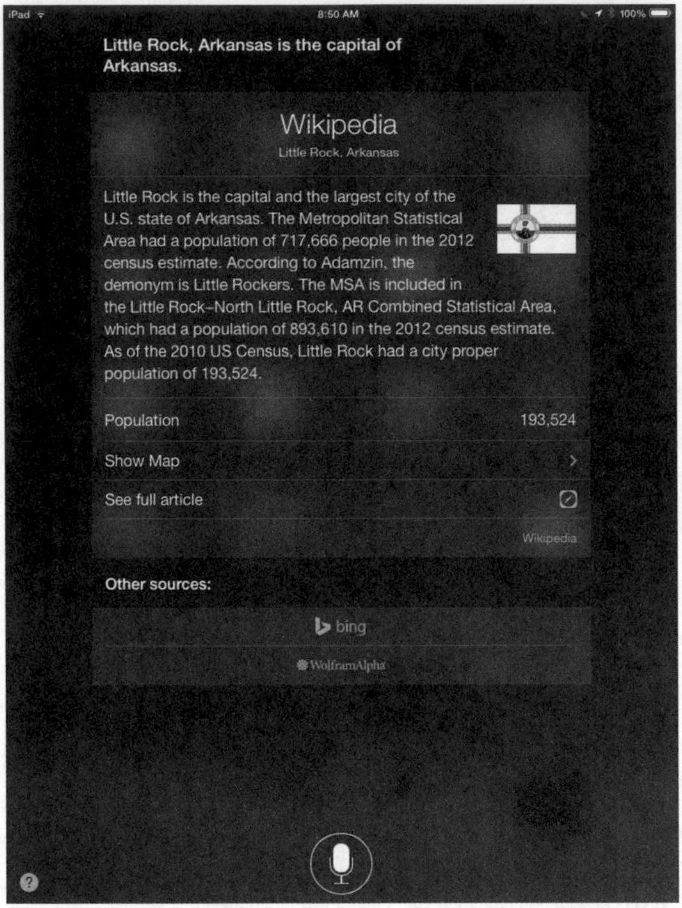

Figure 19-1

Siri should be active when you get your iPad, but if for some reason it's been deactivated, you can use Settings to turn Siri on by following these steps:

1. Tap the Settings icon on the Home screen.

2. Tap General to display the General Settings (see **Figure 19-2**) and then tap Siri.

iPad 🔋	12:47 PM	📶 🔋 57% 🔋
Settings	**General**	

Settings	
📶 Wi-Fi — earlandnancy	
✴ Bluetooth — On	
🔲 Notification Center	
🔲 Control Center	
🌙 Do Not Disturb	
⚙ General	
🔊 Sounds	

General	
About	>
Software Update	>
Siri	>
Spotlight Search	>
Text Size	>
Accessibility	>

Figure 19-2

3. In the screen that appears (see **Figure 19-3**), tap the On/Off button to turn Siri on.

iPad 🔋	12:47 PM	📶 🔋 57% 🔋
Settings	‹ General **Siri**	

Settings	
📶 Wi-Fi — earlandnancy	
✴ Bluetooth — On	
🔲 Notification Center	
🔲 Control Center	
🌙 Do Not Disturb	
⚙ General	
🔊 Sounds	

Siri ⬤

Siri helps you get things done just by asking. You can make a FaceTime call, send a message, dictate a note, or even find a restaurant. About Siri and Privacy...

Language	English (United States) >
Voice Gender	Female >
Voice Feedback	Always >
My Info	Nancy Muir >

To talk to Siri, press and hold the home button and speak.

Figure 19-3

4. If you want to change the language Siri uses, tap Language and choose a different language from the list that appears.

5. To change the gender of Siri's voice from female to male, tap Voice Gender and then tap Male.

 If you want Siri to respond to your verbal requests only when the iPad isn't in your hands, tap Voice Feedback and choose Handsfree Only. Here's how this setting works and why you may want to use it: In general, if you're holding your iPad, you can read responses on the screen, so you may not want to have your tablet talk to you. But if you're puttering with, say, an electronics project, you may want to speak requests for mathematical calculations and hear the answers rather than having to read them. In such a situation, Handsfree Only is a useful setting.

 Siri is available on the iPad only when you have Internet access, but remember that cellular data charges may apply when Siri checks online sources if that Internet connection is via 3G/4G. In addition, Apple warns that available features may vary by area.

Understand All That Siri Can Do

Siri allows you to interact with many apps on your iPad by voice. You can pose questions or ask to do something like make a FaceTime call or add an appointment to your calendar, for example. Siri can also search the Internet or use an informational database called Wolfram Alpha to provide information on just about any topic. You don't have to be in an app to make a request involving another app.

 With the arrival of iOS 7, Siri also checks Wikipedia, Bing, and Twitter to get you the information you ask for. In addition, you can now use Siri to tell the iPad to work with more features such as controlling iTunes Radio playback.

Siri is the technology behind the iPad's Dictation feature. When you have the onscreen keyboard open, note that it contains a microphone key you can tap to begin or end dictation. This feature works in any app that uses the onscreen keyboard.

Siri requires no preset structure for your questions; you can phrase things in several ways. You might ask "Where am I?" to see a map of your current location, or you could ask "What is my current location?" or "What address is this?" and get the same results.

Siri responds to you verbally; with text information; in a form, as with e-mail (see **Figure 19-4**); or in a graphic display for some items, such as maps. When a result appears, you can tap it to make a choice or open a related app.

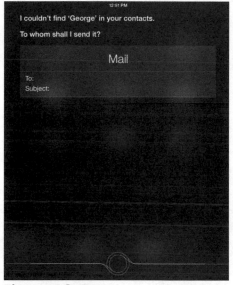

Figure 19-4

Siri works with FaceTime, Music, Messages, Reminders, Calendar, Maps, Mail, Clock, Contacts, Notes, and Safari, as well as with several third-party apps. In the following tasks, I provide a quick guide to some of the most useful ways you can use Siri.

Note that no matter what kind of action you want to perform, first press and hold the Home button until Siri opens (see **Figure 19-5**). Remember that this feature works only on an iPad mini, third- or fourth-generation iPad, or an iPad Air with iOS 6 or iOS 7 installed. The rest of this chapter assumes that you're working with an iPad mini, a third- or fourth-generation iPad, or an iPad Air running iOS 7.

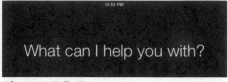

Figure 19-5

Call Contacts via FaceTime

1. First, make sure that the people you want to call are entered in your Contacts app and have their phone numbers included in their records. If you want to call somebody by stating your relationship to her, such as "Call sister," be sure to enter that relationship in the related field of her contact record, and make sure that the settings for Siri (refer to **Figure 19-3**) include your contact name in the My Info field. (See Chapter 18 for more about creating contact records.)

2. Press and hold the Home button until Siri appears.

3. Speak a command such as "Make a FaceTime call to Earl" or "FaceTime Mom." Siri initiates the call (see **Figure 19-6**). If you have two contacts who might match a spoken name, Siri responds with a list of possible matches. Tap one in the list or state the correct contact's name to proceed.

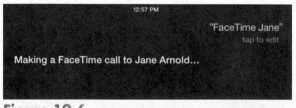

Figure 19-6

4. To end the call before it completes, you can press the Home button and then tap End.

To cancel any spoken request, you have four options: Say "Cancel," tap the microphone key on the Siri screen, press the Home button, or tap anywhere on the screen outside the Siri panel.

Create Reminders and Alerts

1. You can also use Siri with the Reminders app. To create a reminder, press and hold the Home button and then speak a command, such as "Remind me to call Dad on Thursday at 10 a.m." or "Wake me up tomorrow at 7 a.m." A preview of the reminder is displayed (see **Figure 19-7**).

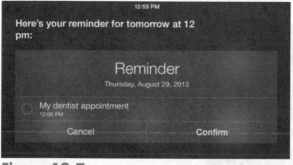

12:59 PM

Here's your reminder for tomorrow at 12 pm:

Reminder
Thursday, August 29, 2013

My dentist appointment
12:00 PM

Cancel   Confirm

Figure 19-7

2. Siri asks you whether it should create the reminder. Tap or say "Confirm" to create it, or tap or say "Cancel."

3. If you want a reminder ahead of the event you created, activate Siri and speak a command such as "Remind me tonight about the play on Thursday at 8 p.m." Siri creates a second reminder, which you can confirm or cancel.

Add Tasks to Your Calendar

1. You can also set up events on your Calendar by using Siri. Press and hold the Home button and then speak a phrase such as "Set up meeting at 5 p.m. on July 23rd." A sample calendar entry appears, and Siri asks if you want to confirm it.

2. If there's a conflict with the appointment, Siri tells you that there's already an appointment at that time (see **Figure 19-8**) and asks whether you still want to set up the new appointment. You can say "Yes" or "Cancel" at that point or tap the Yes or Cancel button.

Figure 19-8

Play Music

1. You can use Siri to play music from the Music app and iTunes Radio. Press and hold the Home button until Siri appears.

2. To play music, speak a command, such as "Play music" or "Play 'As Time Goes By'" to play a specific song or album.

3. When music is playing, use commands such as "Pause music," "Next track," and "Stop music" to control playback.

One of the beauties of Siri is that you don't have to follow a specific command format, as you do with some other voice-command apps. You could say "Play the next track," "Next track," or "Jump to the next track on this album," and Siri will get your meaning.

Get Directions

You can use the Maps app and Siri to find your current location, find nearby businesses (such as restaurants or banks), or get a map of another location. Be sure to turn on Location Services to allow Siri to know your current location (tap Settings⇨Privacy⇨Location Services, and make sure Location Services are on and that Siri is turned on farther down in that dialog).

Here are some of the commands you can try to get directions or a list of nearby businesses:

➡ **"Where am I?"**

Siri displays a map of your current location. If you have a Wi-Fi–only iPad, this location may be approximate.

➡ **"Where is Apache Junction, Arizona?"**

Siri displays a map of that city.

➡ **"Find restaurants."**

Siri displays a list of restaurants near your current location, as in **Figure 19-9**; tap one to display a map of its location.

iPad 🔋   1:07 PM   🔋 61% ▬▶

I found seven restaurants fairly close to you:

7 Restaurants

San Juan Taqueria 1.0 mi >	**Manresa Castle** 1.3 mi >	**The Cup** 1.3 mi >
1440 F St	Sheridan St & 7th St	600 West Sims Way
Mexican, $	Bed & Breakfast, Hotels, $$$	Diners, $$
★★★★★ 2 Reviews	★★☆ 21 Reviews	★★★☆ 11 Reviews
McDonald's 1.3 mi >	**Castle Key Seafood & S...** 1.3 mi >	**The Blue Moose Cafe** 1.4 mi >
310 W Sims Way	651 Cleveland St	311 Haines Place
Burgers, Fast Food	Breakfast & Brunch, Seafood, $$	American (Traditional), $
No Reviews	★★★☆ 3 Reviews	★★★★☆ 37 Reviews
Sea J's Cafe 1.6 mi >		
2501 Washington St		
Seafood, $		
★★★☆ 18 Reviews		

yelp

Figure 19-9

➠ **"Find Bank of America."**

Siri displays a map indicating the location of that business (or, in some cases, several nearby locations, such as a bank branch and all ATMs).

◎ After a location is displayed in a map, tap the Information button on the location's label to view its address, phone number, and website address, if available.

Ask for Facts

Wolfram Alpha is a self-professed online computational knowledge engine, which means that it's more than a search engine because it provides specific information about a search term rather than multiple search results. If you want facts without having to spend time browsing websites to find those facts, Wolfram Alpha is a very good resource.

Siri uses Wolfram Alpha and sources such as Wikipedia and Bing to look up facts in response to questions, such as "What is the capital of Kansas?", "What is the square root of 2003?", and "How large is Mars?" Just press and hold the Home button, and ask your question; Siri consults its resources and returns a set of relevant facts.

You can also get information about the weather, stocks, or the time. Just say a phrase like one of these to get what you need:

➠ **"What is the weather?"**

Siri shows the weather report for your current location. If you want weather in another location, just specify the location in your question.

➠ **"What is the price of Apple stock?"**

Siri tells you the current price of the stock or the price of the stock when the stock market last closed. (Let's hope that you own some.)

➠ **"What time is it?"**

Siri tells you the time in your time zone and displays a clock (see **Figure 19-10**).

Figure 19-10

 Note that with the arrival of iOS 6, Siri could understand more languages than before, and continuing with iOS 7 works in still more countries. If you love to travel, Siri could help make your next trip much easier.

Search the Web

Siri can use various resources to respond to specific requests, such as "Who is the Queen of England?", but it searches the web if you ask more general requests for information. Siri can also search Twitter for comments related to your search.

If you speak a phrase such as "Find a website about birds" or "Find information about the World Series," Siri can respond in a couple of ways. The app can simply display a list of search results by using the default search engine specified in your settings for Safari, or it can say "If you like, I can search the web for such-and-such." In the first instance, just tap a result to go to that website. In the second instance, you can confirm that you want to search the web or cancel.

Send E-mail, Tweets, or Messages

You can create an e-mail or an instant message with Siri. If you say "E-mail Jack Wilkes," a form already addressed to that contact opens. Siri asks you what the subject is and what to say in the message. Speak your message and then say "Send" to speed your message on its way.

Siri also works with the iMessage feature. Tap Siri and say "Message Sarah." Siri creates a message and asks what you want to say. Say "Tell Sarah I'll call soon," and Siri creates a message for you to approve and send.

 It's hard to stump Siri. Siri can't tweet unless you've downloaded and set up the Twitter app, for example. But if you speak a tweet without having Twitter installed, she gives you a link to tap to install the app!

Get Helpful Tips

I know that you're going to have a wonderful time learning the ins and outs of Siri, but before I close this chapter, here are some tips to get you going:

➡ **Making corrections if Siri doesn't understand you:**
When you speak a command and Siri displays what
it thought you said but misses the mark, you have a
few options:

- To correct a request that you've made, you can tap
the Tap to Edit button below the command Siri
heard; then edit the question by typing or tapping
the microphone key on the onscreen keyboard and
then dictating the correct information.

- If a word is underlined in blue, that word is a possible error. Tap the word and then tap an alternative that Siri suggests.

- You can also simply speak to Siri and say something like "I meant Sri Lanka" or "No, send it to
Sally."

If even corrections aren't working, you may need to
restart your iPad to reset the software.

➡ **Using a headset or earphones:** If you're using the
iPad with earphones or use a Bluetooth headset to
activate Siri, instead of pressing the Home button,
press and hold the center button (the little button
on the headset that starts and stops a call).

➡ **Using Find My Friends:** You can download a free
app from the App Store called Find My Friends that
allows you to ask Siri to locate your friends geo-
graphically, if they're carrying devices with GPS and
Location Services turned on.

➡ **Getting help with Siri:** To get help with Siri features,
just press and hold the Home button, and ask Siri
"What can you do?"

Making Notes

*N*otes is the bundled app that you can use to do everything from jotting down notes at meetings to keeping to-do lists. It isn't a robust word processor (such as Apple Pages or Microsoft Word) by any means, but for taking notes on the fly, jotting down to-do lists, or dictating a poem with the Dictation feature while you sit and sip a cup of tea on your deck, it's a useful option. With iOS 7 the font used in Notes changed so if you used it with an earlier iOS, you can see whether it's a look you prefer.

In this chapter, you see how to enter and edit text in Notes, as well as how to manage notes by navigating among them; searching for content; and sharing, deleting, and printing notes.

Open a Blank Note and Enter Text

1. To get started with Notes, tap the Notes app icon on the Home screen. If you've never used Notes, it opens with a blank notes list displayed. (If you've used Notes, it opens to the last note you were working on. If that's the case, you may want to jump to the next task to create a new, blank note.) Depending on how your iPad is oriented, you see the view shown in **Figure 20-1** (landscape) or **Figure 20-2** (portrait).

Get ready to...

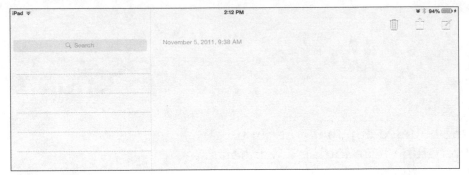

Figure 20-1

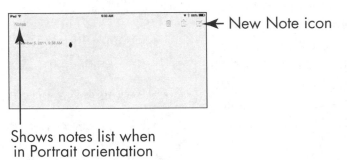

← New Note icon

Shows notes list when
in Portrait orientation

Figure 20-2

2. Tap the blank page. The onscreen keyboard, shown in
Figure 20-3, appears.

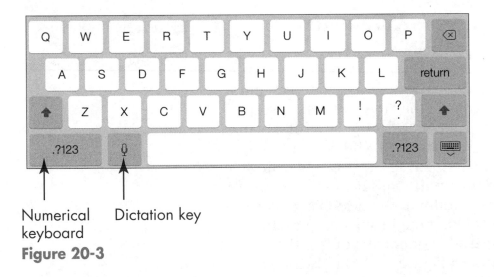

Numerical   Dictation key
keyboard

Figure 20-3

3. Tap keys on the keyboard to enter text (or, if you're using a third- or fourth-generation iPad, an iPad Air, or an iPad mini, tap the Dictation key to speak your text).

 If the Dictation key isn't available on your third-generation or later iPad or your iPad mini, tap Settings⇨General⇨Keyboard and then tap Dictation to turn it on.

4. If you want to enter numbers or symbols, tap either of the keys labeled .?123 on the keyboard. The numerical keyboard, shown in **Figure** 20-4, appears. Whenever you want to return to the alphabetic keyboard, tap either of the keys labeled ABC.

Figure 20-4

5. To capitalize a letter, tap a Shift key (one with the upward-pointing arrow on it) at the same time as you tap the letter. If you activate the Enable Caps Lock feature in General Keyboard Settings, you can also turn Caps Lock on by double-tapping the Shift key; tap the key once again to turn the feature off.

6. When you want to start a new paragraph or a new item in a list, tap the Return key.

7. To edit text, tap to the right of the text you want to edit and then either use the Delete key to delete text to the left of the cursor or enter new text.

If you use the Dictation feature, everything you say is sent to Apple to be changed into text. If you're not comfortable with that, you may want to disable the Dictation feature. For more about Dictation, see Chapter 4.

 When you have the numerical keyboard displayed (refer to **Figure 20-4**), you can tap either of the keys labeled #+= to access more symbols, such as the percentage sign or the euro symbol, or additional bracket styles. Pressing and holding certain keys displays alternative characters.

 There's no need to save a note; it's kept automatically until you delete it.

 You can choose among a very small selection of fonts for your notes by tapping Settings⇨Notes.

Create a New Note

1. With one note open, to create a new note, tap the New Note icon — the one that looks like a small page with a pen hovering over it — in the top-right corner. The current note is saved and a new, blank note appears.

2. Enter and edit text as described in the previous task.

 If your iPad is in portrait orientation, and you want to display the list of saved notes beside the current note, switch to landscape orientation. You can also tap the Notes button in portrait orientation to see a drop-down list of notes.

Use Copy and Paste

1. The Notes app includes two essential editing tools that you're probably familiar with from word processors: copy and paste. With a note displayed, press and hold your finger on a word. The toolbar shown in **Figure 20-5** appears.

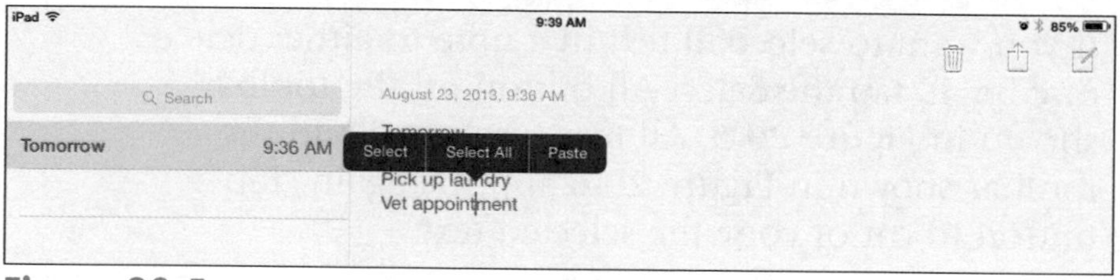

Figure 20-5

2. Tap the Select button. The toolbar shown in **Figure 20-6** appears.

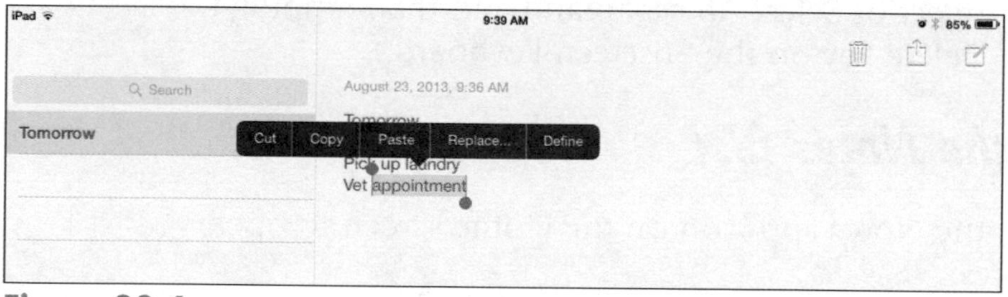

Figure 20-6

3. Tap the Copy button.

4. Press and hold the spot in the document where you want to place the copied text.

5. On the toolbar that appears (see **Figure 20-7**), tap the Paste button. The copied text appears.

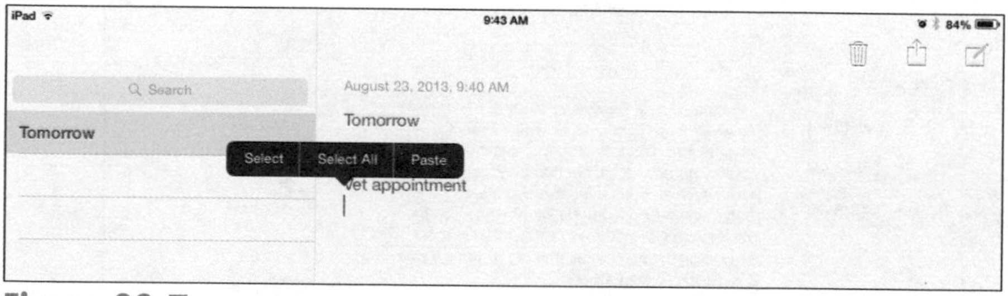

Figure 20-7

If you want to select all text in a note to either delete or copy it, tap the Select All button on the toolbar shown in **Figure 20-5**. All text is selected and the toolbar shown in **Figure 20-6** appears again. Tap a button to cut or copy the selected text.

 To extend a selection to adjacent words, press one of the little handles that extend from the selection and drag to the left or right or up or down.

 To delete text, you can also choose text by using the Select or Select All command and then tapping the Delete key on the onscreen keyboard.

Display the Notes List

1. Tap the Notes app icon on the Home screen to open Notes.

2. In landscape orientation, a list of notes appears by default on the left side of the screen. In portrait orientation, you can display this list by tapping the Notes button in the top-left corner of the screen (refer to **Figure 20-2**); the notes list appears.

3. Tap any note in the list to display it, as shown in **Figure 20-8**.

iPad ᚎ	9:48 AM	ᚎ ᚎ 83% ▭

August 23, 2013, 9:46 AM

"That mou'd pale Cassius to conspire? And what
Made all-honor'd, honest, Romaine Brutus,
With the arm'd rest, Courtiers of beautious freedome,
To drench the Capitoll, but that they would
Haue one man but a man, and that his it
Hath made me rigge my Nauie. At whose burthen,
The anger'd Ocean fomes, with which I meant
To scourge th' ingratitude, that despightfull Rome
Cast on my Noble Father
Caesar. Take your time

Pool rules	9:48 AM
Tomorrow	9:46 AM
"That mou'd pale Cassi...	9:46 AM

Figure 20-8

Notes names your note by using the first line of text. If you want to rename a note, display the note, tap before the current initial text, enter a new title, and press Return. This new text becomes the name of your note in the notes list.

Move among Notes

1. To move from one note to another in earlier versions of Notes you could tap a Next and Previous button at the bottom of a note. With iOS 7, that feature is gone, and in portrait orientation, you have to return to the notes list to move from one note to another. If you want to look for a note based on how long ago you created it, you should know that notes are stored with the most recently created or modified notes at the top of the notes list. Older notes fall toward the bottom of the list. The date and/or time you last modified a note also appear in the notes list to help you out. You have a couple of ways to move among notes you've created. Tap the Notes app icon on the Home screen to open Notes.

2. With the notes list displayed (you can either turn your iPad to landscape orientation or tap the Notes button in portrait orientation; see the previous task for more on viewing the notes list), tap a note to open it.

3. To move among notes in portrait orientation, tap the Notes button and then tap another note in the list to open it. In landscape orientation, just tap another note in the notes list.

 Notes lets you enter multiple notes with the same title — which can cause confusion, so it's a good idea to name your notes uniquely!

Search for a Note

1. You can search for a note that contains certain text. The Search feature lists only notes that contain your search criteria and highlights the first instance of the word or words you enter in each note. Tap the Notes app icon on the Home screen to open Notes.

2. Either hold the iPad in landscape orientation or tap the Notes button in portrait orientation to display the notes list (refer to **Figure 20-8**).

3. Tap the Search field at the top of the notes list (see **Figure 20-9**). The onscreen keyboard appears.

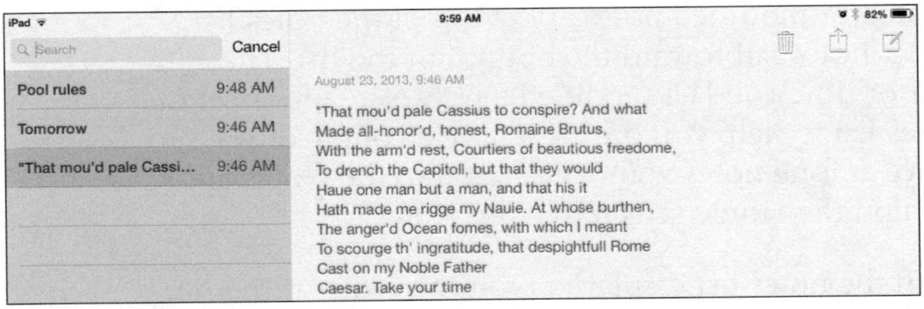

Figure 20-9

4. Begin to enter the search term (see **Figure 20-10**). All notes that contain matching words appear in the list.

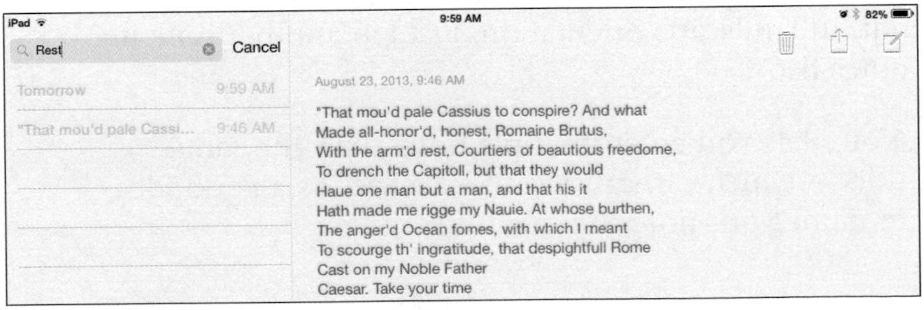

Figure 20-10

5. Tap a note to display it and then locate the instance of the matching word the old-fashioned way: by skimming the text to find it.

Share a Note

1. If you want to share what you wrote with a friend or colleague, you can easily use AirDrop or Mail to do so. With a note displayed, tap the Share icon at the top of the screen, as shown in **Figure 20-11**.

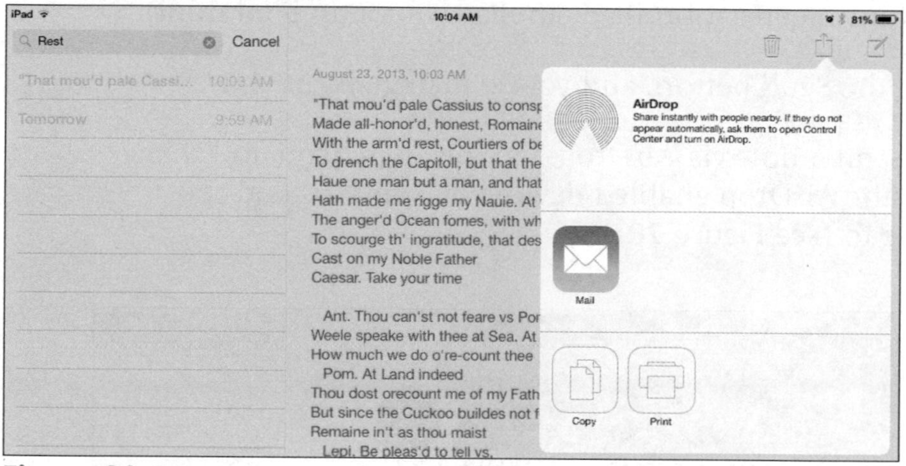

Figure 20-11

2. Tap Mail.

3. In the e-mail form that appears (see **Figure 20-12**), type one or more e-mail addresses in the appropriate fields. At least one e-mail address must appear in the To: field.

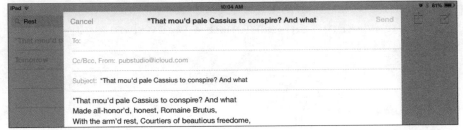

Figure 20-12

4. If you need to make changes in the subject or message, tap either area and make the changes by using either the onscreen keyboard or the Dictation feature (on a third- or fourth-generation iPad, an iPad Air, or an iPad mini).

5. Tap the Send button, and your e-mail goes on its way.

6. To send a note via AirDrop, tap the Share icon and then tap the AirDrop-enabled device you want to send the note to (see **Figure 20-13**).

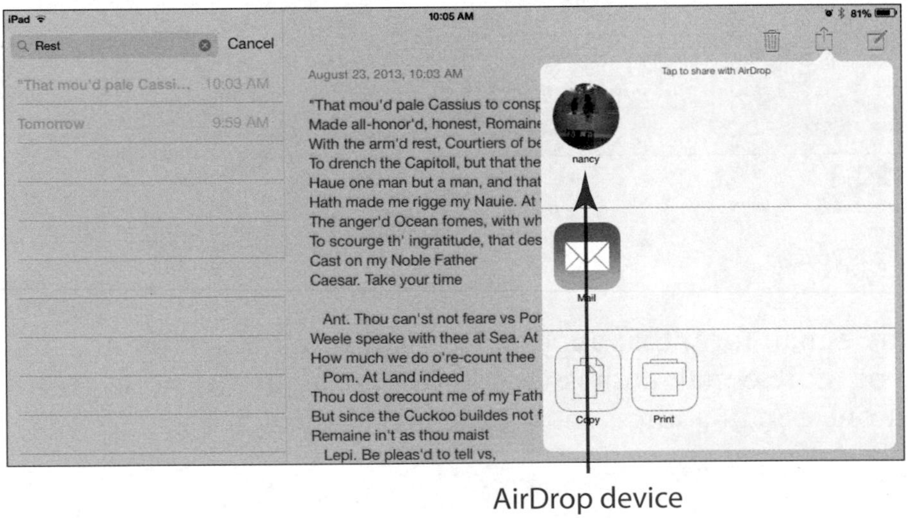

AirDrop device

Figure 20-13

To cancel an e-mail message and return to Notes without sending it, tap the Cancel button in the e-mail form and then tap Delete Draft on the menu that appears. To leave a message but save a draft so that you can finish and send it later, tap Cancel and then tap Save Draft. The next time you tap the e-mail button with the same note displayed in Notes, your draft appears.

Delete a Note

1. There's no sense in letting your notes list get cluttered, making it harder to find the ones you need. When you're done with a note, it's time to delete it. Tap the Notes app icon on the Home screen to open Notes.

2. With the iPad in landscape orientation, tap a note in the notes list to open it.

3. Tap the Trash icon, shown in **Figure 20-14**.

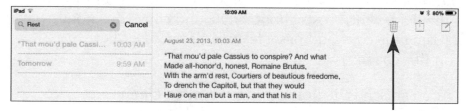

Trash icon

Figure 20-14

4. Tap the Delete Note button that appears (see **Figure 20-15**). The note is deleted.

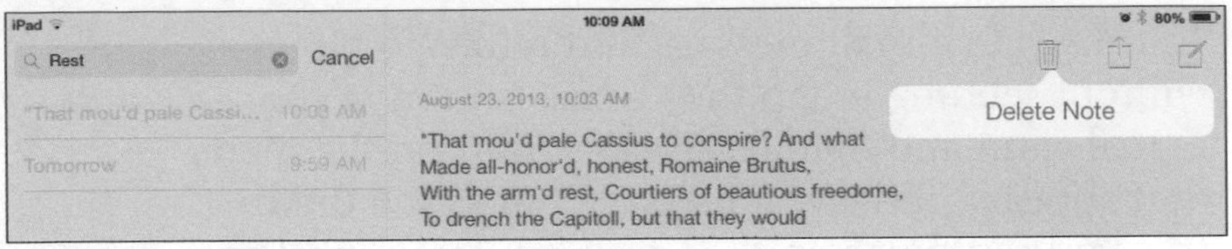

Figure 20-15

Notes is a nice little application, but it's limited. It offers no formatting tools or ways to print the content you enter unless you have an AirPrint-compatible printer. You can't paste pictures into Notes (you can try, but it won't work; only the filename appears, not the image). So if you've made some notes and want to graduate to building a more robust document in a word processor, you have a few options:

→ You can let iCloud sync your iPad notes with the Notes app on your Mac if it uses the Mountain Lion or Mavericks version of the Mac OS and then work with the text from there.

→ You can buy the Pages word processor application for the iPad, which costs about $9.99, and copy your note (using the copy-and-paste feature discussed earlier in this chapter).

→ You can send the note to yourself in an e-mail message. Open the e-mail, and copy and paste its text into a full-fledged word processor, and you're good to go.

Print a Note

1. If you have an AirPrint-enabled printer, you can print your notes. With Notes open and the note you want to print displayed, tap the Share icon at the top right of the screen.

2. Tap the Print icon (see **Figure 20-16**).

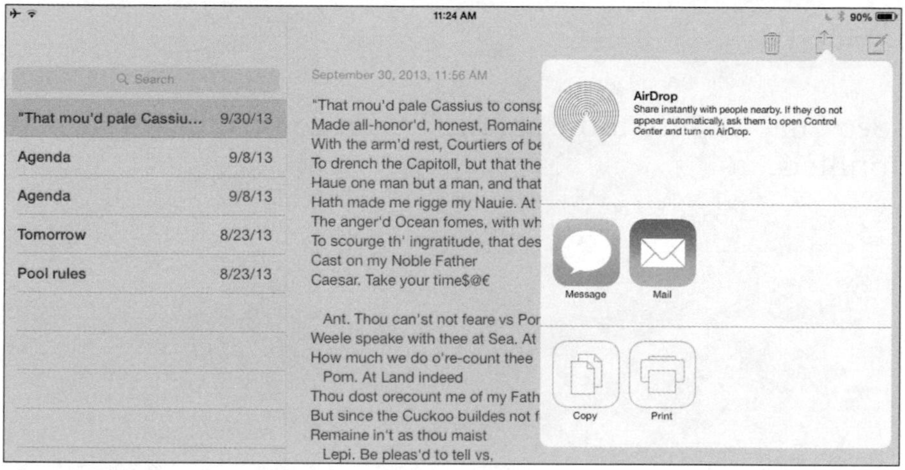

Figure 20-16

3. In the Printer Options dialog that appears, shown in **Figure 20-17,** tap Select Printer to display a list of available printers.

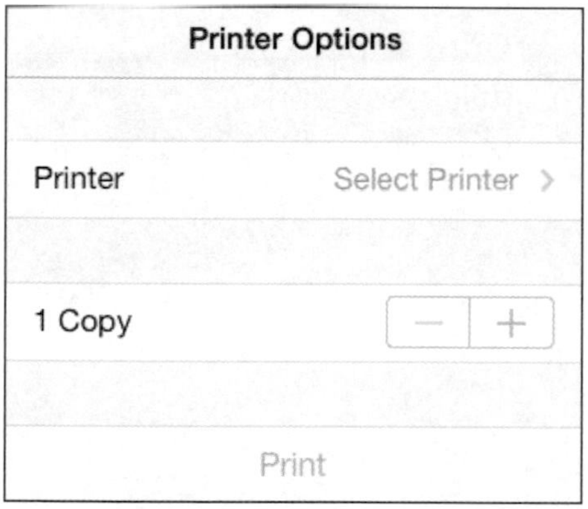

Figure 20-17

4. Tap the printer you want to use.

   5. Tap the + button in the Copy field to print more than
      one copy.

   6. Tap Print.

 See Chapter 5 for more about AirPrint-compatible
   printers.

Troubleshooting and Maintaining Your iPad

Chapter 21

*i*Pads don't grow on trees; they cost a pretty penny. That's why you should learn how to take care of your iPad and troubleshoot any problems it might have so that you get the most out of it.

In this chapter, I provide some advice about the care and maintenance of your iPad, as well as tips about how to solve common problems, update iPad system software, and even reset the iPad if something goes seriously wrong. In case you lose your iPad, I even tell you about a feature that helps you find it, activate it remotely, or even disable it if it has fallen into the wrong hands. Finally, you get information about backing up your iPad settings and content by using iCloud.

Keep the iPad Screen Clean

If you've been playing with your iPad, you know that it's a fingerprint magnet (despite Apple's claim that the iPad has a fingerprint-resistant screen). Here are some tips for avoiding fingerprint marks and cleaning your iPad screen:

⟶ **Use a stylus instead of your fingers.** You can buy a stylus for about $1 (or even less) and use it to tap the screen. You may even find that a stylus is more accurate than your fingers when you're using the onscreen keyboard.

⟶ **Use a dry, soft cloth.** You can get most fingerprints off with a dry, soft cloth such as the one you use to clean your eyeglasses or a cleaning tissue that's lint- and chemical-free. Or try products used to clean lenses in labs, such as Kimwipes or Kaydry, which you can get from several major retailers, such as Amazon.

⟶ Use a stand or dock to hold your iPad. With a stand or dock, you spend less time picking up your tablet, which cuts down on finger smudges.

⟶ **Use a slightly dampened soft cloth.** To get the surface even cleaner, very slightly moisten the soft cloth. Again, make sure that whatever cloth material you use is free of lint.

⟶ **Remove the cables.** Turn off your iPad and unplug any cables from it before cleaning the screen with a moistened cloth.

⟶ **Avoid too much moisture.** Avoid getting too much moisture around the edges of the screen, where it can seep into the unit.

⟶ **Never use household cleaners.** They can degrade the coating that keeps the iPad screen from absorbing oil from your fingers.

 Do *not* use premoistened lens-cleaning tissues to clean your iPad screen. Most wipe brands contain alcohol, which can damage the screen's coating.

Protect Your Gadget with a Case

Your screen isn't the only element on the iPad that can be damaged, so consider getting a case for it so you can carry it around the house or around town safely. Besides providing a bit of padding if you drop the device, a case makes the iPad less slippery in your hands, offering a better grip when you're working with it.

Several types of cases are available for the iPad and iPad mini, and more are showing up all the time. You can choose the Smart Cover, from Apple, for example ($39 for polyurethane or $69 for leather), which covers the screen only; the Smart Case from Apple, which covers both the front and back ($49 in polyurethane); or a cover from another manufacturer, such as Tuff-Luv (www.tuff-luv.com) or Griffin (www.griffintechnology.com), that comes in materials ranging from leather to silicone (see **Figures 21-1** and **21-2**).

Cases range from a few dollars to $70 or more for leather, with some outrageously expensive designer cases costing upward of $500. Some provide a cover for the screen and back; others protect only the back and sides or, in the case of Smart Cover, only the screen. If you carry your iPad around much, consider a case with a screen cover to provide better protection for the screen, or use a screen overlay, such as InvisibleShield from Zagg (www.zagg.com).

Figure 21-1

Figure 21-2

Extend Your iPad's Battery Life

The much-touted 10-hour battery life of the iPad is a wonderful feature, but you can do some things to extend it even further. Here are a few tips to consider:

➡ **Keep tabs on remaining battery life.** You can estimate the amount of remaining battery life by looking at the Battery icon at the far-right end of the Status bar, at the top of your screen.

➡ **Use standard accessories to charge your iPad most effectively.** When connected to a Mac computer for charging, the iPad can charge slowly; charging the iPad on certain PC connections, on the other hand, *drains* the battery slowly. Even so, the most effective way to charge your iPad is to plug it into a wall outlet by using the Lightning to USB Cable (or Dock Connector to USB Cable with pre-iPad fourth gen tablets) and the 10W USB Power Adapter that comes with your iPad (see **Figure 21-3**).

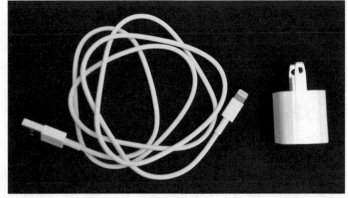

Figure 21-3

➠ The fastest way to charge the iPad is to turn it off while charging it.

➠ Your battery may *lose* power if you leave it connected to the USB port on an external keyboard.

➠ The Battery icon on the Status bar indicates when charging is complete.

 Your iPad battery is sealed in the unit, so you can't replace it, as you can many laptop or cellphone batteries. If the battery is out of warranty, you may have to fork over more than $100 to get a new one. See the "Get Support" task, later in this chapter, to find out where to get a replacement battery.

 Apple has introduced AppleCare+. For $99, you get two years of coverage, which protects you even if you drop or spill liquids on your iPad. (Apple covers up to two incidents of accidental damage.) If your iPad has to be replaced, it will cost you only $49, rather than the $250 it used to cost with garden-variety AppleCare. That means $148 versus the $299 price Apple offered me to replace my iPad 5 when it died 14 months into its life (and Apple advised me that they couldn't service it). You can purchase

AppleCare+ when you buy your iPad or within a month of the date of purchase. See www.apple.com/support/products/ipad.html for more details.

Find Out What to Do with a Nonresponsive iPad

If your iPad goes dead on you, the problem is most likely to be a power issue, so the first thing to do is plug the Lightning to USB Cable (or Dock Connector to USB Cable) into the 10W USB Power Adapter, plug the 10W USB Power Adapter into a wall outlet, plug the other end of the Lightning to USB Cable (or Dock Connector to USB Cable) into your iPad, and charge the battery.

Another thing to try — if you believe that an app is hanging up the iPad — is to press the Sleep/Wake button for a couple of seconds. Then press and hold the Home button. The app you were using should close.

You can always try the tried-and-true reboot procedure. On the iPad, press the Sleep/Wake button on top until a red slider appears. Drag the slider to the right to turn off your iPad. After a few moments, press the Sleep/Wake button to boot up the little guy again.

If the situation seems to be drastic and none of these ideas works, try to reset your iPad. To do this, press the Sleep/Wake button and the Home button at the same time until the Apple logo appears onscreen.

Make the Keyboard Reappear

When you're using a Bluetooth keyboard, your onscreen keyboard doesn't appear. The physical keyboard has in essence co-opted keyboard control of your device.

To use your onscreen keyboard after connecting a Bluetooth keyboard, you can turn off your connection to the Bluetooth keyboard by turning off Bluetooth in iPad Settings, or by moving the keyboard out of range or switching the keyboard off. Your onscreen keyboard should reappear.

Update Software

1. Apple occasionally updates the iPad system software to fix problems or offer enhanced features. You can also tap Settings⇨General⇨Software Update to update your software. If you're not using the iCloud feature, which updates your iOS automatically, or if you prefer to look for updates yourself in iTunes, you should start by connecting your iPad to your computer.

2. On your computer, open the iTunes software that you installed. (See Chapter 3 for more about this topic.)

3. Click your iPad in the iTunes Source list on the left.

4. Click the Summary tab, shown in **Figure 21-4**.

Figure 21-4

5. Click the Check for Update button. iTunes displays a message telling you whether a new update is available.

6. Click the Update button to install the newest version.

If you're having problems with your iPad, you can use the Update feature to try to restore the current version of the software. Follow the preceding set of steps, but click the Restore button instead of the Update button in Step 6.

 You can also use the iTunes Wi-Fi Sync feature (tap Settings⇨General) to sync wirelessly to a computer that has iTunes installed.

Restore the Sound

On the morning I wrote this chapter, as my husband puttered with our iPad, its sound suddenly (and ironically) stopped working. We gave ourselves a quick course in sound recovery, so now I can share some tips with you. Make sure that

➡ **You haven't touched the volume-control keys on a physical keyboard connected to your iPad via Bluetooth.** They're on the right side of the top row. Be sure not to touch one and inadvertently mute the sound.

➡ **You haven't flipped the Side Switch.** If you have the Side Switch set up for the Silent feature, moving the switch mutes sound on the iPad.

➡ **The speaker isn't covered up.** It may be covered in a way that muffles the sound.

➡ **A headset isn't plugged in.** Sound won't play over the speaker and the headset at the same time.

➡ **The volume limit is set to Off.** You can set up the volume limit in the Music settings to control how loudly your music can play (which is useful if you have teenagers around). Tap the Settings icon on the Home screen; then tap Music on the left side, tap the

Volume Limit control (see **Figure 21-5**), and move the slider to adjust the volume limit.

iPad 🛜	3:37 PM	⌁ 🔋 ⚡ Not Charging 🔋
Settings	‹ Music	**Volume Limit**
📱 iCloud		
✉️ Mail, Contacts, Calendars	MAX VOLUME	
📝 Notes	━━━━━━━━━━━━━━━━━━━━━━━━○	

Figure 21-5

When all else fails, reboot. (This strategy worked for us.) Just press the Sleep/Wake button until the red slider appears; then press and drag the slider to the right. After the iPad turns off, press the Sleep/Wake button again until the Apple logo appears, and you may find yourself back in business, sound-wise.

Get Support

Every new iPad comes with a year's coverage for repair of the hardware and 90 days of free technical support. Apple is known for its helpful customer support, so if you're stuck, I definitely recommend that you try it out. Here are a few options you can explore for getting help:

➡ **The Apple Store:** Go to your local Apple Store (if one is handy) to see what the folks there may know about your problem.

➡ **The Apple support website:** It's at www.apple.com/support/ipad (see **Figure 21-6**). You can find online manuals, discussion forums, and downloads, and you can use the Apple Expert feature to contact a live support person by phone.

➡ **The *iPad User Guide:*** You can use the bookmarked manual in the Safari browser to visit http://manuals.info.apple.com/en_us/ipad_user_guide.pdf and open a more robust version of the user guide that comes with your iPad.

Figure 21-6

→ **The Apple battery replacement service:** If you need repair or service for your battery, visit www.apple. com/batteries/replacements.html. Note that your warranty provides free battery replacement if the battery level dips below 50 percent and won't go any higher during the first year you own it. If you purchase the AppleCare service agreement, this service is extended to two years.

 Apple recommends that you have your iPad battery replaced only by an Apple Authorized Service Provider.

Find a Missing iPad

You can take advantage of the Find My iPad feature to pinpoint the location of your iPad. This feature is extremely handy if you forget where you left your iPad or someone walks away with it. Find My iPad not only lets you track down the critter, but also lets you wipe out the data contained in it if you have no way to get the iPad back.

Follow these steps to set up the Find My iPad feature:

1. Tap the Settings icon on the Home screen.

2. In the Settings pane, tap iCloud.

3. In the iCloud settings that appear, tap the On/Off button for Find My iPad to turn the feature on.

4. Tap OK in the Find My iPad dialog that appears (see **Figure 21-7**). From now on, if your iPad is lost or stolen, you can locate it on your computer.

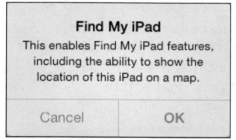

Figure 21-7

5. To use Find My iPad, go to `http://icloud.com` on your computer and then enter your ID and password. The Find My iPad screen appears.

6. Click the Devices button and then click the device you want to locate to display a map of its location and some helpful tools (see **Figure 21-8**).

7. To erase all information from the iPad in a process called *wiping,* click the Erase iPad button. Remember that this process will erase all content — contacts, music, notes, and so on — for good.

Figure 21-8

8. To lock the iPad against access by others, click the Lost
Mode button.

 You can also click Play Sound to help you find your
iPad if you've left it nearby. If you choose this option,
the sound plays for two minutes, helping you track
down anybody who's holding your iPad within
earshot.

Back Up to iCloud

You used to be able to back up your iPad content only via iTunes,
but since Apple's introduction of iCloud with iOS 5, you can back up
via a Wi-Fi network to your iCloud storage. You get 5GB of storage
for free (not including iTunes-bought music, video, apps, and electronic books or music you've copied to the cloud via the paid sub-
scription service, iTunes Match), or you can pay for increased levels
of storage (10GB for $20 a year, 20GB for $40 a year, or 50GB for
$100 a year).

1. To perform a backup to iCloud, first set up an iCloud
account (see Chapter 3 for details on creating an iCloud
account) and then tap Settings on the Home screen.

2. Tap iCloud and then tap Storage & Backup (see **Figure 21-9**).

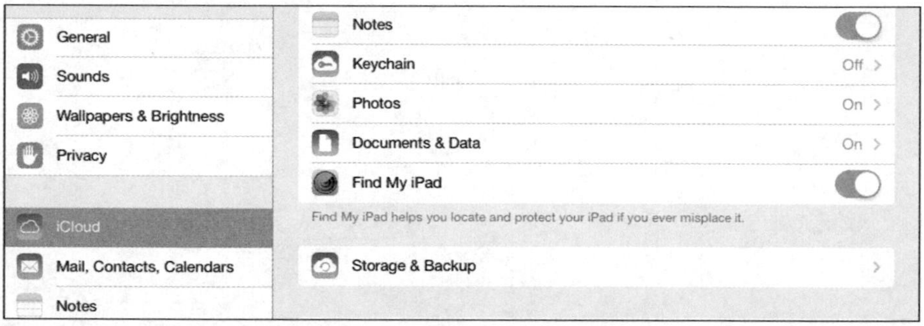

Figure 21-9

3. In the pane that appears (see **Figure 21-10**), tap the iCloud Backup On/Off switch to enable automatic backups.

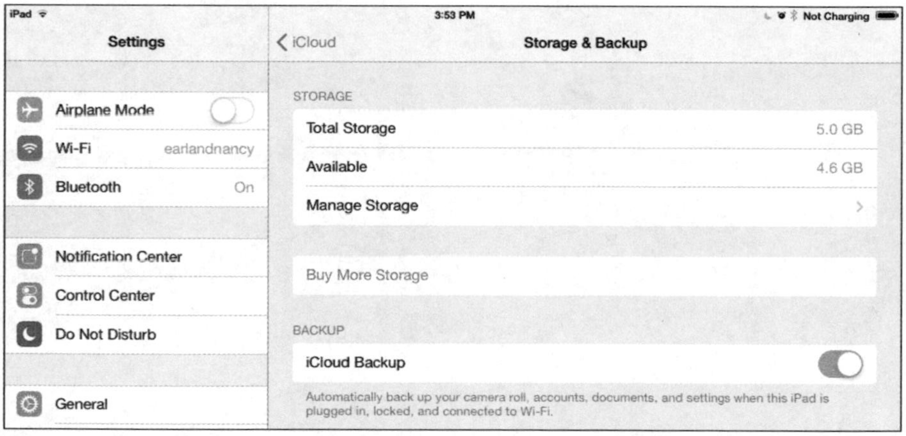

Figure 21-10

4. To perform a manual backup, tap Back Up Now. A progress bar shows how your backup is moving along.

Index

• V •

• W •

Notes

Notes

About the Author

Nancy Muir is the author of over 100 books on technology and business topics. In addition to her writing work, Nancy runs a companion website for her iPad books in the For Dummies series, `iPadMadeClear.com`. She has written a regular column on computers and the Internet on `Retirenet.com` and is Senior Editor for the website `Understanding Nano.com`. Prior to her writing career, Nancy was a manager at several publishing companies and a training manager at Symantec.

Dedication

To world peace.

Author's Acknowledgments

With this book I began to work with Brian Walls who was assigned to lead the team on this book. Brian, you filled BP's shoes admirably and I hope we work together often. Thanks also to Dennis Cohen for his able work as technical editor, and to Kathy Simpson, the book's copy editor. Last but never least, thanks to Kyle Looper, Acquisitions Editor, for giving me the opportunity to write this book.

Publisher's Acknowledgments

Acquisitions Editor: Kyle Looper

Project Editor: Brian H. Walls

Copy Editor: Kathy Simpson

Technical Editor: Dennis Cohen

Editorial Assistant: Anne Sullivan

Sr. Editorial Assistant: Cherie Case

Project Coordinator: Patrick Redmond

Cover Image: ©iStockphoto.com/Kris Hanke